THE HURRIED WOMAN SYNDROME

A Seven-Step Program
to Conquer Fatigue,
Control Weight,
and Restore Passion
to Your Relationship

BRENT W. BOST, M.D., FACOG

McGraw·Hill

New York   Chicago   San Francisco   Lisbon   London   Madrid   Mexico City
Milan   New Delhi   San Juan   Seoul   Singapore   Sydney   Toronto

Library of Congress Cataloging-in-Publication Data

Bost, Brent.
The hurried woman syndrome : a 7-step program to conquer fatigue, control weight, and restore passion to your relationship / by Brent Bost ; foreword by Annette Smick.— 1st ed.
p.   cm.
Includes index.
ISBN 0-07-144577-3
1. Stress management for women.   I. Title.

RA785 .B68   2005
155.9′042′082—dc22   2004017958

3 4 5 6 7 8 9 0   FGR/FGR   0 9 8 7 6 5

ISBN 0-07-144577-3

McGraw-Hill books are available at special quantity discounts to use as premiums and sales promotions, or for use in corporate training programs. For more information, please write to the Director of Special Sales, Professional Publishing, McGraw-Hill, Two Penn Plaza, New York, NY 10121-2298. Or contact your local bookstore.

The information contained in this book is intended to provide helpful and informative material on the subject addressed. It is not intended to serve as a replacement for professional medical advice. Any use of the information in this book is at the reader's discretion. The author and the publisher specifically disclaim any and all liability arising directly or indirectly from the use or application of any information contained in this book. A health care professional should be consulted regarding your specific situation.

This book is printed on acid-free paper.

CONTENTS

FOREWORD

Dr. Annette Smick
of Mayo Health System

DEPRESSION OCCURS twice as often in women as it does in men. Many theories attempt to explain this female predominance: biological differences in brain structure and function; genetic transmission (women are more likely to have daughters who also suffer from depression); and a higher risk of depressive symptoms premenstrually, postpartum, and perimenopausally. Psychosocial risk factors include a lack of social supports, a history of sexual abuse or physical victimization, the presence of three or more young children at home, the absence of a job outside the home, the juggling of multiple caregiver roles, and anxiety (which typically precedes the onset of depressive symptoms).

With so many risk factors, it is understandable that one in five women will experience depressive symptoms at some point in their lives. As they try to multitask too many responsibilities in too little time, maintain relationships, and keep the (household) boat afloat, they are left feeling stressed, with the symptoms of Hurried Woman

Syndrome. The fatigue, weight gain, low sex drive, and moodiness that characterize this condition may not meet the criteria for clinical depression, but they are not minor or insignificant. They can negatively affect self-esteem and lead to changes in behavior and conflicts in relationships. Hurried Woman Syndrome symptoms can interfere with psychosocial functioning and if left unaddressed, can lead to hopelessness, clinical (major) depression, suicidal thoughts, substance abuse, eating disorders, or divorce.

One in four women will experience Hurried Woman Syndrome symptoms at some time during their lives. If you are one of these women, you don't deserve to suffer. You owe it to yourself to learn how to recognize and manage the symptoms and regain a balance in your life.

You are not alone—help is available. Dr. Brent Bost, a gynecologist with a holistic approach, will guide you through the classic symptoms of Hurried Woman Syndrome, providing understanding, support, and a little humor to neutralize the guilt and encourage action through his medically sound seven-step program.

You have nothing to lose and improved self-acceptance and quality of life to gain.

Take the journey. If not now, when?

Happy trails.

INTRODUCTION

THE WOMEN WHO visit my ob-gyn office often come for a standard checkup, their annual appointment. It's only when they're actually in my office that many mention, almost as an afterthought, how exhausted and stressed out they've been. The interesting thing is that once they start talking, they don't want to stop. The comments that follow are typical of the exchanges I have with these women.

> *It's crazy. I don't have time to relax with my kids, let alone my husband. I've got to do the housework, drive the kids to soccer and baseball, and volunteer each week with my church group. Now I've found out I'm pregnant again. Doctor, what am I going to do? I'm so tired already I could just cry!*
>
> *—Rachel, age 35*

> *I'm a commuter. I spend an hour taking the train to and from work each day and even that time is spent doing tasks for my job!*

I always seem to have an e-mail to write or a work contact to call. Can you be too connected? Then when I get home in the evening, I have to pick the kids up from day care, rush home, and get something on the table. After I help the kids finish their homework, it's time for bed—for them and for me. I've been on the go so much that I have to eat to keep my energy levels up. Now I'm gaining weight, and frankly, I just don't feel the same anymore. It's gotten to the point where . . . well, our sex life is suffering! Sure, my husband still asks, but I'll find myself just turning wearily over in bed and going to sleep or giving in and feeling resentment afterward. Is there something wrong with me?

—Miranda, age 42

As an ob-gyn, my formal medical training prepared me to take care of women with high-risk pregnancies, pelvic pain, hormonal imbalances, and bleeding. These were the problems I expected women to ask me about when I entered private practice eighteen years ago. Little did I know back in my training days that the toughest problems women were struggling with out in the real world weren't bleeding, pregnancy complications, or pain but fatigue, moodiness, weight gain, and low sex drive. These are the problems that plague millions of women in America today, and until recently, they were either approached in a disjointed, ineffective fashion with unproven home remedies, crazy diets, and the wrong medications or—worse—thoughtlessly brushed aside as "normal suffering" by doctors and well-meaning friends alike.

It took me a while to see the pattern, but a few years ago I began to realize that about one in five of my patients was complaining of one or more of these symptoms and that if I asked the right questions, I would usually find the other symptoms lurking in the shadows. Patient after patient, day after day, more and more women kept coming in complaining of these problems. I figured there had to be a link between them—some common thread that tied them all together. But what was it? As I began doing research to find out what condition this group of symptoms might indicate was overwhelming so many of my patients, things got worse—I realized that my wife, LaNell, was beginning to experience the same symptoms. Now it was personal. I simply had to figure this out.

LaNell and I had been married for more than twenty years. We had four great children, ages seven through fifteen, who were as energetic and busy as those of our friends. LaNell and I were living our dreams back in our hometown of Beaumont, Texas, along with our parents, a great church family, a good circle of friends, and a very prosperous medical practice. How could things be better—or more normal, for that matter? Of course, as a busy ob-gyn, I often found myself working twelve- to fourteen-hour days, caught up in the successes and struggles of my patients, which also meant that for most of the day and sometimes into the evening, my wife was at home alone, managing the house and the needs of our four children. But as time passed, I realized that she was beginning to struggle with the same physical and emotional symptoms my patients—and many of our friends—were.

As I talked with hundreds of women about their symptoms and circumstances, I began to see the common thread that linked the vast majority of my patients: chronic stress. Sometimes the stress was unavoidable, such as that caused by caring for a sick child or maintaining a high-powered career. However, for the majority of women, much of the stress was avoidable, or at least, it could be managed better. Of course, when I told them that chronic stress was causing their symptoms, they thought I was crazy: "Come on, doctor, stress can't cause all of these physical symptoms."

However, we all now know that stress can block your coronary arteries and cause a heart attack; it can tighten up your blood vessels and give you high blood pressure; it can even burn a hole in the lining of your stomach and give you an ulcer. The negative energy that stress represents somehow gets transformed into physical changes in our bodies that we recognize as disease. So, why do we find it so hard to believe that stress can change our appetite, energy levels, mood, or interest in sex? There's no doubt that it can. In any event, I conducted a formal survey of over twelve hundred ob-gyn physicians from across the country and found that 94 percent of them felt that chronic stress is the primary cause of Hurried Woman Syndrome.

I'm often asked what I mean by "avoidable" stress. Avoidable stresses are those that come from the busy, hectic schedules and lifestyle choices that many of us embrace as completely routine. Yet the effects of this kind of stress, what I call "hurry," can have very significant long-term and wide-reaching consequences, especially for women. These consequences can include physical illness and emotional problems, including depression.

The effects of life stresses are primarily manifested in four symptom areas: (1) fatigue, often reported as an overwhelming sense of tiredness; (2) a low mood or wide mood swings; (3) problems controlling weight; and (4) a lack of interest in physical intimacy. The symptoms brought on by hurry often begin as fatigue or moodiness but then spill over into the other areas as time goes by. The pressure often comes from activities in which stress appears to be low at first and then builds steadily until it overflows and becomes a problem. It's like a cup under a dripping faucet: at first each drop seems to have little effect on the amount of water in the cup, but eventually the cup fills up and the water spills over the edges.

Many of the things that bring stress into your life are "good" things in themselves: family events, entertainment, kids' sports, volunteer work, and church activities. Yet when they overwhelm you, they can become dangerous to your health and to your relationships. Water is an essential element of life, but too much water can drown you!

LaNell managed to turn it all around without medication. That, plus the research I did, helped me realize that Hurried Woman Syndrome is a significant medical problem and that there are safe and effective ways to treat it. Not everyone needs medication to get positive energy back in their lives, although antidepressants may offer critical assistance for some and a wise adjunct for others.

I've found that some very simple strategies can be used to bring back the vitality, joy, peace, and health to hurried women's lives. This book presents an integrated, medically sound treatment program based on my research and that of other experts, validated by literally thousands of physicians, nurses, and psychologists to whom I've spoken over the last few years. The response has been fantastic: not only have my patients begun to respond, but as I began to share this information with my colleagues, they found that once they started asking their patients the right questions and treating this host of symptoms in a more holistic way, their patients have responded as well. I've written this book to help women identify whether or not they are suffering from the syndrome I've been discussing—Hurried Woman Syndrome.

Part One will help you understand the syndrome, and most importantly, it will help you figure out whether you are a victim of it. Part Two offers a seven-step treatment program based on a two-pronged approach. The first four steps will help you not only improve your sex life but control your weight and jump-start your mood. You'll feel younger, look younger, act younger, and even think younger! The last three steps look at lifestyle choices and empowers you to begin making the right day-to-day choices to lower your stress level and regain control of your life. Many women say they feel hopeless or helpless when they're suffering from Hurried Woman Syndrome. However, after reading this book, you'll discover the time and energy you need to recapture your lost joy, address weight concerns, and rebuild a fulfilling relationship with your partner. In essence, you will meet and defeat Hurried Woman Syndrome.

part one

UNDERSTANDING HURRIED WOMAN SYNDROME

1

LIFE AS A HURRIED WOMAN

WHO ARE HURRIED WOMEN, anyway? Hurried women are busy, productive people. Movers and shakers, they are generally at the top of the ladder both socially and professionally, if they have chosen to have a career outside the home, or in their community and volunteer work. They've got what it takes, and they are getting things done, but what used to seem easy for them is becoming harder and harder to manage. The sense of joy that living life used to bring has mysteriously evaporated. Many say they feel frazzled, even dazed and disorganized at times. They often feel lonely, whether or not they're surrounded by people. They are worn out and moody, feeling underappreciated and on edge even at times when they should be able to relax. Some begin to feel they are trapped by their circumstances—unable to make things change or get better. Many still manage to fake a smile, clinging to the belief that once a particular deadline or challenge has passed, things will get better. But it never does. When one problem drops off the radar screen, another pops up. There's always something making them feel pressured, as if they're falling behind, losing control, or slipping. Does this sound familiar?

- Do you feel stressed out much of the time?

- Is there always someplace you're running to?

- Do you feel like you never have any time for yourself?

- Do you frequently find yourself irritated by things that never used to get under your skin?

- Is there always a whirlwind of thoughts and to-do lists running through your mind, particularly when you're trying to sleep?

- Do the things that used to give you pleasure in life fail to excite you anymore?

- Is your energy so low most of the time that you find yourself struggling to make it through the day (and who has the time or energy to exercise)?

- Has your weight been creeping up in spite of your best efforts with your old "it-always-worked-in-the-past" formula of diet and exercise? Or have you tried one of those fad diets that worked at first but failed to keep the weight off?

- Does your husband's or partner's interest in sex turn you off instead of turn you on these days?

If you've already talked to friends about this, you know that almost everyone is struggling with the same problems (if they're honest). And it's not just you and your friends who are wrestling with these problems. Just look at all the popular women's magazines in the grocery checkout aisle. They are brimming with articles on raising energy levels, coping with stress, following the latest diet fad, and improving your sex life. Realizing all of this may lead you to the popular conclusion that all of these troubles—the fatigue, moodiness, weight gain, and lack of interest in sex—are normal and just the way life is.

Unfortunately, nothing could be further from the truth. Fatigue, moodiness, weight gain, and low sex drive are actually symptoms of a condition that I call Hurried Woman Syndrome. This condition is, indeed, quite common—almost thirty million women in the United States are dealing with it—but it is anything but normal. We have a terrible habit in today's society of confusing *common* with *normal*, and just because we see something frequently doesn't mean we can't change it or that it's okay. Look at obesity. Over two-thirds of Americans are overweight or obese by government standards. It's actually more common to be overweight than to be fit these days! Should we therefore call it "normal" to be overweight? Of course not! To do so would ignore the long-term health consequences of being overweight. Similarly, Hurried Woman Syndrome is associated with a lot of other illnesses, such as migraine headaches, irritable bowel syndrome, ulcers, and chronic fatigue syndrome, as well as diabetes, heart disease, and high blood pressure. Clinical research indicates that, if left untreated, over 30 percent of women with Hurried Woman Syndrome will develop major depression. Sure, feeling this way is common, but don't be fooled: it is by no means normal.

Let's start by looking at what comprises Hurried Woman Syndrome and hear what Hurried Women have to say about themselves. We'll then focus on whether you are experiencing this condition and what you can do about it.

PROFILE OF THE HURRIED WOMAN

The Hurried Woman is right in front of you. She may be your spouse, your friend, your coworker, your daughter; she might even be you! She's usually on the young side, between twenty-five and fifty-five, and often has a few children. She's hurried (or "harried," as the British might say) by the many struggles that complicate her life. Her spouse (or perhaps lack of one), her children, and her work all tend to pull her in different directions, causing a lot of internal stress. She doesn't want to fail any of the people in her life. This constant conflict of needs, both hers and theirs, can wear down even the strongest woman and ultimately lead to the symptoms of Hurried Woman Syndrome and to major depression.

Although children are a frequent source of stress for the Hurried Woman, they aren't required for symptoms of the syndrome to occur. Professionals, business owners, and women in high-powered, stressful careers who are childfree also experience the syndrome.

CLASSIC SYMPTOMS

FATIGUE

I'm tired all the time and I don't know why.

—Jean, age 26

I used to have so much energy for the things in my life—my husband, my kids, my career as an attorney. Now, I'm struggling to stay on top of everything. It's overwhelming.

—Toni, age 41

Fatigue is the most common feature of Hurried Woman Syndrome, and it's usually the first sign of it. However, a common variant is to be overly anxious instead. Many women who experience anxiety find themselves avoiding social situations or feeling fearful but can't put a finger on what they're afraid of. In fact, many Hurried Women are anxious about not having enough energy. It's the worst of both worlds. Almost 40 percent of my patients complain of fatigue at any given time, and in a recent survey of ob-gyn physicians I conducted (the results of which were presented at the annual clinical meeting of the American College of Obstetricians and Gynecologists in May 2002), fatigue was the most common reason women sought help from their doctors.

Most women realize that they should be tired after a long day at work or with the kids, and they expect that they will feel better after they rest. This kind of fatigue is predictable, and it's temporary. If you really do feel better after resting, you probably do not have Hurried Woman Syndrome. However, the fatigue that the Hurried Woman feels is *pervasive*. It's hard to shake, and it doesn't ease up much, even after a good night's rest or a three-day weekend.

As the tiredness builds into an obvious lack of energy, the Hurried Woman begins losing her desire to participate in life. Things that were previously fun or interesting are no longer perceived that way, and what was once an enjoyable activity may now be almost dreaded. Certainly other medical conditions such as anemia or an underactive thyroid can produce these same symptoms. We'll cover these conditions in more detail in Chapter 3 so that it's clear whether they should be ruled out as a source of your fatigue.

MOODINESS

I feel "down" a lot of times, even when things seem to be going okay.

—Miranda, age 37

I've got such a short fuse lately. I seem to snap at people all the time these days—and for a not-very-good reason. Then I feel guilty. Is this really normal?

—Pat, age 48

It's sometimes difficult to separate low mood, or moodiness, from fatigue. When there's no energy left, your mood tends to drop, and you often become irritable or disagreeable. If you feel constant pressure to perform yet have to struggle against tiredness to get the job done, this aggravation can spill out as being "down" or moody. It's an inevitable consequence of fatigue. Sadly, it also produces a lot of hurt feelings and guilt, which only serve to worsen the problem. It's a vicious cycle.

One of my patients described the moodiness of Hurried Woman Syndrome as "PMS that lasts all month long," while another described it as "that rainy day feeling that stays with you like a dark cloud, even when the sun's shining." Sometimes the down feeling can dull your ability to think straight and juggle all the details in your busy schedule. Hurried Women find that they become more forgetful—misplacing car keys, relying more and more on Post-it notes and to-do lists, forgetting those important little details that seem to pile up all the time.

Weight Gain

I'm eating like I used to, but I keep putting on weight.
—Sara, age 44

I'm too tired to exercise. Besides, I don't have the time, particularly with work and the kids.
—Meghan, age 29

Weight gain is a common problem for my patients and a growing number of people in this country. It can be an isolated problem for many, but it is also one of the cardinal symptoms of Hurried Woman Syndrome. Either way, being overweight can have serious health consequences, both physically and emotionally. According to the most recently published statistics from the Centers for Disease Control and Prevention (CDC), about 35 percent of American women are classified as overweight and another 30 percent are obese.

For the majority of women, and in particular those who fit the profile of the Hurried Woman, weight gain can stem from many sources. Extreme fatigue makes it hard to exercise, as does a very busy schedule. Many women simply won't take time out from meeting everyone else's needs to fulfill their own need for exercise. Unfortunately, this lack of aerobic physical activity makes fatigue levels increase in intensity, compounding the problem further. To make matters worse, a hectic schedule often makes meals on the run seem like a necessity, but this wreaks havoc on your diet, which drives your weight up and your mood down.

LOW SEX DRIVE

I'm too tired to have sex most nights.

—Andrea, age 34

I don't feel sexy anymore.

—Amy, age 41

Most Hurried Women can identify with these comments. In fact, a recent survey of ob-gyn physicians reveals that about one-third of all women who come to the doctor's office express concern about low libido (a lack of desire), and there are likely more who don't feel comfortable mentioning it. A marriage and family therapist practicing in a Chicago suburb heard about Hurried Woman Syndrome on her local news and wrote me that she suspected this condition was the major reason couples came to see her. Of course, they didn't call it that, but she thought it was clearly the problem that had caused trouble in their relationship and made them seek help. Indeed, I saw so many Hurried Women in my own medical practice that I felt compelled to research the problem and write a book about it.

A woman's sex drive can be influenced by several different factors, including the following:

• **Physical factors.** A woman's physical health (particularly if she suffers from a chronic illness), general energy levels, and comfort issues (such as pain during intercourse) can all affect her desire for physical intimacy.

• **Hormonal factors.** Estrogen and testosterone seem to set the stage for a normal sexual response in women. However, they are not the main characters in planting the "seeds of desire" in a woman's mind. Less than 20 percent of women actually respond to testosterone replacement. Other (emotional and situational) factors are usually more important than hormones in determining a woman's sexual energy.

• **Emotional factors.** Women tend to need to feel emotionally connected to their partner before sex becomes desirable. If there's trouble in the relationship or unresolved issues between them, she will most likely be the first to turn away physically until the problems are resolved.

• **Situational factors.** When they're under pressure in their day-to-day lives, sex goes from a low- to a no-priority activity for many women. The desire simply vanishes. For most men, the opposite is true—they tend to view sex as a way to relieve stress.

Popular culture assumes that poor lovemaking techniques and low testosterone levels are the key elements causing the epidemic of low sex drive seen in women today. However, in the survey I conducted, ob-gyn doctors identified the primary causes of low sex drive for women as (1) not enough time in a busy schedule for sex to be fun and (2) a strained primary love relationship—often a result of the same busy lifestyle. Most couples are struggling with trying to carve time out of a crowded schedule to have a better relationship, not just sexually but emotionally as well.

In addition, couples struggle with the differences in the way men and women approach the issue of sex, which adds to the problem. Concern about low sex drive generally represents one of two possible situations: one partner's sex drive is lower than it used to be, and/or the other partner is complaining about it. And it's affecting their relationship.

So what is the cause of all this misery? Why do so many women lack energy, have low moods, gain weight, and have a diminished interest in sex? The answer may surprise you: 94 percent of ob-gyns in my survey identified chronic stress as the cause of Hurried Woman Syndrome. Your first impression may be to think, "Impossible! There's no way stress can cause all of these physical problems." However, Chapter 2 will show you how chronic stress can make an indelible impact on your health, your life, and your relationships, as well as lead you down the path to major depression if you don't do something about it now. Stress is the root of Hurried Woman Syndrome.

2

STRESS AND HOW IT AFFECTS YOUR BRAIN AND YOUR LIFE

STRESS-RELATED ILLNESS. It's a term that was once rarely if ever heard, but now it's familiar to almost everyone. Much recent scientific research has been directed at identifying illnesses that are caused or significantly worsened by stress. The Centers for Disease Control and Prevention (CDC) estimates that stress-related illnesses account for 75–90 percent of all patient visits to a health care professional each year. This may seem outrageous at first glance, but the list of illnesses that either primarily result from or are aggravated by stress includes heart disease, stroke, diabetes, high blood pressure, ulcers, irritable bowel syndrome, infertility, headaches (particularly migraines), and depression. And the list is growing rapidly.

STRESS AND THE BODY-BRAIN CONNECTION

Stress is defined in physiologic terms as an internal response to an external stimulus. There are all types of stimuli outside of us that are waiting to get in. A stimulus usually enters our bodies through one or more of the five senses—we smell something, we hear the boss calling, we see someone on the street—and is then processed by the brain, or internalized. The brain categorizes the stimulus as good or bad, pleasant or unpleasant, and also decides the relative value of the stimulus—whether it's a "biggie" or barely worth noticing. Indeed, the brain is so powerful a filter that it can simply choose to disregard a stimulus altogether. When you get dressed in the morning, you know exactly where your shirt touches your shoulder and where your shoes put pressure on your feet. However, within just a few seconds, the brain shuts these signals out (unless your shoes hurt, that is). The nerves in your shoulders and feet continue to feel the garments (the external stimulus) and still send sensory information upstream to headquarters, but the brain decides that these signals aren't worth tracking any longer and simply tunes them out as unimportant. They are disregarded.

Through an amazingly complex set of chemical reactions and electrical discharges, the brain uses our memory of past experiences, clues from the surrounding environment, and our present mood to process the external stimulus into one that's now internal. It then determines what our response will be on multiple levels.

- **Physical**—to run or fight, to tense up or relax

- **Emotional**—to feel joy or sadness, anger or remorse, love or hate

- **Expressive**—to say something or keep quiet, smile or frown, reach out or pull away

These are the responses we can actually experience and recognize consciously if we are looking for them. Not all stressors are bad in themselves. Exercise is an example of a positive stressor that can strengthen our bodies. However, when the brain decides to respond negatively to a stressor, a great deal goes on in the body beneath the surface on a microscopic, cellular level.

The brain has been termed the *master gland* because it modulates and regulates virtually every organ system in the body. Everything from the highest order of thinking to our emotions and our bowel movements is regulated or at least markedly affected by what goes on in the brain. When "headquarters" decides to react to a stressor, our senses become more acute, our muscles tense up, and the body prepares to respond to the stimulus. The brain orchestrates the body's response through the release of several chemicals into the bloodstream.

Cortisol and Epinephrine

The two most important of these chemical signals are epinephrine (adrenaline) and cortisol, both of which come predominantly from the adrenal gland. Epinephrine increases the heart rate and blood pressure, releases sugar into the bloodstream to supply extra energy, and sharpens our senses to meet the (perceived) immediate threat. Similarly, the cortisol that is released into the system enables the body to sustain this type of response for extended periods of time but not indefinitely. The release of epinephrine and cortisol is the so-called "fight-or-flight" response, which enables us to react to or run away from an immediate threat. Obviously, this complex reaction was built into our system to help us cope with hardship and physical danger in our environment, so it's certainly a normal response. However, if the body is forced to sustain this fight-or-flight response for a long time, the action of these hormones, particularly cortisol, will begin to have some very negative physical effects. Much recent research has pointed to cortisol as the primary hormone involved in the physical changes that occur in our bodies in response to prolonged stress.

CUSHING'S SYNDROME AND THE BRAIN

Cushing's syndrome provides the perfect model to study the long-term effects of chronic stress on humans. Cushing's syndrome is a disease usually caused by an overgrowth of cells or a tumor in the adrenal gland that produces excessive amounts of cortisol. The primary symptoms of Cushing's syndrome are fatigue, low mood or irritability, weight gain, low sex drive (impotence in men), sleep disturbance, and skin changes. You probably recognized the first four symptoms on the list as those of Hurried Woman Syndrome. Hurried Women rarely have Cushing's syndrome, yet the symptoms look remarkably similar.

If left untreated, Cushing's syndrome carries a high risk for developing the same diseases as those related to stress: high blood pressure, heart disease, obesity, diabetes, ulcers, infertility, and depression. However, the vast majority of people who suffer with one or more of these ailments don't have Cushing's syndrome and usually have normal levels of cortisol. How can cortisol be the cause of these stress-related illnesses yet not be elevated on a blood test? There are many theories to explain this phenomenon.

Most likely, chronic stress causes cortisol to be released into the body in short bursts, or pulses. These pulses are probably small and occur at odd times throughout the day, making it unlikely that a random blood test will catch a modest elevation in cortisol level. However, these pulses could cause significant changes in body function and ultimately tissue damage, particularly if they occur over a long period of time. Think about being thumped on the nose. Your eyes water and it hurts for a second, but then you're okay. Although annoying, it's fairly innocuous. Now imagine being thumped on the nose once every minute. Over and over, hour after hour, day after day, week after week. How long do you think it would be before your nose was sore, bruised, even bloodied? Although there are holes in the cortisol theory, small bursts of cortisol from chronic stress over an extended period could add up and have a similar effect on your body and health.

Hurried Women don't have Cushing's syndrome because their cortisol levels are normal, but cortisol is still one of the hormones implicated in causing stress-related illnesses like Hurried Woman Syndrome. Fortunately, most of us have finally begun to recognize that stress can cause physical illness and imperil our health. It is still hard for us to believe that stress can also affect our mood, our appetite, our energy levels, and our interests, but it does. This leads us to the most important part of the discussion on stress and its effect on our physiology—the link between stress and depression.

THE BASIC FACTS ABOUT DEPRESSION

Major depression is a significant medical illness, accounting for more than twenty thousand deaths yearly from suicide in America alone, an estimated $47 billion in annual health care costs, plus an estimated $44 billion decline in worker productivity each year. Major depression affects women twice as often as men, and the National Institute of Mental Health estimates that 20 percent of women will have a major depressive episode in their lifetime. Although there are many theories, the reason for this difference in depression rates between men and women is unclear. The fact is major depression is a major health concern, particularly for women.

The official criteria for a diagnosis of major depression, as described in the *Diagnostic and Statistical Manual of Mental Illness-IV (DSM-IV)* of the American Psychiatric Association, requires that five or more of the nine possible symptoms of major depression be present; that the symptoms persist for at least two weeks' duration without a break; and that the symptoms create a significant negative impact in the patient's life at home, at work, or in relationships. The nine possible symptoms of depression are:

- Sad or irritable mood

- Loss of interest/lack of desire for pleasure (low sex drive)

- Fatigue

- Sleep disturbance

- Significant change in weight/appetite

- Impaired concentration/inability to make decisions

- Feelings of guilt, self-blame, worthlessness

- Physical agitation (restlessness)/slowing (lethargy)

- Suicidal thoughts

At this point, most women think, "Looking at this list, I'm depressed and so are all my friends!" *Everyone* has some of these symptoms at one time or another. But before you get depressed about the possibility of being depressed, let's look at the criteria more fully.

The symptoms of depression are frequently experienced by healthy people, usually springing up when you are under pressure. You often recognize the cause of the stress, fix it (or at least live through it), and then get back to normal. This is not major depression. The number of symptoms, their duration, and the degree to which they disturb your daily functioning are not long enough or bad enough to qualify as depression. You may feel more tired than you used to feel, perhaps you've gained a few pounds over the last few years, and you've had more restless nights or taken an unexpected nap occasionally while waiting in the carpool line, but this is not depression—at least not yet. Why? Because you can still go to work every day, take care of your family, and muster up the energy to get up early and do something fun *when you want to*. Although you do have some of the symptoms of depression, you don't have enough of them, they haven't lasted long enough, and they're not severe enough to stop you from doing what you need to do and much of what you want to do. This is why you are not depressed. But you may feel it's getting more and more difficult to keep it all going.

Many people say "I'm depressed" when they really mean they're upset about something or just in a blue mood. This is not depression either. Unfortunately, we throw the word *depression* around pretty carelessly, which is one reason there's so much confusion about what depression really is—and isn't.

DEPRESSION AND BRAIN CHEMISTRY

Depression is caused by a chemical imbalance in the brain and has nothing to do with being a "wimp" or "not trying hard enough to get happy." Although many of us heard these opinions about depression when we were growing up, they are very inaccurate. Unfortunately, these erroneous ideas on the nature of depression are still held by many people and often keep those who need help from seeking it.

The human brain functions much like an exceptionally complex chemistry set. Chemicals in the brain, called neurotransmitters, are used by nerve cells to communicate back and forth. These neurotransmitters—specifically serotonin, dopamine, and norepinephrine—are responsible for regulating anxiety and depression and also have an indirect effect on energy levels, appetite, mood, sleep, and sex drive. When these neurotransmitters are in balance, people feel good, healthy. However, when the brain chemistry is too far out of balance, the end result is major depression.

The brain has its own natural rebalancing system that keeps the levels of serotonin, dopamine, and norepinephrine in the right concentrations to maintain a healthy equilibrium. If the rebalancer is functioning properly, we have few if any symptoms of depression.

When things get tough, the rebalancer system helps us bear up under the pressure and keep going with only an occasional depressive symptom for a brief period. However, when stress levels get turned up even higher or last too long, the system may get overwhelmed and we experience more symptoms that seem to worsen. Thankfully, the rebalancer can still put the chemicals back in order fairly quickly once the stress has passed. However, the natural rebalancer doesn't always function like we want.

There are three basic types of rebalancer problems. First, some people have a rebalancer that is genetically defective and are plagued by depression most of their lives—essentially, a long-term rebalancer problem. Generally, these people have a strong family history of depression, and most will likely need help keeping their rebalancer operating effectively. Second, many women experience a short-term rebalancer problem—premenstrual syndrome (PMS), which will be discussed later (see the Index). However, the Hurried Woman is affected by the third type of chemical rebalancer problem—one caused by chronic stress or "hurry." This one runs parallel with stress levels. You can have PMS in addition to Hurried Woman Syndrome, which will make both of them worse during the premenstrual time, but let's focus on the Hurried Woman Syndrome alone for now. Medical research has clearly established that stress, particularly chronic stress such as that experienced by the Hurried Woman, can cause physical illness—ulcers, high blood pressure, heart disease, cancer—and even depression.

DEPRESSION VERSUS PREDEPRESSION

The chemicals in our brain obey the law of entropy—that is, all things in the universe tend toward disorder. An abandoned house is a good example of how entropy works. Even though the same forces of nature—wind, rain, and sun—pound on both a vacant house and one in which people live, the vacant house will begin to deteriorate and look terrible much faster than the home that's occupied. Shingles will go missing, the paint will begin to crack, and grass will grow up in the cracks in the driveway. The concept of entropy means that any system, whether it's a household or a brain, will deteriorate if it isn't tended regularly. And the more complex the system, the more likely deterioration will occur faster and have a more pronounced effect on performance. The brain must constantly rebalance its serotonin, dopamine, and norepinephrine levels in the appropriate compartments of the brain for us to feel normal.

Stress causes our natural rebalancer to function at less than 100 percent efficiency, and more stress reduces efficiency even further. When the efficiency level drops low enough, the rebalancer can no longer keep up and the chemical imbalance worsens, producing more and more symptoms that become more intense. The number and severity of symptoms parallels the level of chemical imbalance in the brain. This is a critical point. You don't go to bed one night with your brain chemistry 100 percent balanced, feeling totally normal, and then wake up the next morning in a major depression with your brain chemistry way out of balance (perhaps only 65 percent balanced) and complaining of five or more depressive symptoms. The explanation is not that something "breaks" and you're suddenly in a major depression, but rather that as the neurotransmitters in your brain become more and more unbalanced, you develop more symptoms and they become more severe. The opposite is true when it comes to treatment. As the brain chemistry becomes more balanced, your symptoms begin to lessen in severity and number. In other words, there are different degrees of brain chemistry imbalance—from "normal" all the way to "major depression"—and where a woman is on that continuum will determine how many symptoms of depression she has and how severely they impact her life. The brain chemistry balance is not like a light switch—"on versus off," "balanced versus unbalanced," "depressed versus normal"—but more like a dimmer switch that can raise and lower the amount of light (in this case, symptoms of depression) through multiple levels.

Let's say that most of the time, Lisa's brain chemicals are 90 percent balanced or better (10 percent or less out of balance), and she feels pretty good. She's functioning well on a daily basis. She notices a mild symptom or two—being more tired than usual or feeling a bit crabby—when her brain chemistry dips below the 90 percent level because of a stressor. For example, when her mother-in-law, with whom she has a tense relationship, comes for a three-day visit or when an important deadline is looming at work. When Lisa's mother-in-law returns to her lair or the project at work is completed, her levels return to the normal range and she feels good again within a few days. Most experts would consider this situation, which is illustrated graphically in Figure 2.1, to be normal. When Lisa's brain chemistry balance drops below 90 percent, she begins to have symptoms, but when the pressure falls off, she bounces back quickly.

However, if she faced a situation in which the stresses were greater or lasted longer (or both), such as if her mother-in-law became ill and moved in with Lisa's family, the balance of brain chemistry might drop lower, perhaps to the 80 percent range (20 percent out of balance), and stay there for a while. If this happened,

✤ FIGURE 2.1: LISA'S BRAIN CHEMISTRY AROUND A STRESSFUL EVENT

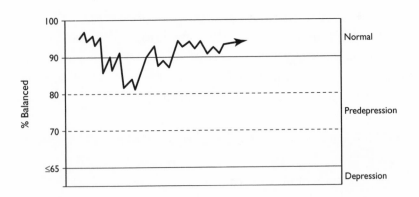

the fatigue would probably be worse. Lisa might even decide to skip her aerobics class or bow out of activities with friends because she was just too tired. Perhaps she'd begin to do what a lot of us do and "comfort" herself with food. The combination of decreased activity and increasing food intake would cause weight gain. Figure 2.2 demonstrates what her brain chemistry balance might look like in this situation.

Instead of turning around, let's say the stresses in Lisa's life continued to push her brain's chemical balance further down to the 70 percent level (30 percent out of balance). The fatigue would get much worse and her energy level would fall noticeably again. She'd begin having more and more trouble getting out of bed in the morning and would either fall asleep at her desk in the afternoon or wish she could. Her weight would climb steadily, and she'd start to dress differently to hide it. Furthermore, her desire for intimacy would start to trail off due to critically low energy levels, self-consciousness about her continued weight gain, an irritable mood, or all three. Whatever the explanation, the loss of desire would probably cause problems between her and her partner. Finally, to top it

☝ FIGURE 2.2: THE EFFECT OF ADDITIONAL STRESS ON LISA'S BRAIN CHEMISTRY

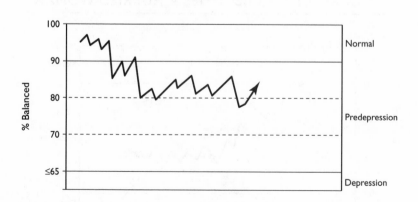

all off, the whole situation would make Lisa frustrated, confused, and perhaps a bit angry about what has happened to her energy, her figure, her mood, her sex drive—her happiness. These symptoms would result from the imbalance in brain chemistry as shown in Figure 2.3.

If she reached this point, Lisa would clearly not be in a healthy situation. It would have gone on too long and negatively affected too many areas of her life for her to not want to get better. She would probably already have tried to get back to her exercise routine and a diet strategy that worked in the past (but doesn't seem to work anymore). She'd be frustrated and probably feel guilty about not being the mother, wife, friend, worker, boss, and volunteer she'd always been in the past. She'd be searching for answers but not know where to find them. At this point, she would have Hurried Woman Syndrome. But, how do we know? Let's count the symptoms of depression that Lisa would experience if she were only at 70 percent balance:

1. Fatigue

2. Moodiness (or low mood)

✿ FIGURE 2.3: LISA BECOMES A HURRIED WOMAN

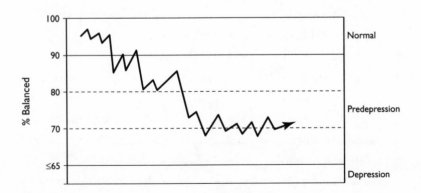

3. Weight gain

4. Low sex drive

With four symptoms of depression and the negative impact they're having on her life, we'd have trouble saying that she is feeling "normal." But she doesn't meet the criteria for major depression either, because that would require five symptoms and she's only got four. She's one symptom short of major depression—only one! This is what I call a "predepression," or Hurried Woman Syndrome.

Hurried Woman Syndrome is caused by the same chemical imbalance as major depression (that's why it has the same symptoms), but the imbalance is not quite as severe (that's why there is one less symptom). Because the chemical balance of Hurried Woman Syndrome lies just short of major depression, I feel it is appropriately described as a predepression. Couple this with the fact that over 30 percent of women who suffer with Hurried Woman Syndrome will progress to major depression unless there is intervention, and the term *predepression* makes a lot of sense.

To make the picture of predepression clearer, let's look at the same model we used earlier but describe each condition by the number of symptoms encountered. Figure 2.4 illustrates the relationship between the number of symptoms a woman experiences, the level of her brain chemistry balance, and where she is on the continuum between being normal and depressed. When she has one or no symptoms, she feels good; she's happy and normal. However, when she consistently has two symptoms, she starts to feel the pressure and begins to notice difficulty in certain areas of her life; she feels "stressed out" but is still considered normal. If the pressure grows and she gets a third or fourth symptom, she's crossed over into Hurried Woman Syndrome; she is in a predepressed state. Finally, if she develops a fifth symptom she will be in a major depression. Many women float back and forth between these different symptom levels. This is why milder cases of Hurried Woman Syndrome seem like ordinary stress and the worst cases seem like major depression. The lines between each of these different situations can be blurry at times.

TAKING STEPS TO COMBAT PREDEPRESSION

As we've discussed, when a woman has five or more symptoms of depression, she has major depression and needs to seek medical attention. Self-help books are wonderful as adjuncts, but suicide is a real concern with this condition. Since over 15 percent of depressed people kill themselves, no one can afford to take the very real threat of self-destruction lightly. When a woman has three or four symptoms, she is not depressed but is in the predepression of Hurried Woman Syndrome. Because medical research estimates that Hurried Women have a 1:3 chance of becoming depressed, they must take positive action to prevent major depression. Women with

🌸 FIGURE 2.4: THE CONTINUUM OF SYMPTOMS AND BRAIN CHEMISTRY BALANCE BETWEEN NORMALCY AND MAJOR DEPRESSION

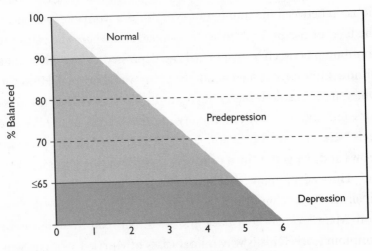

Number of Symptoms

one or two symptoms are still considered normal, perhaps best labeled "stressed out, but recoverable." They feel the effects of stress, which can be very significant depending on how much aggravation the symptoms are causing, but they still feel in control of the situation—at least for now. These women should be aware that they could become Hurried Women and will hopefully take measures to avoid this progression. I feel we should be as concerned about preventing Hurried Woman Syndrome and major depression as we are in treating them.

Technically, the *DSM-IV* classifies what I call Hurried Woman Syndrome as "minor depressive illness" (three to four symptoms of at least two weeks' duration), but I don't find this terminology helpful for two reasons. First, the word *minor* implies to both doctors and patients that this is an insignificant problem that isn't worth much attention, which is far from true. Second, the word *depression* has such negative connotations that many women refuse to pursue any kind of treatment for it because they are afraid of being labeled "crazy" or "weak." Let's face it; no one wants to be depressed. This is another reason I prefer the term *predepression*. Many women, once they understand the relationship between Hurried Woman Syndrome and major depression, perceive the benefit of not waiting until they get their fifth symptom (along with the diagnosis of major depression) before trying to fix the problem. They see the wisdom of viewing Hurried Woman Syndrome as a precursor, or warning sign, and are therefore willing to take positive steps to get better and prevent major depression.

"IT'S SO COMMON" . . . BUT IS IT NORMAL?

I've lectured all over the country to both health care providers and consumers on Hurried Woman Syndrome. Most people recognize the truth of what I'm saying and the importance of identifying and treating this condition immediately. However, some remain skeptical. "Isn't this condition really just 'life'? Everyone is under stress and pressure. This all looks pretty 'normal' to me." But just because something is common doesn't mean it's normal. Remember our example from Chapter 1 of how common it is to be overweight. Just because two-thirds of Americans are obese by government standards doesn't mean this condition is or should be considered normal.

The same holds true for Hurried Woman Syndrome. We could decide that it's normal as we age or experience chronic stress to be tired, feel moody, gain weight, and be indifferent toward sex. But to do so would doom one-third of the thirty million women who experience Hurried Woman Syndrome to develop major depression (that's ten million women who have the power to prevent major depression if they see the importance of doing something now). And it would leave the other twenty million to struggle with these problems, hoping to fight their way back to feeling good again— perhaps with their health and their relationships intact. Let's not make the error of mistaking what we see as common for normal. They are decidedly not the same thing.

CHALLENGES TO THE IDEA OF HURRIED WOMAN SYNDROME

I find that skeptics fall into three categories when it comes to accepting the reality of Hurried Woman Syndrome. First, there are women who want to deny that it's a medical condition because they are afraid to admit they might be having problems coping with the stress they're under. This common attitude is expressed in the following letter.

I heard about Hurried Woman Syndrome from a friend and I've got all the symptoms, but I don't have any major stress in my life, so I'm not sure why I've got this problem. . . . I'm finishing up law school after six years. It took me longer because I'm a single parent trying to raise my nine- and seven-year-old sons while working full-time at my teaching job. . . .

—Shanna

So many Hurried Women, like Shanna, don't see themselves as under pressure, even though they obviously are. It's denial. These women don't want to be labeled with a problem, particularly depression or something like it. Many people will agree that an acute stressor like finding out your seven-year-old child has diabetes or your mother has breast cancer can cause a lot of disruption in your life, adversely affect your brain chemistry, and cause major depression. However, they don't see the connection between continuous lower levels of everyday stress, such as Shanna's raising two boys on her own while working full-time at a demanding job and attending school at the same time. The chronic stress of today's hectic lifestyle is enough to cause the predepression of Hurried Woman Syndrome.

Of course, there's nothing new about denial. It stands in the way of treating all sorts of illnesses, particularly those that come from lifestyle choices such as smoking, alcoholism, drug addiction, and obesity. Many Hurried Women are afraid they will be viewed as weak or defective. They are neither, but they can't accept that yet. Sometimes they're afraid they will have to change the way they approach life in order to get well, and that scares them. None of us wants to be drawn out of our comfort zone, even when there's no comfort there anymore. Sadly, many of these women struggle with the syndrome until it's too late to salvage much of the life they knew before.

I feel very similar to many of your readers and scored in the depressed range on your mood test. These feelings have plagued me for about three years now. I did seek help a couple of years ago, and the doctor prescribed Prozac, which I refused to take. I don't think a pill can solve life's problems. I also went to a therapist a couple of times, but it just became a cry fest and never achieved anything. I'm thirty-eight, single, and have been living with the same boyfriend for seven years. Granted, we've been through some difficult times (failed business, his divorce, business lawsuits, me going back to school and working, etc.), but we've stayed together. Though we don't have sex nearly as much as we once did, I think what is really affecting me the most is the inability to make decisions—I can't think clearly anymore—and not having control over my own life. A feeling of hopelessness and that nothing really matters is overwhelming. How can you start to take control of your life when you have no direction, no energy, no love?

—Julia, age 38

Does this sound like a happy person to you? She is obviously suffering from Hurried Woman Syndrome (or perhaps, major depression) but doesn't want to be thought of as sick or having a problem. She longs to feel better but has decided it's not right for her to take medicine and that counseling is a waste of time. Even worse, she doesn't make the connection between her lifestyle and how she feels. But can anyone really blame her? Isn't the life she describes pretty typical for many women today?

I am twenty-six and have two children, four years and eleven months old. My husband has been telling me I need to see someone for a while and I blow him off. I constantly stress about the kids, the future, everything. My husband works more than full-time so I can stay home, so it's just me and the kids at home, along with another four-year-old and a three-month-old baby I keep. Anyway, I constantly feel rushed, rushed to do everything, no time to rest. I think the line I use most at home is "Hurry up!" I dread going to bed at night because I already know that I don't want to get up the next morning. As for a sex drive—what is sex?

I have no drive at all and I know it frustrates my husband, but I have no control over it. Also, I haven't gained weight, but regardless of all the exercise and watching what I eat, I can't get the baby weight off after almost a year. Please help!
—Tasha, age 26

It's clear that Tasha and her husband have made some lifestyle choices that have raised her stress levels—her husband is working longer hours so she can stay at home with her kids, but she's also watching two other small children to make extra money, presumably to make ends meet. Most couples today make these kinds of life choices all the time. But inherent in this type of decision is a series of trade-offs that makes the choice more difficult. For example, if you pick choice A, you'll be giving up the benefits of choice B. If you choose B instead, you'll lose the benefits from choice A. Life is full of trade-offs, which is what makes these decisions so difficult. They become even tougher when you must look at long-term versus short-term trade-offs. Choice A may have good benefits and minimal costs in the short run but create devastating losses down the road. Choice B may have few benefits and significant cost now but reap a huge reward later. We'll discuss the specifics of how these choices affect us, and particularly how the hidden costs can be significant, later in this book. For now, I want you to see how the hurried lifestyles that most of us have adopted and come to view as routine can have a significant impact on our health and relationships. And continuing to ignore the problem is not the correct solution.

The second type of skeptic actually thinks women with depression are weak and should stop whining, "pull themselves up by their bootstraps," and get on with the business of life. Some of these skeptics are men and some, surprisingly, are women. These people are laboring under a primitive assumption about the nature of depression and don't understand the scientific basis of the illness. They have never experienced depression first-hand. If they had, they would know better than to be critical of those who suffer with major depression or the predepression of Hurried Woman Syndrome. These people need to be educated.

The third type of skeptic, like the first, is also afraid. However, these critics—who are usually women—don't want to acknowledge Hurried Woman Syndrome because they feel it might be seen as the price women pay for attempting to "have it all"—pursuing a high-powered career and having a family, too. They don't want to say that women can't handle it all, perhaps feeling it would be a sign of weakness. Of course, this isn't true either. We've recognized that men need to find a balance between work and home to remain healthy (or regain their health). Why should it be any different for women? It's not an easy task; but it's also not an impossible one. Everyone needs to find an equilibrium between career (whether paid or volunteer or both) and family life. An important key to success is to give women the knowledge they need to recognize when things are becoming unhealthy so they can fix the problem and maintain the balance they need.

CHILDREN AND FAMILIES OF HURRIED WOMEN

Not only do Hurried Women suffer, but many of the people around them suffer, too. Friends, coworkers, employers, and the people who love and need them the most—family—struggle with the effects of Hurried Woman Syndrome. A woman who was about thirty years old came up to speak with me after one of my lectures and related the following story.

About four years ago, I was forging ahead as an accountant with a medium-sized firm in Dallas, Texas. I had finally passed the CPA exam after studying hard for about six months and was looking forward to maybe becoming a partner one day. My hus-

band is a teacher and, since they have the same schedule, he helps a lot with our girls who are both in elementary school now. Even so, tax season (January 15 to April 15) is still brutal. I often work twelve to fourteen hours a day during those three months and see the kids only when I can sneak away from the office for a dinner break. One evening during the last (and worst) week of tax season, I came home from work exhausted and found the kids were still up about two hours past their bedtime. I was furious! I told my husband I was looking forward to getting home with the girls already in bed so I could soak in the tub because "today has been the rottenest day of my life!" My youngest, about three then, burst into tears and ran to her room, while the six-year-old withdrew to the couch. After the furor, my husband explained to me that he had allowed the girls to wait up late so they could see me—which hadn't happened for more than an hour over the last three days—and give me the special card they had spent much of the afternoon creating for me with their own little hands. It was a beautifully decorated card which read, "To the Best Mommy in the Whole World. We Miss You So Much!"

—Rita in Dallas

She told me that after she assuaged the hurt feelings, she decided then and there to make some changes in her life. After hearing her story and realizing I had been lecturing away from home too much lately, I decided to do the same thing. The good news is that much of the damage described in Rita's story can be undone quickly, particularly if the situation doesn't go on too long. However, some of the emotional scars borne by the loved ones of Hurried Women can run deep.

We've been married for fifteen years and have two great kids. My wife is the perfect mother. She goes to all the kids' programs at school, makes all of their ball games, serves as homeroom mother, and is even on the board of the PTA. I know it sounds selfish, but what happened to me? She is never interested in being intimate anymore. We had a great sex life before the kids came, but now it's as though I am repulsive to her. She doesn't even want to hug me because she says, "It leads to other things." I'm forty-three and have tried to keep myself in good physical shape, but she on the other hand has gained about thirty pounds and says the reason she doesn't want to be intimate is that she's self-conscious about her weight. Her usual excuse is "I'm too tired." What I need to understand is this: If she is willing to spend so much time and energy sacrificing to please our children, why won't she put even half of that same effort into our relationship? I love her just like she is and tell her that often, but it's like it doesn't matter. I can't stand to feel this way, but I'm jealous of my own children! I feel abandoned emotionally. What can I do to fix this problem?

—Dave in Memphis

What comes through clearly in this scenario is that two of the symptoms of Hurried Woman Syndrome, fatigue and weight gain, have played a dominant role in creating problems with intimacy—the symptoms perpetuate each other.

MOTHERHOOD, AGING, AND THE HURRIED WOMAN SYNDROME

I am forty-eight and have three children from ages nine to fifteen. They are all active in at least two sports, and between my work, their schoolwork, and checking on my mother who is in a nearby nursing home, we don't have time for much fun these days. We usually eat meals on the run and my husband, who also works full-time, often carts one child to one activity while I take the other two kids somewhere else. I don't have time to exercise and my weight has been steadily climbing (I won't tell you how much I weigh!). I don't know why I'm having so much trouble

coping with all of this now, because I've been doing it for years.
What's going on here?

—Dana, age 48

This question is frequently asked by many Hurried Women—why is this happening *now*? There are two answers: one that applies to this woman's situation and another that applies to women—and everyone—in general. Dana was able to successfully juggle all of these things in her life a few years ago for a lot of reasons. First, she was younger. I can attest to the fact that I'm not nearly as energetic at forty-seven as I was at thirty-seven. And I've even noticed a difference between forty-seven and forty-five. Satchel Paige said, "Age is a question of mind over matter. If you don't mind, it doesn't matter." However, the baseball legend was not talking about raising children! Age does matter when it comes to energy levels.

Second, I think time itself is a factor in causing fatigue. Mothering is a 24/7 job. There's a sign in my office that says, "Motherhood ain't for sissies," and believe me, it's not. Raising a family is hard work, particularly if it's your second job. Let's say on an average day you crank out eight or nine short, fun-filled hours at "the plant," then you come home to prop your feet up, read the newspaper, and be served a wonderful dinner that someone else prepared for you. Right? Wrong! Instead, you come home to begin your second shift—cooking, cleaning house, washing clothes, helping with homework, paying bills, and shuttling kids from baseball to band rehearsal to wherever else they want to go. And then, at the end of a very tiring day, you need to be sure to have saved some time and energy to be intimate with your husband—who's been looking a little purple around the collar lately. Are you tired yet? Anyone would be. But, this fatiguing lifestyle is not confined to women who work outside the home.

Stay-at-home moms also get tired because they often pick up the slack at school and extracurricular activities for the parents who work all day. There is a sisterhood among mothers. Stay-at-home moms usually get sixteen hours a day of uninterrupted pleasure at their chosen profession—motherhood—particularly when the children are of preschool age. I love my four children very much, but if I had stayed at home with them every day, sixteen hours a day, seven days a week, for about 358 days a year (as my wife did), they would have been stuffed and mounted on the living room wall, particularly in those early years. I don't have the mental and emotional stamina to do my wife's job, and believe it or not, my kids are really good children. The chronic stress of raising kids through their teens can wreak havoc on anyone's brain chemistry.

THE STRESS OF TODAY'S LIFESTYLE

There has been much speculation about why Hurried Woman Syndrome has become such an epidemic in recent years. Dana, from the preceding letter, typifies three major demographic shifts that have occurred over the last few decades. These sociologic changes have dramatically raised stress levels for women.

The first of these stressors is work. U.S. Department of Labor statistics reveal that twice as many women with school-age children were working full-time jobs in 2000 as did in 1964. Women are also in much more stressful employment situations, both physically and emotionally, than they were thirty or forty years ago. I'm not saying that women shouldn't work or hold high-stress jobs. But balancing work and home must be a priority for working women, just as it should be for working men. To ignore the importance of maintaining this balance can have severe health and even social repercussions.

The second major stressor comes from a combination of delayed childbearing and increasing longevity. The later in life a woman starts having children, the more likely she is to have older, needier parents while she is still trying to raise her own children. This is the so-called sandwich generation phenomenon.

Third, with divorce rates still hovering around 50 percent, many women are attempting to balance all of the competing needs in their lives alone. High levels of stress, particularly when they remain high for long periods of time, will often lead to the adverse changes in brain chemistry of Hurried Woman Syndrome and major depression. Given the present social situation, it is little wonder that so many women—almost 1:4—are experiencing Hurried Woman Syndrome. It is a modern epidemic.

3

ARE YOU A HURRIED WOMAN?

As discussed in the earlier chapters, the symptoms that plague Hurried Women are symptoms of depression. Yet, the difference between the two is not the *type* of chemical imbalance in the brain—the levels of serotonin, dopamine, and norepinephrine are out of balance in both depression and Hurried Woman Syndrome—but the *degree* of that imbalance. Make no mistake; they are very similar problems. Indeed, for most women, the road to major depression passes through Hurried Woman Syndrome. The Attitude and Mood Self-Assessment Quiz that follows will help you find out whether you are on this road and, if so, how far down it.

☸ ATTITUDE AND MOOD SELF-ASSESSMENT QUIZ

Instructions

1. Either photocopy this form or use a separate sheet of paper and write the numbers 1 through 20 down the left margin.

2. Read each statement carefully and answer each question on your answer sheet in the way that best describes how frequently you have felt this way *during the past month*. The answer scale is as follows: A = much or most of the time; B = often, but not a lot; C = occasionally; and D = little or very rarely.

3. Try to answer the questions honestly and don't look ahead to the scoring until after you've finished. If you are presently on a diet, answer questions 6 and 16 as you would have before you began dieting.

Statements

	ANSWER	SCORE
1. I feel sad or blue.	A	5
2. I still find joy in the things I do.	C	3
3. I cry (or feel like crying) more than I used to.	A	4
4. I get a good night's sleep.	C	3
5. I feel useful.	D	4
6. I eat as much as I always have.	A	1
7. I can make decisions easily.	D	4
8. I feel that some people would be better off if I were gone.	D	1
9. I feel good about the future.	D	4

		42	Yo
10.	I feel restless and need to keep moving.		
11.	I feel lonely or like to be alone.		
12.	I get tired for no reason.	A	5
13.	I can think clearly.	D	4
14.	Mornings are my best time of day.	A	1
15.	I don't feel good.	B	4
16.	I've been gaining (losing) weight.	A	5
17.	I am happy with my sex life.	D	5
18.	I find it easy to do things.	D	4
19.	I look forward to a challenge.	C	3
20.	I just don't want to get out of bed.	B	5
	TOTAL		70

Using the scoring guide in Appendix A, tally each answer, total your score, and check the table below to see where you are on the depression scale:

SCORE	*Attitude/Mood Assessment*
< 30	Normal
30–39	Stressed but recoverable
40–55	Hurried Woman Syndrome
56–64	Hurried Woman Syndrome with possible depression creeping in
≥ 65	Significant depression likely

If your score is less than 30, you're normal or at least as normal as most of us can hope to be. If your score is between 30 and 39, re feeling the effects of stress on your brain chemistry, but you an reverse these changes with some rather simple adjustments. You don't have enough symptoms to be a Hurried Woman, but if things get worse instead of better, you'll be there.

If you scored between 40 and 64, you definitely have Hurried Woman Syndrome. Your brain chemistry is far enough out of balance to cause trouble—at home, at work, in your relationships—but not far enough to qualify as major depression. The various recommendations in this book will help you ease the stresses in your life that are making you feel less than 100 percent. Although antidepressants can be very helpful in reversing the ill effects that stress causes in your brain chemistry, they won't get rid of the stress that threw your chemicals out of balance in the first place. Only you can do that.

If your score is 65 or higher, it's extremely likely that you are experiencing major depression or will very soon. Medical research shows that it's in your best interest to consult your doctor as soon as possible. Major depression is a serious health threat, and medication will most likely be helpful in getting you back to feeling like yourself again. Besides, there are several medical conditions other than Hurried Woman Syndrome that look a lot like depression, and the possibility of these conditions need to be investigated before you assume that your symptoms are definitely depression.

MEDICAL CAUSES OF DEPRESSION SYMPTOMS

Many medical conditions can cause symptoms of depression, particularly fatigue. If your score placed you in the Hurried Woman Syndrome range or higher, you owe it to yourself to go to your doctor and at least rule out other common health problems. The following discussion cannot replace a conference with your doctor, but

I include it to help you organize your thoughts before you have your appointment. You can't expect to cure all your medical problems by reading a book or two and having a brief visit with whoever happens to be behind the counter at the health-food store. You've got to trust your physician to help you sort this stuff out. However, some doctors aren't familiar with the terms *Hurried Woman Syndrome*, *predepression*, or *minor depressive illness*. Remember that although most practitioners are up-to-date on major depression, many have not heard of the milder forms of this illness and may not recognize them without some gentle prodding. You should become very familiar with Hurried Woman Syndrome because you may need to describe it briefly to your doctor. Now, let's discuss other common medical causes of fatigue.

ANEMIA

Anemia is a very common cause of fatigue in women, particularly those who are still menstruating. About 5–7 percent of women in their reproductive years will be anemic on a screening test. If you have long periods (more than five to seven days of flow) or heavy cycles (pass large clots or experience flooding), be certain to mention this to your physician. If the fatigue seems much worse during or immediately after your menstrual cycle, or if you have been anemic in the past, then anemia is much more likely than depression to be the cause. A complete blood count (CBC) is a simple and inexpensive test to screen for anemia. Besides checking your iron status, it may also give a hint to nutritional problems such as a deficiency in folic acid (folate) or vitamin B_{12} (cyanocobalamin) or to underlying problems with blood formation that can cause anemia. Some chronic diseases like lupus, thyroid disturbances, stomach ulcers, and even cancer can cause anemia as well. If your periods are heavy and your CBC comes back normal, you may want to repeat the test right after a menstrual cycle. Some women are anemic for only a few days after their cycle but feel fatigued for much longer, even though their blood count rebounds pretty quickly.

THYROID DISEASE

Thyroid disease is very common in women. About 12 percent of women have either too much (hyperthyroidism) or—more commonly—too little thyroid hormone (hypothyroidism). Thyroid hormone directly regulates our metabolism and indirectly controls many other body functions. Symptoms associated with hypothyroidism are fatigue, weight gain, intolerance to cold, constipation, mental dullness, and menstrual irregularities. This is why hypothyroidism is so easily confused with depression and Hurried Woman Syndrome—the symptoms are very similar. Overall, more than 10 percent of American women are estimated to have hypothyroidism. Hyperthyroidism, an excess of thyroid hormone, causes agitation and anxiety, a racing pulse, heat intolerance, and weight loss. If hyperthyroidism is left untreated for an extended period of time, the person will "burn out" from the high thyroid levels and begin to tire out and experience fatigue and weight gain, which can be confusing.

The only way to accurately screen for thyroid disease in women, particularly those taking hormones such as birth control pills or hormone replacement therapy, is to test the thyroid-stimulating hormone (TSH) level. TSH is the chemical signal the brain uses to make the thyroid gland produce more thyroid hormone. So when TSH is up, thyroid levels are low and the brain is asking the thyroid gland for help. Thyroid screening in women can be confusing because sex hormones, particularly estrogen, affect the way thyroid hormone is carried throughout the body and make the "traditional" thyroid level (T_4) inadequate to assess thyroid status fully.

Some women may benefit from low doses of thyroid hormone, even when their lab tests come back normal. The normal range of thyroid hormone in humans is very wide. In most labs, the acceptable range for TSH is between 0.5 and 4.5 ng/dl. You're just as normal when your TSH is 0.5 as when it's 4.5; however, you may weigh five pounds more at 4.5 than at 0.5. Many women with fatigue or weight concerns who also have a "high normal" TSH (low normal thyroid hormone level) will see five to seven pounds come off when they start a low dose of thyroid hormone. You shouldn't expect a remarkable turnaround from low-dose replacement, but it does happen occasionally. It is important not to push people out of the normal range artificially to encourage unhealthy weight loss, but if your TSH is in the high normal range, ask your doctor if you would benefit from a low dose of thyroid hormone.

MENOPAUSE AND PERIMENOPAUSE

Most women have heard a lot of information about these two conditions recently and are much more aware of them now than they were a few years back. But there is still confusion regarding what to do about the symptoms and how to preserve long-term health. Many physicians are also confused about the conflicting information. The symptoms of menopause and perimenopause not only look like those of Hurried Woman Syndrome, but they can also interfere with treatment. It's important to assess your perimenopausal or menopausal status when suspecting a diagnosis of Hurried Woman Syndrome to avoid this potential confusion.

Menopause is defined by two specific events: cessation of menstruation (your periods stop because your ovaries no longer produce eggs), and cessation of estrogen production (because your ovaries no longer produce eggs, they no longer produce estrogen, specifically estradiol). Small amounts of estrogen do come from the adrenal glands and from fat cells, which convert other hormones into weak estrogens after menopause. However, these estrogens (estriol and estrone) are much weaker than the estradiol produced by the ovaries before menopause and are produced in much lower quantities. The drop in estrogen action that occurs in menopause accounts for most of the symptoms many women experience—hot flushes (often called "flashes"), night sweats, insomnia or restlessness, emotional lability (the technical term for moodiness), decreased ability to concentrate, and fatigue.

Follicle-stimulating hormone (FSH) is the test used to diagnose menopause. It is the chemical signal the brain uses when it wants more estrogen. Like its cousin TSH, FSH is an "inverted test." When estrogen levels are low, FSH will be high and vice versa. Unfortunately, FSH level only shows whether a woman is in menopause at the time of the test. It cannot predict when menopause will occur in the future. Thus, an FSH that's normal today may be in the menopausal range in a few weeks. Even more frustrating, FSH levels can sometimes be equivocal—somewhere between the normal and menopausal ranges.

The best way to handle the latter situation is to assume that you are not in menopause yet and repeat the test in a month or two. This is important for a number of reasons, the most significant of which is pregnancy protection. Women in menopause cannot become pregnant because they no longer ovulate, but women who aren't in menopause—even if it's coming very soon—can and do become pregnant. I've had many patients who thought they were through having children twenty years earlier, only to find themselves pregnant again at age forty-seven! Needless to say, reactions to this vary quite a bit. Although natural fertility wanes steadily after the age of thirty, it's best to assume you can become pregnant until menopause is officially diagnosed.

Perimenopause is the time between when you experience regular menstrual cycles and the menopause itself. Perimenopause can last anywhere from two to three months to two to three years. This time of life is often marked by all of the familiar menopausal symptoms—mood swings, hot flashes, and night sweats—but you still have menstrual cycles, although they become more and more irregular. They can be closer together (but no less than twenty days apart) or further apart. Many women skip two or even three cycles at a time. Irregular menstrual cycles and mood swings are the hallmark symptoms of perimenopause.

The reason for all of these symptoms is not a lack of estrogen—that's menopause—but rather, fluctuating levels of estrogen. Perimenopause is something of an estrogen roller coaster. Estrogen levels wax and wane irregularly, which produces the irritating and often unpredictable symptoms. We will discuss menopause and perimenopause more thoroughly in Chapter 6 and cover the good, the bad, and the ugly effects of hormone replacement and how they impact the Hurried Woman. For now, it's important to realize that menopause and perimenopause can mimic both depression and predepression.

Autoimmune Diseases and Arthritis

Lupus, rheumatoid arthritis, ankylosing spondylitis, polymyalgia rheumatica, and polyarteritis nodosa are not only diseases that are hard to pronounce but also tend to cause fatigue, bone pain, muscle aches, odd skin rashes, and other unusual symptoms. A full discussion of these illnesses is too involved for this book, but it's important to tell your doctor if you have any of these symptoms in addition to fatigue, moodiness, weight gain, and low sex drive. Most doctors will screen for these illnesses with an antinuclear antibody (ANA) test and a sedimentation rate (sed rate) as a minimum. Suspicious results on these tests or other symptoms peculiar to one of these conditions often lead to more sophisticated screening.

Infections

Most infections cause fatigue. Acute infections, both viral and bacterial, are typically recognized by patients because the associated symptoms are readily apparent. Most women know something's wrong when they have a fever, chills, nausea, vomiting, diarrhea, and so on. However, some more chronic viral infections, low-grade upper respiratory and sinus infections, and urinary tract infections can drag you down over time. Even allergies can do this. Some viral infections can be followed by an extended postviral syndrome that may persist for several weeks or months after the acute infection is gone, and relapses are common. Mononucleosis is probably the most well-known among this group of infections. Sometimes the time that elapses since the acute infection is so long that the patient doesn't see the connection. Broad-based screening tests are often used to pick up the telltale signs of low-grade, persistent or recurrent infections.

OTHER ILLNESSES

Many other conditions include fatigue as a symptom, including cancer, heart disease, lung disease, kidney failure, diabetes, high blood pressure, Addison's disease (adrenal gland insufficiency), multiple sclerosis, and Parkinson's disease to name a few. Since fatigue is such a pervasive symptom for a wide variety of ailments, you need a doctor to help sort it out.

GOING TO THE DOCTOR

The main point of this discussion is to help you organize your thoughts and create a list and time line of your symptoms before visiting your doctor. Write down any over-the-counter (OTC) medicines or home remedies you may have tried or (more importantly) are still taking. Also, gather a little family history about the diseases discussed earlier. Think about your menstrual history, weight gain or loss over the last year or two, and any changes in your appetite or diet, and write them down in note form so you can take it with you to your appointment.

Now, can you guess which of the other medical causes of fatigue is the most common? About 12 percent of women have thyroid problems and about 5 percent of menstruating women are anemic, but recent research shows that almost 30 percent of women in America suffer either from the collection of symptoms that comprise Hurried Woman Syndrome or from major depression. This is a huge problem. If your score on the Attitude and Mood Self-Assessment Quiz was 40–64, your fatigue, moodiness, weight gain, and lack of sexual interest are coming from the brain chemistry imbalance of Hurried Woman Syndrome—nowhere else. And if you don't do something about it, you are placing yourself in significant danger of developing major depression.

Skeptics often ask, "Why is treating Hurried Woman Syndrome so important?" There are several answers to this question, but the most important reason is that it is a predepressed state and avoiding major depression can have huge payoffs—both physically and emotionally—for you and also for society in general.

WHY MAJOR DEPRESSION IS A SERIOUS HEALTH PROBLEM

Depression is a major medical illness. World Health Organization statistics show that rates of depression and suicide are increasing rapidly in virtually every civilized culture throughout the world, and the first episode of depression is also occurring at an earlier age. Government health agencies estimate that nineteen million adults in the United States will experience a depressive illness this year and that every American has a 1:6 risk of developing major depression in their lifetime. Even worse is the news that more than half of those people who experience depression never seek medical attention and therefore often suffer devastating outcomes with regard to health, employment, and quality-of-life issues, as do the people around them.

Lasting Changes in the Brain and Body

Many people, both health care professionals and the public at large, believe depression is only a "mental" illness, meaning "it's all in your mind." This is why many people fail to see the connection between depression and physical symptoms like fatigue, weight gain, and low libido, as well as other major medical illnesses. Depression and chronic medical conditions like heart disease, diabetes, and high blood pressure share a two-way relationship in that they may cause or worsen each other. Not only does depression make us more vulnerable to other illnesses, it actually causes physical changes in the brain that can be permanent.

Modern brain imaging techniques have not only verified the cause of depression to be a chemical imbalance in the serotonin-dopamine-norepinephrine system in the brain, but they have also documented that permanent structural changes occur in the brains of depressed people. Depression leaves "footprints" or scars in the brain, particularly the hippocampus. This area of the brain is particularly important to perception, memory, and mood. Depression causes shrinkage, or atrophy, of the hippocampus and the amount of atrophy is directly related to the severity of the depression.

Unfortunately, the changes in brain structure caused by depression appear to be permanent. Just as a heart attack leaves permanent scars in the heart muscle, depression leaves permanent scars in the brain tissue.

HURRIED WOMAN SYNDROME: ONE STEP SHORT OF MAJOR DEPRESSION

We've already discussed the difference between major depression and Hurried Woman Syndrome on the basis of what we see clinically. Brain imaging techniques have shown that Hurried Women demonstrate the same atrophy and tissue loss in the hippocampus as women with major depression. The amount of tissue loss is less than that seen in major depression, but the hippocampus of a woman with Hurried Woman Syndrome is measurably smaller than normal. Is it "all in your head" as some skeptics believe? Yes, in the sense that it's in your *brain*. Remember, the loss of brain tissue worsens the longer the symptoms last and becomes much more pronounced if the Hurried Woman develops more symptoms and becomes depressed. In other words, treating Hurried Woman Syndrome as early as possible can help prevent the progression of permanent brain damage.

COMMON MISCONCEPTIONS ABOUT HURRIED WOMAN SYNDROME

Whenever I present my research on Hurried Woman Syndrome, whether to a group of health care professionals or to the general public, there are usually a few doubters. There are three common misconceptions that I hear repeatedly.

MISCONCEPTION #1: THIS IS THE BODY'S NORMAL REACTION TO STRESS. WHY TREAT IT?

It seems logical to some that if the body is supposed to react to stress this way—increased levels of norepinephrine and cortisol, causing the symptoms of Hurried Woman Syndrome—then we shouldn't intervene in this normal process.

I like to look at an analogous situation in the body. Imagine taking a sharp knife and rubbing it lightly over your forearm. The knife scratches your skin but doesn't draw any blood. You can see the red line where the skin was scratched, but with a little time, your forearm returns to the exact state it was in before the knife touched it. Your arm reacted appropriately to an external stressor (the knife) and was able to fix the minimal changes it experienced.

Imagine if you repeated the maneuver, but this time you applied a little more pressure with the knife. You would now see small drops of blood on your skin following the path of the blade. Without any intervention, your forearm would still heal back to the state it was in before the knife touched it, but a thin scar would remain. Is your forearm still normal? Many of our skeptics would say that it is because it healed without any intervention. However, I would argue that although the forearm responded "normally" to the stress it endured—healing with a scar—it is not exactly the same as it was before the knife stressed it. Now there's a scar.

Next imagine applying enough pressure with the knife to cut into the deeper layers of skin. The knife severs veins, arteries, nerves, and muscle tissue. Three fingers no longer move, and the pain is excruciating. Your arm responded in the normal, expected fashion to the stress it encountered, but it is clearly no longer "normal." Indeed, in this example, the tissue did react "normally" to the level of stress inflicted on it, but the tissue has been transformed by the event and is now clearly abnormal. And depending on the level of damage, it may have lost forever some important functioning because of the injury caused by the stressor.

Similarly, the changes in brain chemistry we recognize as Hurried Woman Syndrome are the expected result from chronic stress. Whether the woman suffering from it can return to totally normal function depends on how severe the disturbance in brain chemistry is and how long it has lasted.

Misconception #2: This Is So Common, It Must Be Normal.

I don't want to beat a dead horse, but I hear this over and over. Part of it depends on your definition of *normal*. If you mean frequently occurring, it's true that Hurried Woman Syndrome is that. I tend to define *normal* as healthy. It is evident that Hurried Woman Syndrome isn't a normal, healthy circumstance from the amount of disruption it causes in people's lives. Duke University researchers David Beck and Harold Koenig, in their 1996 literature review in the *International Journal of Psychiatric Medicine*, identified minor depression, or Hurried Woman Syndrome, as (1) the third leading cause of lost time from work for women, (2) a major contributor to marital discord and divorce, and (3) a significant risk factor for progression to major depression. According to Wolfgang Maier and associates in their 1997 article published in the *Journal of Affective Disorders*, the degree of life disruption from this condition parallels that of major depression, "and the need for treatment is comparable."

I think that women with the syndrome and the people who live with them, work with them, and love them deserve to know that the problem can be fixed before it escalates and before it causes damage to their lives.

MISCONCEPTION #3: IF MY CHANCES ARE ONLY 1:3, WHY NOT JUST WAIT AND SEE?

Hurried Women have the power to turn their situation around with a variety of techniques, including cognitive-behavioral coping strategies, medication, or a combination of these approaches (which we'll discuss in Chapters 4 and 5). However, ignoring the problem will allow one-third of women with the syndrome to lapse into major depression where all treatment options are much less effective, particularly those that don't involve medication.

I suspect that if better data were available, we'd be pleased to find that a significant portion of women with Hurried Woman Syndrome actually do get better on their own over time. They either realize something's wrong and take steps to slow down and get better, or the stressors in their life become less stressful—the kids grow up, the troubled marriage ends or improves, they change jobs, and so on—but at what cost? How long does it take to hurt feelings, scar relationships, lose a job, or alienate a spouse? I'm afraid that "wait and see" ends up being "delay and pay" for most Hurried Women. Preventing major depression is a worthy goal in itself, but it's important to remember that women who are one symptom short of major depression aren't particularly happy people. They deserve to feel better.

PARTIAL SOLUTIONS

Women who decide to do something to get better often start with a do-it-yourself approach. They usually go to the health-food store or pick up a self-help book or two, looking for a plan. Unfortunately, the herbal supplement route doesn't work very well for most Hurried Women and self-help books, at least up until now, are focused on only one facet of the Hurried Woman Syndrome—a diet book, a book on relationships, or a primer on reducing stress—thereby missing the forest for the trees and resulting in only a partial solution and, ultimately, frustration.

Other women appropriately view their symptoms as a possible medical problem and go to their doctor or nurse practitioner for help. Many health care providers will recognize the syndrome immediately and offer appropriate medical therapy. However, unless you are aware of Hurried Woman Syndrome and can explain it in fifty words or less, doctors and nurse practitioners who are locked into the "chief complaint model" will start focusing on just one symptom and will likely miss the diagnosis of Hurried Woman Syndrome or predepression.

In a 1993 study by Laurence Kirmayer and others published in the *American Journal of Psychiatry*, it was found that 69–80 percent of outpatients with major depression visited their health care provider with a complaint related exclusively to a physical symptom. In other words, the doctor or nurse practitioner was not aware of a mood problem at all until depression screening took place. It's also important to recognize that the patient didn't perceive a possible link between his or her chief complaint—a physical symptom—and the other symptoms of depression.

Unfortunately, some health care providers don't begin to think of major depression until the patient stops showing up for work, can't get out of bed, or starts writing suicide notes. We must become more aware of the fact that major depression often exists in people who outwardly appear very functional. Of course, if we have trouble spotting major depression among our patients, imagine how much more trouble we have properly identifying minor depression. People with minor depression are usually more functional than those with major depression and their symptoms are fewer and less severe. Yet as we have discussed before, both need attention.

4

USING COGNITIVE-BEHAVIORAL COPING SKILLS

Whenever I introduce the term *cognitive-behavioral coping strategies* at a lecture—unless I'm in a room full of mental health professionals such as psychiatrists, psychologists, therapists, social workers, and counselors—I always get a deer-in-the-headlights response from the audience. The term sounds intimidating and terribly "psychological." But if you break it down into its component parts, it makes more sense. *Cognition* means "thinking." In this sense, it's not the action of having a thought, but the content of the thought itself. Our thoughts and perceptions to a great extent determine our behavior and, on a more philosophical level, the way we view ourselves and the world around us. Similar to the notion "you are what you eat," people are what they *think* they are. Each of us views our surroundings from our own unique perspective and from that perspective comes our own personal sense of reality. If I think I'm fat, then I am fat. It really doesn't matter what I actually weigh or how others view me. That's my personal reality and my perception of that reality.

The attitudes and thoughts that come from our inner perception determine our behavior. An adolescent with anorexia nervosa looks in the mirror at her undernourished skeleton and thinks she is fat and unattractive. That is her reality. And although everyone tells her that she's obviously wrong, based on her own personal reality, she is grossly overweight and therefore will not eat. This is an extreme example, but it shows that what we think (cognition) definitely influences what we do (our behavior).

Cognitive-behavioral coping therapy focuses on changing our behavior by altering the way we think, particularly correcting our errors in logic ("If I lose this job, I'll never find another one"), false beliefs ("No one listens to me"), and negative thinking ("I should have accomplished more by this point in my life"). It seeks to shine a flashlight on these monsters in our mind's closet and help us to recognize and remove them from our thinking. We can then learn new ways to deal with situations we previously dreaded or found difficult and defeating. Variations on cognitive-behavioral therapies include rational-emotive behavior therapy, relaxation training, cognitive restructuring, and others. A similar approach that has become quite popular is called coaching therapy, or simply coaching. It sounds a lot less intimidating but appears to offer similar benefits.

Coaching is action oriented and focuses on a person's current life and plans for the future in contrast to traditional psychotherapy, which often focuses on the past in an attempt to heal old emotional wounds. In a 2001 study by James Barrett and colleagues of 114 primary care patients, cognitive-behavioral coping strategies were just as effective as antidepressants in treating minor depressive illness (Hurried Woman Syndrome). Similar results were reported by Martin Keller and others in a report published in the *New England Journal of Medicine* on 681 patients with chronic depression. It would appear that identifying what causes stress and worry in your life, developing a different perspective on these stressors, and making some adjustments in your approach to life to lower your stress levels is a reasonable alternative to medication in curing Hurried Woman Syndrome. And without the potential side effects of medication.

THE STRESS EQUATION

With all the stress of modern life piling up these days, why do some women get Hurried Woman Syndrome while others don't? We can look at the "stress equation" to explain this:

$$(\text{Genetics} + \text{Stressors} - \text{Resources}) \times \text{Duration} = \text{Effect of stress on brain chemistry balance}$$

GENETICS

Our genetic makeup determines who we are physically. The strands of DNA within each cell contain the entire genetic code necessary to make a complete human being. This is why the concept of cloning is possible. Our genes determine our hair color, height, and blood type. They also dictate to a large extent how our bodies function— our metabolism, how fast we can run, how far we can see. Science is coming to understand that heredity also determines our susceptibility to diseases like diabetes, alcoholism, heart disease, and depression. In Chapter 2 we discussed the natural rebalancer system and how it keeps the brain's critical neurotransmitters in line to avoid symptoms of depression. One proposed explanation for why some women develop Hurried Woman Syndrome and others don't is that the attributes of the natural rebalancer system, like the other systems in the body, are determined by our genetic makeup. It may be that some rebalancers are more susceptible to the effects of stress than others and perhaps that different kinds of stress have more effect on one type of rebalancer system than another. Genetic susceptibility has been demonstrated in many other stress-related illnesses, and it is very likely that genetic susceptibility plays a role in the development of Hurried Woman Syndrome as well. Of course, we can change our *jeans*, but we can't change our *genes*—we have to learn to live with them.

We've all heard about the healthy lifestyle choices people with a family history of heart disease can make to avoid suffering the same fate as their forbearers—avoid smoking, stay fit through exercise and diet, and keep cholesterol under control.

We have long recognized that bad lifestyle choices can cause disease, but we are just beginning to realize that good lifestyle choices can help us treat diseases and, even more important, prevent them. It's critical to choose a healthier lifestyle when confronted with an illness, but it's even more critical to choose that lifestyle before the damage begins. Prevention can be a more powerful tool than treatment. And as we've already discussed, Hurried Woman Syndrome is largely a preventable illness—as is major depression.

STRESSORS

Benjamin Franklin said that the only two things that are certain in this world are death and taxes. The third one we have today is stress. We all must deal with stress on a daily basis. It comes to us in many forms and through many different circumstances.

Whether a stressor is perceived as positive or negative depends on the perception of the recipient. The amount of stress one experiences from a given stressor also depends on how the stress is perceived. Many factors affect the perception of a stressor. One is the amount of emotional investment one has in the situation. Leaving for work and being unable to locate your umbrella would probably cause less stress than being unable to locate your car.

Another factor is previous experience. For example, when your husband tells you he's invited his boss over for dinner at the last minute, you're more likely to feel extra negative pressure if the last time this happened the evening was a fiasco. If, instead, it was followed by his getting a promotion, you might feel stressed but look forward to the evening as another opportunity to help your husband advance his career and perhaps as an enjoyable social occasion. We use our memory of prior experiences to process each external stimulus and assign meaning to it.

Another factor in perceiving the impact of a stressor is the circumstances surrounding it. When the telephone rings at my house after midnight, it startles me and I might become a little anxious because it's usually either a call to run to the hospital or someone saying a family member is in trouble. The same ring earlier in the evening may be an annoyance, but it doesn't make my heart race.

Finally, the amount of stress we perceive from a stimulus can be altered or amplified by the stress burden we are laboring under already. In other words, a little stressor can become a big stressor if we're already stressed out. Once we reach a certain level of feeling pressured, it's as if each additional stressor gets blown up out of proportion as opposed to what it would have been under different circumstances. Let's say you're already behind schedule getting ready for work, where you're due to make a big presentation to an important client, when your seven-year-old spills grape juice all over his only clean school uniform shirt—white, of course— and you explode. If not for the big presentation, you would have had seven hours of sleep instead of three, gotten the other uniform shirts washed the night before, not been so tired that getting up and ready for work took you thirty minutes longer than usual, and not blown up at a seven-year-old who loves you more than life itself over a simple careless act of childhood. This is the stress amplifier effect. Once your level of stress reaches a critical point, additional stress doesn't just increase on a 1:1 ratio; it is multiplied two, three, or more times.

Interestingly, the only factor that determines how much additional stress a new stressor brings over which we don't have positive control is the stressor itself. We determine our perspective by the way we think—we decide how much emotion to invest in any given situation. We interpret the surrounding circumstances to suit our view of life. We catalog our memories and cast them in the emotions of our choosing. We have made almost all of the decisions about family, career, activities, and how to prioritize them that have brought us to our current level of stress. In great measure, we set our level of stress; no one does it for us. Yes, other people often throw stressors our way, but we decide how to perceive them and we place the relative value on each one. This also means *we* can change the level of stress!

RESOURCES FOR STAVING OFF HURRIED WOMAN SYNDROME

Resources are the tools we possess to lower our stress levels. The more resources we have, the more likely we are to be able to handle stress without encountering physical or psychological symptoms. Resources include people, money, experience, and time.

• **People.** Although the people in our lives often bring us more stress, they can also be very helpful in coping with it. Grandparents can babysit. Church friends cook meals for each other when there's a death in the family. Work friends gather at lunch to catch up on reactions to world events and to share what else is happening in each other's lives. Women who have a strong social support system are often able to cope with stress more effectively than those who are isolated and don't experience the emotional and psychological benefits of talking and interacting with friends.

• **Money.** Money is a resource not because it can "buy happiness," but because it can be used to hire a housecleaning service or buy an extra restaurant meal now and then. It can hire a babysitter for an afternoon or a night out on a regular basis. Money can also provide the means for much-needed "retail therapy" (men call it shopping). It's amazing how a new pair of shoes or a new CD by a favorite artist can disperse dark clouds. Of course, money can cut both ways if it isn't handled properly; debt can be a major stressor. But generally women who have access to money and use it wisely tend to cope better with stress.

• **Experience.** Experience helps take a lot of the anxiety out of many situations. When a patient is having her first baby, her prenatal visits last almost three times longer than those of women who are having their second or third child. Experience and training are much the same idea. Once a colleague has shown you how to handle a sticky situation successfully, the new confidence you acquire keeps your anxiety levels down when a similar situation arises and you can handle it on your own. In broader terms, we might call the sum of training and experience the ability to cope. It's important to realize that our ability to cope comes from learning not only through experience but also through education. Coping skills can be taught quite effectively.

• **Time.** Time can be a major resource to lower the effects of stress, but who's got it? In particular, women who have lots of stress don't feel they have enough time to do everything. Time is a precious commodity, and it's important to use it wisely. I don't say this to urge you to cram more stuff into your already busy day but rather to encourage you not to spend the time you have on things that aren't important to you. This may seem obvious, but many of us find ourselves doing things not because they are important or fulfilling but because we feel obligated to do so. The most frequent complaint of Hurried Women, other than being fatigued, is that they lack time or at least have the feeling that they're short on time. That's the reason I chose to call this condition Hurried Woman Syndrome—the perception of always being short on time, or hurried, is one of its key features.

DURATION

The longer we must deal with a stressor, the more effect it has on our overall stress levels and physiology. This means that even small stressors endured for an extended period can have the same overall effect on our brain chemistry as a major stressor endured for a much shorter time. While a Hurried Woman probably recognizes her big stressors, she is also dealing with innumerable small stressors that often pass under her conscious radar yet still have a cumulative effect on her overall stress level. In fact, many Hurried Women can't identify any major stressors that caused the syndrome; the little ones simply added up over time.

IN SUMMARY

All of this may seem obvious, but the following key points are worth repeating:

• We determine how "big" a stressor is through the way we think about ourselves and the perceptions we hold about the situations in which we're involved. This means we can lower the effect stress has on us by changing our thinking and perceptions.

• Eliminating unnecessary stressors, particularly the small ones, will have a positive effect on our overall level of stress. For most Hurried Women, the small stressors are the only ones that can be removed easily.

• Maximizing the use of our resources can minimize the effects of stress on our bodies and brain chemistry. This includes not wasting precious resources on things that aren't that important in reaching our goals. Obtaining more resources through experience, training and education, better time management, improved networking, and better money management can lower the effect of all types of stressors.

• Shortening the time a stressor acts on us will improve our overall stress level. We must learn to make decisions quickly and move on rather than worrying over one decision for days, even though it isn't that crucial in the overall scheme of things. Also, we can't disregard the additive effect time has in making small stressors act like big stressors.

Because they are so effective and because they attack the root cause of the syndrome—stress—I feel that cognitive-behavioral coping strategies are clearly the best approach to curing Hurried Woman Syndrome and should be an integral part of any long-term treatment plan. However, many women find that when they are struggling with the syndrome they cannot hope to implement these strategies effectively without help. Indeed, many of them are teetering on the edge of major depression and must get their brain chemistry back in balance before they will be able to find the physical and emotional strength necessary to focus on using cognitive-behavioral coping strategies to get better and stay well. Antidepressant medications can provide this assistance and their proper use will be discussed in Chapter 5.

5

THE ROLE OF ANTIDEPRESSANTS

THE ANTIDEPRESSANTS available for use today are much better than those we had a little more than a decade ago. I remember as a kid my mother relating how people she knew had been "drugged out" by medications such as Valium. Although you may feel rotten at times being a Hurried Woman, being overly sedated or getting hooked on something is not a solution. The newer antidepressants, while still causing side effects in some people, don't have such extreme adverse reactions. It's not a perfect science, but we've come a long way in the past few years.

NEUROTRANSMITTERS REVISITED

Before making treatment recommendations about specific antidepressants, it's important to understand how each symptom of Hurried Woman Syndrome directly relates to the balance of each of the three main neurotransmitters in the brain: dopamine, serotonin, and norepinephrine. Balancing the three is much like balancing the legs of a camera tripod. All three legs need to be equal if the world is to look "level," or normal, as pictured in Figure 5.1.

The three legs of the neurotransmitter tripod are in balance—they all touch the dotted line which represents the normal, level situation. But when any one of the legs drops down below the other two, the tripod is no longer level. The following table lists the symptoms caused by a relative deficiency (low level) of each of the neurotransmitters:

Relative Serotonin Deficiency	Relative Dopamine Deficiency	Relative Norepinephrine Deficiency
Anxiety/panic	Low sex drive	Fatigue
Agitated mood	Weight gain	Weight gain
Excessive worry	Low mood	Decreased alertness
Obsessive behavior	Apathy	

✿ FIGURE 5.1 NEUROTRANSMITTERS IN PROPER BALANCE

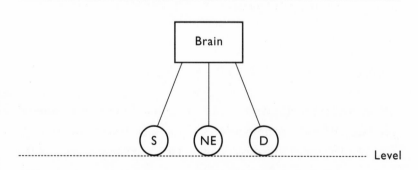

SEROTONIN DEFICIENCY

When serotonin becomes low relative to the other two neurotransmitters, it makes us anxious, irritable, and moody. Some people will have panic attacks—a racing heart rate, an overwhelming sense of fearfulness or doom, shortness of breath—and interestingly are often unable to identify what exactly is worrying them. This used to be termed *agoraphobia*, which means a fear of open spaces in Latin, but really was meant to describe a free-floating anxiety. People with low serotonin levels tend to dwell on things that annoy or worry them and may have trouble sleeping at night. Those who have exceptionally low levels of serotonin may even engage in obsessive-compulsive behavior. Serotonin deficiency is represented graphically in Figure 5.2.

DOPAMINE DEFICIENCY

When dopamine levels fall too low compared to those of the other two neurotransmitters, we are unable to experience pleasure normally. Things that used to be fun just don't excite us anymore. A lack of desire for physical intimacy is a symptom of low dopamine.

✿ FIGURE 5.2 SEROTONIN DEFICIENCY CAUSING ANXIETY

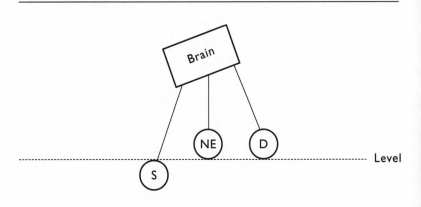

Figure 5.3 depicts the chemical imbalance caused by a deficiency of dopamine. Since the sensation of pleasure eludes them, people with low dopamine aren't motivated to participate in pleasurable activities. They often appear to be apathetic, distant, down, and unable to focus their attention and energy (what's left of it) on even the most simple of tasks. People with a dopamine deficiency also tend to gain weight because exercise seems unrewarding and staying focused on a diet becomes too big a chore to handle as their appetite increases.

NOREPINEPHRINE DEFICIENCY

The best way to view the action of norepinephrine in the brain is to think of it as "central adrenaline." It activates and excites nerve cells throughout the brain. Norepinephrine makes us feel excited, heightens our senses, helps us focus our attention, elevates our mood, and energizes us. Conversely, when norepinephrine levels are too low—the norepinephrine leg drops lower than the other two, as seen in Figure 5.4—it causes feelings of sluggishness, fatigue, and even sleepiness.

✤ FIGURE 5.3 DOPAMINE DEFICIENCY REDUCING SEX DRIVE AND INCREASING APPETITE

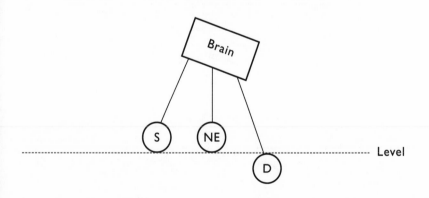

✦ FIGURE 5.4 NOREPINEPHRINE DEFICIENCY CAUSING FATIGUE

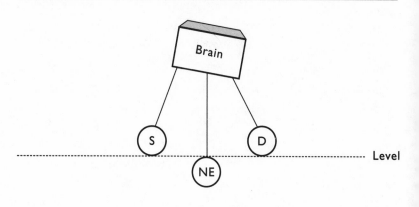

A lack of mental energy often translates into a lack of physical energy, and the desire for exercise usually drops off rapidly, which aggravates weight gain. To make matters worse, appetite usually increases—remember that most over-the-counter (OTC) diet pills at one time contained ephedra and caffeine, both of which are stimulants like norepinephrine, which curbs appetite. In contrast, when someone has too much norepinephrine relative to the other two, he or she becomes jittery, nervous, irritable, and unable to sleep. This is the situation depicted in Figure 5.5.

Does this remind you of someone with too little serotonin? It should, because in relative terms, when norepinephrine levels are too high, the tripod is out of balance—the norepinephrine leg is too high relative to the serotonin and dopamine legs. We could just as easily consider the serotonin leg—or perhaps both the serotonin and dopamine legs—to be too low, at least lower than the norepinephrine leg. When it comes to balancing neurotransmitters, relativity counts. In other words, it's not necessarily the absolute amount of each neurotransmitter that determines which symptoms the Hurried Woman experiences, but rather the relative balance between them.

✦ FIGURE 5.5 EXCESS NOREPINEPHRINE CAUSING ANXIETY

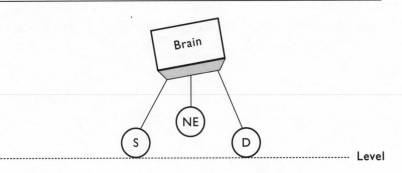

THE RELATIVE BALANCE OF NEUROTRANSMITTERS

We talk about "normal" levels of neurotransmitters to understand the concept of each one's action in the brain, but it's really more accurate to say that the relative balance between them is what determines whether the world appears level or not. To simplify the matter, it's helpful to divide Hurried Women into two basic groups: those with "high anxiety" and those with "low energy." Looking at these two groups separately will allow us to discuss specific recommendations about medications.

HIGH-ANXIETY HURRIED WOMAN SYNDROME

Hurried Women in this category usually don't sleep well at night. They lie down and then find themselves attempting to mentally solve all their current problems, all their past problems, and the problems that may come tomorrow or anytime in the future. Sound familiar? High-Anxiety Hurried Women tend to be worriers. Many tell me that they can't seem to sit still. They often find themselves pacing the floor, wringing their hands, fidgeting in their seat, or constantly thinking about something in their life that's troubling them. Many of them collapse into bed at night exhausted from a busy day only to awake before the alarm goes off, unable to fall back to sleep. They often feel on edge, even when things appear to be going okay. Jamie's story is typical:

> *I guess it started about two years ago when I turned forty. I began to notice I was always on edge, moody and irritable. My husband and the kids just couldn't do anything right. I couldn't rest at night because I had a million things running through my mind. I couldn't stay focused and kept falling asleep at work because I couldn't sleep at night! I'm a nervous eater so I would often snack, but I was too tired to keep up my walking (which I had to do after the kids went to bed), so I gained about twenty-five pounds over a year or so. My doctor started me on Zoloft [a selective serotonin reuptake inhibitor] and within two to three weeks I felt much better. I quit lying awake in bed at night, blowing up over little things at home, and just felt a lot better about myself. I started eating better and have gone back to walking for about a month now. I've lost eight pounds so far and can tell the difference in the way my clothes fit. I feel like I'm back in control again.*

The high-anxiety version of Hurried Woman Syndrome comes from a relative deficiency of serotonin, a relative excess of norepinephrine, or some combination of the two. The high-anxiety variant is best treated with a special group of antidepressants called selective serotonin reuptake inhibitors (SSRIs). The SSRIs allow levels of serotonin in the brain to rise by helping the natural rebalancer system function more efficiently. A similar effect would be achieved if we could force norepinephrine levels to fall, but we currently have no medication that accomplishes this successfully, so SSRIs remain the best treatment approach for the High-Anxiety Hurried Woman. The following table lists the SSRIs currently available and the primary neurotransmitter(s) they affect:

SSRI (Generic)	Neurotransmitter(s)
Zoloft (sertraline)	Serotonin and dopamine
Prozac (fluoxetine)	Serotonin
Lexapro (escitalopram) formerly Celexa (citalopram)	Serotonin
Paxil CR (paroxetine)	Serotonin

Selective serotonin reuptake inhibitors all work to elevate serotonin in the brain, which is why they soothe anxiety so well. However, over time (usually six months or longer) they tend to lower dopamine levels in relative terms. Remember the tripod example—as we raise the serotonin leg of the tripod, one or both of the other two legs may become "lower" relative to the improved level of serotonin (see Figure 5.6).

Unfortunately, lower relative levels of dopamine can result in a blunting of sex drive or even anorgansmia—the lack of ability to

✾ FIGURE 5.6 SSRI CORRECTING SEROTONIN DEFICIENCY AND LOWERING DOPAMINE OVER TIME

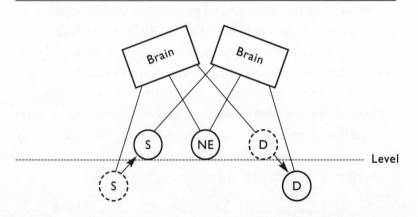

achieve an orgasm or climax. About 40–50 percent of women who take SSRIs for an extended period will complain of less interest in sex and about 3 percent will experience anorgansmia. Of course, this is aggravating to someone who likely already has a low sex drive!

The good news is fourfold. First, from the table you can see that Zoloft tends to elevate dopamine as well as serotonin, which translates into less loss of sex drive than most of the other SSRIs, so Zoloft makes a good first choice among this group of medications. Second, in most cases, virtually all of the other symptoms of which the Hurried Woman was complaining are remarkably better after a few months of treatment; life overall seems much more balanced, and she can feel the improvement. Third, the problem of low sex drive can be improved by fine-tuning the dosage of the medications. Fourth, and probably most important, there are other ways of improving sex drive in women that are more potent and can counteract this side effect of SSRI therapy. These methods will be discussed later.

Much of what appears to be a side effect from SSRI therapy may actually be explained by the phenomenon of "objects that are closer appear larger." In other words, when all of the other problems the High-Anxiety Hurried Woman was concerned about—irritability, sleeplessness, anxiety, mood swings, anger, crying spells, feelings of hopelessness and doom—are gone a few months after starting the medication, the only remaining symptom—low sex drive—is more noticeable than it was when those other things were demanding so much attention. The truth of the matter is that for most women, particularly those with Hurried Woman Syndrome, the low sex drive was aggravated by the brain chemistry changes brought on by stress, but it may not have been the primary cause. Sex drive in women is a very complex issue that involves not only brain chemistry, but hormonal, physical, psychological, and situational factors as well. We'll discuss the multiple causes of low sex drive and how they interac⸝ with Hurried Woman Syndrome in Chapter 10. For now, it's i⸝ tant to understand that SSRI treatment can sometime⸝

with getting rid of low sex drive, and there are strategies to fix this problem.

Other side effects that often accompany SSRI therapy are as follows:

✡ OTHER COMMON SIDE EFFECTS OF SSRI THERAPY

Side Effect	Percent Affected
Nausea	10%
Diarrhea	7%
Dry mouth	5%
Sleepiness	7%
Insomnia	5%
Fatigue	3%

Many of these side effects will clear up after a few days to a couple of weeks. Most doctors and nurse practitioners try to warn you about them so you'll know to hang on and expect them to dissipate over time. However, it's best to let your health care provider know if you're experiencing unexpected symptoms or side effects after you start any new treatment.

LOW-ENERGY HURRIED WOMAN SYNDROME

This represents the other side of Hurried Woman Syndrome. These women aren't anxious—they don't have enough energy to be anxious. Fatigue is an overwhelming feature of virtually every day. They don't usually have trouble falling asleep; in fact, many say they could fall asleep anywhere—in the carpool line, at work, in church, or doing homework—theirs or the kids'. These women may also tend to wake up before the alarm goes off much like High-Anxiety Hurried Women. Many say that physical intimacy becomes just another chore they must try to work into their already busy schedule, usually at the end of a very hard day. Low-Energy Hurried Women are the first to give up on exercise and the most prone to gain weight. Unfortunately, when exercise falls off, energy levels drop even lower, weight climbs, sex drive slumps further, and over time guilt becomes a major problem. The guilt is fueled by remorse over no longer wanting to participate in activities that used to be fun but are now a headache. My patient, Jennifer, age thirty-seven, came to me with the following complaint:

> *I just can't do it anymore. I stay at home with our three children, ages eight, four, and two. My husband travels with his job about three nights each week and is in the Reserves one weekend a month. I sleep eight hours at night but wake up sometimes before the alarm goes off and can't get back to sleep. When my husband's home, I want to be a good wife and please him, but by the time we get everyone else in bed, I'm exhausted. He says that it's okay, but I feel so guilty about not being interested in sex anymore. It used to be fun, but now it's just another chore. I can't lose the baby weight from my two-year-old because I can't find time to exercise. I'm crabby all the time, and I cry over stupid things like when Jason was leaving for school and couldn't find the math homework he and his dad had done the night before. I don't know what to do anymore.*

Many Hurried Women tell me they feel a sense of loss, almost as if a dear friend had passed away, as they withdraw from their activities and the friends and family involved with those activities. They feel isolated by their lack of energy and frustrated about not being the friend, wife, and mother they used to be before all this tiredness became so overwhelming. This leads to more guilt, sometimes anger that seems to flare up unexpectedly and undesirably, and finally depression. High-Anxiety Hurried Women often struggle with feelings of guilt as well, but this is a dominant symptom for Low-Energy Hurried Women. The root of all the fatigue and lack of energy is a relative deficiency of norepinephrine in the brain.

A small group of medicines called "newer antidepressants" seem to elevate neurotransmitter levels through the natural rebalancer system. These medicines and the neurotransmitters they elevate are as follows:

Newer Antidepressant (Generic)	Neurotransmitters
Wellbutrin XL/Wellbutrin SR (bupropion)	Norepinephrine and dopamine
Effexor XR (venlafaxine)	Serotonin and norepinephrine
Remeron (mirtazapine)	Serotonin and norepinephrine

The most common side effects from these medications are tremors, insomnia, sweating, rapid heartbeat, and anxiety. This makes sense because they all tend to raise levels of norepinephrine and therefore excite the body's fight-or-flight response. A rare complication of medications in this group is seizures. If you have a history of seizures, be sure to tell your doctor and discuss your options before taking any medication, particularly one of the newer antidepressants.

The majority of Low-Energy Hurried Women I treat seem to respond best to Wellbutrin, which is also marketed under the name Zyban for smoking cessation. Because of its effect on norepinephrine, Wellbutrin tends to reenergize Hurried Women and elevate their mood. It also preserves dopamine, which is why it seems to cause less sexual dysfunction than other antidepressants, particularly the SSRIs, and may even have a positive benefit for weight loss. Two forms of Wellbutrin are available: Wellbutrin SR—the "SR" stands for sustained release and is taken twice daily—and Wellbutrin XL—the "XL" indicates a trademarked coating that allows for a smooth, slower release of the medication inside the pill. Wellbutrin XL can be taken once daily.

These medications can make a huge difference in the lives of Hurried Women like Jennifer, who said this about her experience with treatment:

> *After about a month on the medicine [Wellbutrin XL], my energy came back. I didn't feel powerless anymore. I could focus my thoughts and had the energy to get things done again. Life is still hectic at times, but I feel that I'm back in control and can handle it now. My husband says I'm a lot easier to be around and I've even been able to save some for him. I have also started working out three times a week. I haven't lost any weight yet, but my clothes are already fitting better, so I'm happy. I guess it's time to start working on lowering my stress levels.*

Tricyclic and tetracyclic antidepressants were popularly used in the treatment of depression before the SSRIs and newer antidepressants became available. Although these older medications were helpful, the new generation of antidepressant medications appears to be superior—in terms of having fewer and milder side effects and less potential for adverse reactions with other medications—as well as being more effective, particularly in women.

MORE ON ANTIDEPRESSANT THERAPY

Since Hurried Woman Syndrome is caused by the same type of changes in brain chemistry as major depression, Hurried Women respond very well to antidepressant medications. Indeed, most clinical trials reveal that remission rates with antidepressants for patients with Hurried Woman Syndrome are between 60 and 84 percent, whereas remission rates in major depression are only about 35–60 percent. This difference in treatment outcome verifies two important concepts about the relationship between Hurried Woman Syndrome and major depression: (1) they are caused by the same type of chemical imbalance; and (2) it's easier to treat Hurried Woman Syndrome than to treat major depression because the chemical imbalance is not as severe. To me, it also highlights the importance of getting treatment when you are still in the Hurried Woman Syndrome phase rather than waiting to see if you develop major depression. Once major depression begins, the likelihood that treatment will be successful is much lower. *Preventing* major depression is important.

Low-Energy Hurried Women seem to do best on Wellbutrin. It raises norepinephrine levels and preserves dopamine, which explains why it has few side effects. However, it is not the best choice for the High-Anxiety Hurried Woman, who responds best to SSRI therapy because her norepinephrine level is already too high relative to serotonin. Although the majority of women respond well to SSRI therapy, a significant number will complain of low sex drive over time, perhaps from an unintended lowering of dopamine levels. Zoloft is less likely than most of the SSRIs to cause sexual problems because it preserves dopamine to some extent. However, if sexual dysfunction does occur, many experts advocate combining two medications to balance both neurotransmitters. The combination of Wellbutrin and Zoloft—what I call "Well-Oft"—has been tested in several clinical studies and appears to work well. The two medications together provide double support for dopamine, which probably explains their success.

These medications are not addictive and rarely cause sleepiness, so the vast majority of people can take them and work, sign contracts, drive a car, take care of children, and so on without the fear of being out of it or less than fully responsive to what is going on around them. Plus, research shows that the combination appears to be safe for long-term use because of both medication's low toxicity and rare side effects. In contrast to Valium and its many cousins, the new generation of antidepressants are not "feel-good pills." I have had some patients errantly view them as sedatives, skipping them on a good day and taking two of them on a bad day. This is not how these medications work, so please don't make this mistake.

The newer antidepressants work with your body's natural rebalancer system to correct the balance of neurotransmitters rather than artificially taking over the system. This is the main reason you can't take them just when you feel like it. If you use them off and on, you are "shaking up" your rebalancer system rather than helping it work more smoothly and are more likely to have side effects. The best thing about these new medications is that they simply do what they are supposed to do—rebalance chemicals in the brain—and little else, unlike older treatments, such as Valium and tri-/tetracyclic antidepressants, which have lots of side effects.

Most experts recommend taking antidepressants for at least six months to a year before attempting to stop. Remember, these medicines work slowly to balance brain chemistry, so it takes a while for them to rebalance and stabilize the neurotransmitters. Many Hurried Women make the mistake of stopping their medicine as soon as they begin to feel better only to relapse within a few weeks. Taking antidepressants erratically not only causes side effects but can also make the brain chemistry imbalance harder to fix.

While the new breed of antidepressants can offer you a safe and effective strategy to treat Hurried Woman Syndrome and depression, even more exciting is the revelation that nonmedical treatment can be just as effective. There's no doubt that many women need a "jump-start" on the road to recovery and thankfully antidepressants can now provide this safely for most. But after a few months on an antidepressant, when they get their heads back on straight and regain their energy, they need to begin working on the cognitive-behavioral aspects of therapy so they can take back control of their lives and get off medication. Even women who choose to take antidepressants should benefit from adopting cognitive-behavioral therapies as well. Not only is this logical, but the 1997 research by Maier and colleagues (see Chapter 3) showed that combining the two strategies produced much higher response rates in their study of chronic depression.

Part Two will outline a medically sound seven-step program that integrates cognitive-behavioral coping strategies to conquer the emotional and physical effects of stress, regain your lost energy and happiness, teach you the principles to get and maintain a healthier body, and rekindle the passion in your relationships. In other words, not only survive, but meet and defeat Hurried Woman Syndrome forever!

part two

YOUR SEVEN-STEP PLAN
FOR BETTER LIFE BALANCE

6

THE BRAIN IS CALLED the master gland because it directly and indirectly modulates almost every system in the body. And the body's many systems also affect how the brain functions. In other words, you can't really separate the brain from the body. When you have a cold, you "feel bad." This means not only muscle aches, fever, chills, weakness, and a headache, but also being grouchy, irritable, sad, and unable or unwilling to focus your attention on anything but simple tasks. What's going on in your body has a direct impact on how your brain functions as well as how you perceive yourself and your environment. This is why it's important in treating Hurried Woman Syndrome to focus attention on rebalancing both brain chemistry and the body.

There are a few relatively simple things that all women should do to have a healthier body. Of course, men would benefit from most of these recommendations as well, but our primary focus at this point will be a proper body balance for women.

VITAMINS

Not a day goes by that we don't hear a news flash about what this vitamin or that mineral can do to promote health or conquer disease. There certainly is some very good news about what nature has placed all around us to help us stay healthy. However, after twenty years in the medical field, I can tell you that much of what we hear about nutrition that's "new" these days is mostly hype and can be very confusing. The twenty-year debate over dietary fiber—first it was good, then it was bad, and now it's good again—is an excellent example of just how confusing this area of research can be at times. I'll present here what most experts have agreed on and try to keep the recommendations practical.

MULTIVITAMINS

Almost everyone can benefit from taking a good multivitamin each day. In fact, a recent double-blind placebo-controlled clinical trial showed a significant benefit in terms of higher energy levels and an improved sense of well-being in people who took a multivitamin daily versus those who took a placebo. Placebo-controlled trials compare the medication that's being tested against an inactive "sugar pill," also called a placebo. When clinical trials are "blind," it means that the patient does not know whether she is receiving the active medication or the placebo. When a trial is "double-blind," not only does the patient not know whether she received the study drug or the placebo, but neither do the doctors and nurses involved in the study. Blinding helps prevent bias from interfering with the results of the study.

Healthful Vitamins and Minerals

Vitamins and minerals appear to have some benefit in helping Hurried Women balance their bodies. The following is not meant to be an exhaustive list, but it will certainly cover the most important supplements for women. Your doctor or nurse practitioner may recommend others based on your specific health circumstances.

Vitamin A. Look for a multivitamin containing no more than 2,500–5,000 IU (international units) of vitamin A (retinoic acid or retinol). Doctors used to recommend much higher doses because we knew that vitamin A was necessary for good vision and also bolstered the immune system to fight infections and possibly cancer. However, studies have now shown that too much vitamin A may cause certain birth defects and liver toxicity and even encourage some cancers to grow. Like so many other things in life, moderation is best. Additional vitamin A over the amount found in the standard multivitamin is not usually recommended. Recent research suggests that there may be an association between higher retinol intakes (more than 5,000 IU/day) and an increased risk of osteoporosis in older men and women. However, vitamin A from beta-carotene—the vitamin A source found in carrots and dark green vegetables—has not been associated with this risk. So take a reasonable amount of vitamin A in a multivitamin, but don't feel you need to cut back on carrots to compensate.

Vitamin B₆. Double-blind, placebo-controlled trials have shown that vitamin B_6 (pyridoxine) at doses of 200–400 milligrams per day helps women who suffer with premenstrual syndrome (PMS)–related mood swings and irritability. It may also help with similar symptoms in perimenopause. I have patients who felt that 400 milligrams worked so well that they doubled it! Unfortunately, high doses of vitamin B_6 will cause your feet and hands to go numb—

what we in the medical business call a peripheral neuropathy—which obviously indicates too much of a good thing.

VITAMIN B$_{12}$. The recommended daily allowance (RDA) of vitamin B$_{12}$ (cyanocobalamin) is 6 micrograms, and that is the amount included in most multivitamins. Vitamin B$_{12}$ is important in making healthy red blood cells and if levels get too low, a special type of anemia can develop. As we mature, our ability to absorb this vitamin can become impaired, so people over fifty are encouraged to make sure they get enough. A complete blood count (CBC) and serum B$_{12}$ level can be used to diagnose this uncommon problem. I mention this vitamin, not because it's so important, but because some doctors offer patients regular injections of vitamin B$_{12}$ to treat fatigue. However, unless blood levels have been tested and found to be low, I can see no valid scientific reason to administer these shots; any benefit the patient sees is most likely the placebo effect.

VITAMIN C. If you're a Linus Pauling fan, you believe that vitamin C (ascorbic acid) helps prevent everything from colds to cancer. Although some of the claims made about vitamin C are controversial, most experts agree that it can help fight off infections and allergies and is an important antioxidant in the fight against cancer and heart disease. Antioxidants help stop free radicals from damaging our body tissues and even our DNA. Free radicals have also been implicated in causing cancer, heart attack, stroke, and many other diseases. The Linus Pauling Institute at Oregon State University recommends adding 400 milligrams of vitamin C to your standard multivitamin each day. Since most manufacturers package it in tablets of 500 milligrams or more, I recommend taking a single 500-milligram tablet each day along with your regular multivitamin. Dr. Pauling originally recommended much higher doses of vitamin C back in the 1970s (1,500–2,000 milligrams per day), but more recent research suggests that the lower dose is optimal.

VITAMIN D. This vitamin is routinely added to milk and bread and also comes to us through exposure to ultraviolet rays in sunlight. The crippling disease rickets—which we thankfully don't see much of anymore in this country—comes from vitamin D deficiency in children. Vitamin D aids in the absorption of calcium, which is why it's important to women in the prevention of osteoporosis. However, taking a calcium supplement with added vitamin D is often unnecessary, depending on how much sun exposure you get and your intake of fortified foods like bread and dairy products. Vitamin D synthesis in the skin declines with age. This is why some experts recommend that people over the age of sixty-five consider taking an additional 200–400 IU of vitamin D per day.

VITAMIN E. The scientific evidence on the effectiveness of this antioxidant is confusing. There are eight different forms of vitamin E (tocopherol). The two that have received the most attention are alpha-tocopherol and gamma-tocopherol. Alpha-tocopherol is the most abundant and the most active form of vitamin E in humans and has been shown to decrease the breast tenderness associated with fibrocystic breast disease in doses of 400 IU per day. Many experts recommend taking a supplement of 200 mIU (milli-international units) per day of alpha-tocopherol to decrease the chance of heart disease and stroke. Gamma-tocopherol has been shown to decrease the rate of prostate cancer cell development. Interestingly, one recent study showed that alpha-tocopherol worked to prevent heart disease only if gamma-tocopherol levels were high as well. The specific roles of each of these different forms of vitamin E are still not certain. For now, 200–400 mIU per day, preferably of the gamma variety, seems appropriate.

CALCIUM. Women over thirty need to begin supplementing their calcium intake to help prevent osteoporosis later in life. It may also help decrease leg cramps at night. In addition to your multivitamin, taking 1,000 milligrams each day is good in your thirties, then step up to 1,500–2,000 milligrams daily in your forties and beyond. If you have a history of kidney stones, ask your doctor if you should lower the amount of your calcium supplement. TUMS-EX tablets (750 milligrams of calcium per tablet) are an inexpensive and well-tolerated source of calcium. Since it is only 50 percent bioavailable, four tablets will provide 1,500 milligrams of calcium daily. TUMS can also help with acid reflux, so many women like to take them when they go to bed. If you drink calcium-enriched orange juice or milk, look at the amount of calcium you are taking in through these other sources and adjust your calcium supplementation accordingly. Whole milk has about 300 milligrams of calcium per 8-ounce glass, while skim milk has about 150–200 milligrams. Calcium-enriched orange juice usually has about 200 milligrams per glass.

Folic acid. Recent research indicates that folic acid is helpful in preventing heart disease and Alzheimer's disease. Folic acid (folate) supplements may also help prevent some types of cancer, particularly in people who drink alcohol regularly. Folic acid has been shown to reduce the risk of spina bifida (open spine) and congenital heart disease in infants when women begin taking supplemental folic acid prior to becoming pregnant. A regular multivitamin provides 0.4 milligrams (400 micrograms) of folic acid, which is adequate while attempting pregnancy, but most experts recommend switching to a prenatal vitamin containing at least 0.8 milligrams of folic acid once pregnancy has been diagnosed.

Iron. Iron deficiency is common worldwide and is still a significant problem in the United States. Although uncommon in men, about 5–7 percent of women who menstruate have iron-deficiency anemia. This problem can usually be diagnosed with a CBC. I recommend that women with heavy periods, particularly those who feel tired and run-down during and immediately after a menstrual cycle, consider taking a low-dose, over-the-counter (OTC) iron supplement. These supplements come in several forms, including ferrous fumarate, ferrous gluconate, ferrous sulfate, iron dextran, iron polysaccharide complex, iron sorbitol, iron sucrose, and sodium ferric gluconate. The RDA of elemental iron for women is 18 milligrams and is the amount found in most multivitamins. If you choose to add an iron supplement to your daily vitamin, just follow the instructions on the label.

The most common side effect of iron supplements is bowel disturbance—either constipation or diarrhea—and there's no way to predict which one you will have, if either. Taking too much iron can cause a condition called hemochromatosis, which leads to diabetes and liver failure, so don't take more than one tablet of a supplement each day without checking with your health care provider first. If you feel short of breath, have chest pain, or feel faint with menstrual cycles, you should discuss this with your practitioner right away.

EXERCISE

Aerobic exercise is critical to the successful treatment of Hurried Woman Syndrome. Exercise releases chemicals in the brain, called endorphins, which make you feel better. These chemicals give you a sense of well-being and help counteract the fatigue experienced by Hurried Women. Exercise also improves your physical stamina, which allows you to bear up under physical and emotional stress. Just as in the saying "you have to spend money to make money," you have to spend energy to get energy. Regular aerobic exercise gives you more energy. I sometimes have trouble convincing myself to go running in the neighborhood or walk on the treadmill when I get home after a particularly tiring day at work. But I have found over and over again that if I can make myself do it, I feel better the next day. "I'm too tired to exercise" is the start of a vicious cycle and probably the most common excuse people give for not following through on an exercise program. If you don't exercise today, you will be more tired tomorrow, which will further discourage you from exercising and make you even more tired the next day. This continues until you give up on exercise altogether. You must say to yourself, "I'm too tired to *not* exercise. If I don't do it tonight, tomorrow will be worse than today." It's a psychological challenge to convince yourself of this at times, but if you can do it, you will be rewarded in the end.

Exercise is also critical for successful weight management, particularly for women over thirty and men over forty. The minimum amount of exercise I recommend to maintain body weight and fight fatigue is three thirty-minute sessions each week. This is a "maintenance dose" and must be viewed as a starting point. To lose weight effectively, many women must exercise more than this. Realistically, you'll have to find the level and type of exercise that's right for you, considering such things as your age, current level of physical training, willingness to diet, and any physical limitations. The proper role of exercise in weight management has to be balanced with diet and should be tailored to your needs, likes, and abilities. This makes it tough to prescribe a standard "dose" of exercise that works for everyone, particularly when it comes to weight control. The best approach to aerobic exercise in long-term weight management will be discussed more fully in Step 3 (Chapter 8). For now, think of regular aerobic exercise as a fatigue buster.

LIMITING SUGAR, ALCOHOL, AND CAFFEINE

Sugar has become the poster child for the adage "If it tastes good, you know it can't be good for you!" Much of sugar's bad reputation is undeserved—a teaspoon of sugar contains only 15 calories. Obviously, placing reasonable limits on sugar intake is part of any diet effort, but what I'm talking about here is avoiding sugar binges or the sugar rush of a candy bar, soft drink, or frosted doughnut. For many of us, the sugar high we seek is often followed by a sugar low we don't like, which in turn leads us to look for more sugar, and a tumultuous blood sugar roller-coaster ride ensues. Many people bounce back and forth all day between feeling anxious and jittery or sluggish and dull-headed, depending on where they are on the blood sugar scale.

If you feel sluggish and weak in the midafternoon, usually about two hours after lunch, you may indeed be experiencing mild hypoglycemia (low blood sugar). This is not a disease but rather a predictable physiologic phenomenon. There are two ways to approach this problem properly. First, you can eat a snack when you feel your energy drop. Not a candy bar or soft drink, because the rapid rise in blood sugar that these provide will make you feel better within twenty minutes but will cause a surge of insulin that will lower blood sugar an hour or two later. A better snack choice is a piece of fruit or a few whole-grain crackers. These snacks are lower in calories, which will support your weight management program, and release their sugars more slowly, thus avoiding the wide swings in blood sugar that make you feel bad.

The second approach to the midafternoon slump is to be certain that the lunch you ate two hours earlier was not too big and had a good balance of carbohydrates, protein, and fats. In other words, keep it light. When you eat a meal, your blood flow is redirected to the intestinal tract in anticipation of digesting the food and getting the nutrients into your system. This effectively steals blood away from the brain and makes you feel tired or sleepy after a meal, particularly a big one.

Many of us tend to eat more when we're under pressure, but some of us also tend to crave certain foods when we're stressed. Many women acknowledge an overwhelming urge to eat sweets, particularly chocolate, just before their period. Let me clarify that chocolate is not necessarily bad for you. In fact, chocolate can cause the release of endorphins that can improve your mood. (My wife has lobbied for years to have chocolate named the fifth essential food group.) The problem with chocolate is that it often comes linked with a lot of sugar—candy bars, cocoa, etc. If you already feel emotional during this time, you don't need to take a ride on the sugar roller coaster at the same time. Be careful not to give in to the desire for a sugar binge if you have PMS mood swings. This is true of alcohol and caffeine as well.

Now let's talk briefly about sugar substitutes. Many people in our society have a sweet tooth. In fact, Americans consume more processed sugar per person than residents of any other country on the planet. To help compensate for this overindulgence, we have continually sought the perfect sugar substitute. And since demand precedes supply, there is no shortage of alternatives available. Saccharine, affectionately known as "the pink stuff," has finally gotten off the hazardous chemical list. Recent research shows that it is not carcinogenic after all. Aspartame (NutraSweet) is currently the most abundant artificial sweetener in soft drinks and has been commercially available since 1996. In spite of several urban legends that have sprung up over the years that it causes multiple sclerosis, seizures, and brain damage, it has passed the scrutiny of government agencies and scientists alike. I still recommend that it be used in moderation. There are isolated reports that ingesting large quantities of diet drinks containing aspartame may actually block weight loss and that the sweetener may be a trigger for bloating and intestinal cramping in women with irritable bowel syndrome. I recommend limiting yourself to four 8-ounce servings of aspartame-containing beverages (or foods) a day; consider two packets of aspartame the same as one serving.

There is a plethora of scientific research substantiating the claim that drinking small amounts of alcohol on a regular basis is probably a healthy habit. Red wine particularly seems to help ward off stroke and heart disease because it contains the plant pigment resveratrol. However, too much of a good thing can cause tremendous problems. It is estimated that alcohol abuse and alcoholism affects more than fourteen million Americans, often at a high emotional and financial cost. Furthermore, alcohol is involved in over 40 percent of all traffic crashes and accounts for $50 billion in damages each year. Some women under pressure, particularly those with PMS, drink to relax and relieve anxiety. This sounds okay until we remember that alcohol also releases our inhibitions. And if your inhibitions are the only thing stopping you from taking a swing at your spouse or child, you'd probably better think twice about drinking alcohol when your PMS is flaring. Also remember that alcoholic beverages affect women twice as much as men and are usually loaded with calories. Beer, for example, is high in the sugar maltose, which will raise blood sugar levels higher and faster than white bread. The insulin response to the carbohydrates in beer causes fat storage in the abdominal wall and the proverbial beer belly. Consider limiting your alcohol consumption to one glass of wine three days a week, avoiding mixed drinks altogether—most of them are loaded with sweeteners—and being cautious about beer intake, even light beers.

Caffeine is a stimulant found in many of the foods and medications we take in on a regular basis. Caffeine, along with another natural stimulant called ephedra, were both popular ingredients in OTC diet pills until the Federal Drug Administration (FDA) decided that the combination was too dangerous. Caffeine helps us be more alert and energetic in small, infrequent doses, but in higher doses it makes us feel jittery and nervous and causes insomnia. You can also build up a tolerance to the drug, so frequent caffeine users report that the more they use, the more they need to get the same effect. Caffeine is physically addictive and has a withdrawal syndrome that includes irritability, fatigue, headaches, and an inability to concentrate. With gourmet coffee shops on every corner and a wide variety of diet drinks available, many people use and abuse caffeine regularly and probably experience withdrawal symptoms more commonly than they think. Adding caffeine ups and downs to the symptoms of Hurried Woman Syndrome is anything but helpful. Consider limiting your caffeine intake to three 8-ounce servings a day or less, none of them within two to four hours of going to bed, since caffeine can interfere with sleep. If you are currently consuming mass quantities of caffeine, you may need to wean down over a week or two to avoid withdrawal symptoms.

HORMONES AND MENOPAUSE

Menopause is the absence of menstrual cycles and is due to a primary physiological change: the virtual absence of estradiol (the most potent estrogen) and progesterone. These two hormones, which are an integral part of your physiology for about forty years, now depart. Not all of the changes that accompany menopause are bad—no more menstrual cycles and no chance for a surprise pregnancy can be very good news to a forty-eight-year-old woman—but some of the more prominent changes aren't particularly welcomed:

- Hot flushes (or "flashes") and night sweats, which are called vasomotor symptoms

- Vaginal dryness and shrinkage (atrophy), which can make intercourse painful

These are the classic symptoms of menopause and affect almost 90 percent of women at some point. The hot flushes and sweats usually go away over time, but the vaginal dryness and thinning of the skin tend to worsen through the years. Many women in menopause also report the following problems as well:

- Sleeplessness

- Mental dullness or an inability to concentrate

- Lack of interest in sex

Women with frequent night sweats are obviously bothered by a lack of sleep. If you regularly wake up in the middle of the night soaking wet and have to get up and change your clothes, how much sleep are you getting? Medical research shows that women with low estrogen levels get less REM (rapid eye movement) sleep. A chronic lack of REM sleep causes drowsiness during the day, fatigue, and irritability. People who don't get enough REM sleep stop dreaming and also relate that they have trouble remembering and concentrating during the day.

The symptoms of menopause often rob women of their desire for physical intimacy as well. If you're irritable and tired and intercourse is uncomfortable, why would you want to have sex? Add to this the fact that as menopause progresses, testosterone levels fall. This occurs because the majority of testosterone in women comes from the ovaries, and as the ovaries shrink during menopause, testosterone levels decline. Testosterone's role in female libido is similar to that in men but not as significant. Nonetheless, many women will experience a lower sex drive when their testosterone level drops. Finally, women in menopause are at increased risk of developing some significant medical problems, such as osteoporosis, heart disease, Alzheimer's disease, and stroke. Research has shown these risks to be independent of age, implying that estrogen might have some protective effect against these illnesses.

Menopause can obviously have a significant impact on a woman's happiness, her day-to-day functioning, and her long-term health. Even more important to our discussion, the symptoms of menopause and those of Hurried Woman Syndrome overlap to some extent. This fact has three important implications. First, menopause can make it more difficult to assess whether a woman has Hurried Woman Syndrome or not. For example, a woman who is struggling to cope with menopausal symptoms will score higher on the Attitude and Mood Self-Assessment Quiz from Chapter 3. Putting her on the appropriate hormone(s) may improve her symptoms significantly and avoid misdiagnosis or overtreatment.

Second, the presence of Hurried Woman Syndrome, particularly when it is unrecognized, may confound efforts to treat women in menopause and perimenopause. For years, when a woman on hormone replacement therapy called up her doctor and said, "I'm getting more anxious and can't sleep at night," the doctor would simply bump her hormones up a notch. They would both be happy for a while—the patient with the placebo effect and the doctor with a happy patient—but it would rarely last more than a few months because they were treating Hurried Woman Syndrome with higher and higher doses of estrogen rather than the appropriate therapy.

Third, there is a link between estrogen (and to a lesser extent, progesterone) and the balance of serotonin, norepinephrine, and dopamine in the brain. In other words, sex hormones have a direct impact on brain chemistry. A prime example of this interaction is PMS. The mood swings associated with PMS appear to be caused by an acute unbalancing of the brain chemistry that occurs only during the second half of the menstrual cycle. Although it's not clear which hormone is out of balance, the emotional highs and lows of PMS can often be smoothed out with birth control pills. In this case, rebalancing the sex hormones also rebalances the brain chemistry. Since almost 40 percent of Hurried Women are in perimenopause or menopause—or will be soon—it is important to discuss hormone replacement and menopause in more detail.

In twenty years of medical practice, I can't remember a time when there wasn't some type of controversy over hormones. Hormone replacement therapy (HRT), estrogen replacement therapy (ERT), and birth control pills always seem to be dodging some latest research "bullet" that exposes a new side effect, link to cancer, and so on. These scary stories about hormones always make the front page of the newspaper, the cover of women's magazines, and the evening news. The media always sound the alarm loudly when it comes to problems with hormones. The interesting thing is that virtually none of the problems are ever proved to be true in the long run. After the initial panic, the evidence streams in over the next six months to a year that the previously reported problem isn't really a problem after all or was perhaps a bit overstated, and the "all clear" news item usually winds up on page 22 of the newspaper or as a twenty-second sound bite on the radio. I guess the follow-up message that "hormones are okay after all" isn't as exciting as the "your hormones are killing you" one was. This issue is significant because a large number of Hurried Women will need to make the decision about whether or not to start hormones or how long to stay on them, because contrary to what many health care professionals thought a few years ago, they aren't necessarily good medicine for everyone.

The latest controversy surrounding hormones has come from a landmark study called the Women's Health Initiative (WHI), which set out to test the benefits and risks of taking hormones in menopause. Before we get into the details of this study, let's go over some background information on hormones and a few definitions.

MENOPAUSAL HORMONE THERAPY PRIOR TO THE WOMEN'S HEALTH INITIATIVE

Estrogen was first used in menopause to control hot flashes and night sweats and to help with vaginal dryness. It was originally developed in a pill but now comes in many forms: pills, patches, vaginal rings, and creams. When estrogen is given by itself it is estrogen replacement therapy (ERT). Besides controlling the common menopausal symptoms already listed, estrogen stimulates the tissue that lines the uterus (endometrium) to grow. If estrogen is given by itself (called unopposed estrogen) to women in menopause who have not had a hysterectomy, about 10 percent will develop uterine cancer. This is why ERT should only be used in women who have had a hysterectomy. For other women who want to receive the benefits of estrogen replacement, a second hormone, a progestin, must be added to counteract the estrogen's potentially negative effect on the endometrium. This dual hormone treatment is called hormone replacement therapy (HRT). The two hormones may be taken together every day, or the progestin can be taken in an intermittent fashion. Literally hundreds of clinical studies have been conducted over the last forty years to look into the benefits and risks of ERT and HRT. Prior to the release of the HRT results of the WHI trial in 2002 and the release of the ERT results in April 2004, most experts in the field would have agreed on the following benefits of both HRT and ERT, particularly in younger women entering menopause:

- Fewer hot flushes and night sweats.

- A decreased risk of stroke.

- A decrease in heart attack risk by raising "good" cholesterol (HDL) and lowering "bad" cholesterol (LDL). Estrogen also seemed to prevent the coronary arteries from becoming clogged. In younger women, this appeared to equal a 30–50 percent reduction in heart attack risk if the hormones were started before heart disease had been diagnosed.

- A tremendous decrease in osteoporosis and risk of hip fracture by preventing bone resorption. This benefit is obtained only if the hormones are begun within five to seven years after entering menopause. Once bone mass is lost, hormones cannot bring it back.

- A lower risk of colon cancer.

- A 20–40 percent reduction in Alzheimer's disease among women while using the hormones. Previous hormone use did not appear to protect women against Alzheimer's disease.

- Improved sleep.

- Better vaginal elasticity and lubrication during intercourse.

- Improved bladder function, particularly fewer bladder spasms.

- A decreased risk of macular degeneration, the major cause of blindness in postmenopausal women.

- Much less tooth loss.

- Better skin tone and less wrinkling because estrogen preserves collagen in the skin.

The risks of ERT/HRT were felt to be small and consisted mainly of an increased risk of thromboembolism—blood clots that usually form in the legs. No one wants a blood clot or phlebitis (vein inflammation), but these by themselves won't kill you. However, if part of the blood clot breaks away and moves into the lungs it's called a pulmonary embolism. This condition can be fatal. Fortunately, the increased risk of blood clots on ERT/HRT was felt to be very low, estimated to occur in about 1:200 women or 0.05 percent. Also, as discussed earlier, unopposed estrogen could not be used in a woman who still had her uterus because to do so would increase her risk of uterine cancer. Uterine cancer is the only cancer that has been proven to be caused by estrogen. But women who take HRT actually lower their risk of developing this disease. The proper use of progestin reverses this risk almost completely.

The unproven risk associated with ERT/HRT that drew the most controversy was a possible link to breast cancer. Of the many studies that addressed the issue of whether or not hormones cause an increased risk of breast cancer, no link was found in more than 90 percent. In the few studies in which risk was found, it was only a slight risk, one that might be explained by sheer chance or by bias in the research. Women who are taking estrogen when their breast cancer is diagnosed tend to live longer, have smaller tumors, and experience less metastases (spread of the cancer to other areas of the body) than do women who are not taking hormones. This doesn't make sense if estrogen causes breast cancer. Although some zealots argued vehemently against estrogen and hormone replacement because of the fear of breast cancer, they were (and still are) in the minority. The common belief among hormone experts was that the benefits of ERT/HRT outweighed the limited risks and that virtually every woman should consider taking hormones in menopause. The results of the two WHI studies have caused us to reevaluate our approach to ERT and HRT, but the news about hormones is not as bad as you might think.

The next section describes the results of the two WHI trials and a discussion of how to understand the results of clinical research. It will provide a lot of the scientific support for my recommendations about the proper use of hormones.

The WHI Trial Results in Perspective

The Women's Health Initiative was a large, multicenter, clinical research trial to assess the good and bad news about HRT and ERT, particularly their effect on other medical illnesses in menopause. The study was funded by the United States government through the National Heart, Lung, and Blood Institute, a subgroup of the National Institutes of Health (NIH). Beginning in 1995, researchers enrolled more than 26,000 women between the ages of fifty and seventy-nine who had never taken hormones and divided them into two clinical trials. In the WHI-HRT trial, one group of more than 8,000 women received Prempro, the most popular HRT medication at the time, while another group of similar size would receive a placebo. Prempro consists of 0.625 milligrams of Premarin (an estrogen) and 2.5 milligrams of medroxyprogesterone acetate (MDPA, a progestin), and it was to be taken daily over a ten-year period. The designers of the WHI-HRT study wanted to see if HRT could offer primary prevention for medical illnesses like heart disease and osteoporosis without too much risk. The goal of primary prevention is to stop disease before it starts, while the goal of secondary prevention is to slow down the progression of a disease once it has begun.

The WHI-ERT trial consisted of about 10,000 women, whose medical characteristics were similar to those of the women in the HRT group but who had already had a hysterectomy. These volunteers were also divided into two groups—about 5,000 women started taking 0.625 milligrams of Premarin alone, and the other half took a placebo.

The study followed the women carefully to assess the medical benefits and risks of ERT/HRT, specifically in regard to heart disease, stroke, blood clots, breast cancer, osteoporosis, and colon cancer. Control of menopausal symptoms—hot flushes, night sweats, vaginal dryness, and so on—were not followed. The investigators actually kept women with significant menopausal symptoms out of the study. This fact alone casts doubt on the accuracy of the results. Another major cause for concern about the results from both WHI studies comes from the design of the studies. The WHI researchers wanted the trials to assess the primary prevention benefits of the two hormone regimens. Unfortunately, they failed in this task by setting up studies that could only assess secondary prevention.

PRIMARY PREVENTION VERSUS SECONDARY PREVENTION. Primary prevention is taking an organ system that is free of disease, like the heart and blood vessels, and keeping it that way—free of disease. We knew from the Framingham study and other large epidemiologic studies begun more than fifty years ago that women had a much lower mortality rate from heart disease than men at age forty. But by the age of fifty-one, the rates for men and women were the same. It's not that all of the sick men had died off and those that remained had a lower rate of death from heart disease, but that the risk for women had risen rapidly. In other words, the men's risk didn't fall to meet the women's, the women's risk rose to equal the men's.

What was protecting women at age forty but was no longer there to protect them at age fifty-one and beyond? Since the average age of menopause is fifty-one, the researchers felt the obvious answer to this question was estrogen. By age fifty-one, about half of the women in the Framingham study were in menopause, and a significant number had been in it for a few years. This finding led researchers to postulate that estrogen might offer some primary prevention against the development of heart disease in women.

Numerous studies through the years demonstrated that estrogen provided significant primary protection from heart disease, somewhere in the range of a 35–50 percent reduction in the incidence of heart attack. Since heart disease was—and still is—the number one cause of death in women, it made sense to offer this protection to virtually all of them.

Secondary prevention is taking an organ system in which a disease process has already begun and treating it to prevent the damage from getting worse. In this case, if estrogen could prevent women who already had heart problems from getting worse, then it would offer secondary prevention. Many people, even the authors of the WHI study, get confused over the difference between primary and secondary prevention, which can be demonstrated by the following example. If you take a new car off the showroom floor and wax it every three months, the paint will look shiny and new basically forever. This is primary prevention. If, instead, you take an old car with half the paint already gone and begin to wax it, the wax will actually strip the rest of the paint off. If the wax had protected the battered paint job, it would provide secondary prevention, but in this case, the same wax that offers primary prevention to the new car actually damages the already injured paint job on the old car.

A couple of large clinical trials of ERT/HRT in women with known heart disease showed that hormones did not prevent the progression of heart disease once the blood vessels and heart had been damaged. In other words, ERT/HRT does not appear to offer much in the way of secondary prevention, only primary prevention. Although the designers of the WHI trials wanted to assess the possible role of ERT/HRT in primary prevention of cardiovascular disease, they set up a secondary prevention trial instead. How? Remember that the age range in the trials was fifty to seventy-nine years. However, the average age of women in both studies was sixty-three and more than two-thirds of the women were over sixty years old when the studies began in 1995. Since the average age of menopause is fifty-one, this means that more than two-thirds of women in the study had been in menopause for ten years or longer.

The original longitudinal studies showed that a woman's cardiovascular risk becomes the same as a man's within a few years after the onset of menopause unless she takes hormones. This means that the window of opportunity to achieve primary prevention of cardiovascular disease (heart attack and stroke) for the majority of women in the WHI trials had already been closed several years before they entered the studies. The only help these women could have hoped for from ERT/HRT would be secondary prevention and we already knew that ERT/HRT would not provide it. This means that we could not draw any meaningful conclusions about primary prevention from the WHI trials.

The proper study design to assess the primary prevention benefits of ERT/HRT would require enlisting women within the first year of entering menopause, randomly assigning them to receive hormones or placebo, and following them for seven to ten years to see what happened. Unfortunately, the cost of the WHI trials ran into many millions of dollars, and it is unlikely that the government or any private company will take on any research project of this magnitude again in the near future.

RELATIVE RISK VERSUS ABSOLUTE RISK. It is important to understand the types of risk uncovered by research studies and how to properly value the risk-benefit ratio in making decisions about any treatment, particularly ERT/HRT. When medical studies present information about risk, they usually compare the risk of taking a treatment versus taking a placebo (or doing nothing). The risk of treatment is therefore a *relative risk*—the increase in risk of being treated compared to the risk of doing nothing. A statement from a research study such as "people who ate an ounce of peanuts daily were three times more likely to have a heart attack than people who didn't" means that the relative risk of eating the peanuts over not eating them is high—300 percent. If this statement were true, it would appear at first glance that eating an ounce of peanuts each day is very bad for your heart. Who would take such an incredibly high risk just for peanuts? However, we don't know the whole story yet. We do know that it's three times riskier to eat the peanuts than to not eat them, but to make the right decision about the peanuts, we also need to know the absolute risk involved with eating them.

Absolute risk gives us an idea of the magnitude of the risk involved for one person. In other words, analyzing absolute risk allows us to answer the question "What is my individual risk?" In the peanut example, if we find that the absolute risk of heart attack in the "no peanuts" group was only 0.0003 percent to begin with, then the absolute risk of eating the peanuts is only 0.0009 percent! This is an incredibly low absolute risk, and if they like peanuts, most people would go ahead and eat them. Even though the relative risk was very high at 300 percent, the *absolute risk* was exceptionally low at only 0.0009 percent. When absolute risks are very low, calculations of relative risk can be very confusing.

A real-life example of weighing relative risk versus absolute risk in decision making may help further illustrate the difference. When a twenty-year-old woman starts birth control pills, she doubles her *relative* risk of having a fatal blood clot. The relative risk of her birth control pills killing her increases by 100 percent. One might ask, "Who would take such a crazy risk?" But if she stops the analysis here, she may make the wrong choice. In contrast, her *absolute* risk of a fatal blood clot before she started the pill was only 1:100,000 women (0.001 percent). On the pill, it's now 1:50,000 women (0.002 percent). The relative risk did double, but the absolute risk is still very low. In fact, this woman is much more likely to suffer a serious complication from getting pregnant without the pill than by taking it.

So when making the decision to take a medication or not, if the benefits (not getting pregnant) of a treatment (birth control pills) outweigh the risks (blood clots, and so on), then taking the medication makes sense. Conversely, if the benefits don't outweigh the risks, then avoiding the treatment is logical. It is the balancing of risks and benefits that should determine the medical decisions we make.

RESULTS FROM THE WHI-HRT TRIAL

The first of the two WHI trials, the WHI-HRT arm, was halted in the summer of 2002 after 5.2 years because of fear that the combination of Premarin and MDPA might actually increase the risk of heart attack, stroke, blood clots, and breast cancer when started in women already in menopause. The study data showed the following increase in risk for the women who took Premarin and MDPA over the women who didn't take any hormones:

Complication	Relative Risk	Absolute Risk
Heart attack	29% increase	1:1,430 women per year
Stroke	41% increase	1:1,250 women per year
Blood clots	200% increase	1:555 women per year
Breast cancer	26% increase	1:1,250 women per year

A great deal of excitement was generated by the release of this information to the public. The focus of the press release was on the relative risk numbers, which sounded impressive to the media and panicked women on hormones. In my opinion, however, the decision to leave out the discussion of the absolute risks involved with HRT misled the public and created an unnecessary scare for women who were already undergoing such treatment. Even more disconcerting to me is that the editors of the medical journal that released these numbers did little to offer a balanced perspective of the results of the study in terms of absolute risks and benefits—which was their duty to the public. The flurry of news reports and subsequent republishing of the WHI-HRT data in different medical journals—which often appeared to be yet more new studies confirming the worst fears about HRT—caused many women to abruptly stop taking their hormones, suffer all the symptoms of menopause, and give up some very important health benefits simply because they weren't given the whole story.

Dealing with numbers can sometimes be confusing. To put these increases in risk in their proper perspective, let's compare them to another common situation. The likelihood of getting pregnant while taking birth control pills is 1:200 per year. In other words, one woman will get pregnant out of every two hundred women taking the pill. Most women consider this a low risk of failure. Comparing this risk with the data from the WHI-HRT study, the increased risk of having a heart attack from taking HRT over no hormones at all is seven times lower than the risk of getting pregnant on birth control pills. Similarly, the risk of developing breast cancer or having a stroke from taking the combination hormone replacement is also much lower than the likelihood of becoming pregnant while on the pill—six times (600 percent) lower. Even the risk of developing a blood clot is more than two times lower than the likelihood of getting pregnant on birth control pills. The increased likelihood of developing a blood clot on HRT is actually lower than the likelihood that a woman who has had her tubes tied will eventually become pregnant.

Certainly in terms of absolute risk, none of these unfavorable events is very likely to happen to a woman on HRT. In fact, the 26 percent increase in the relative risk of breast cancer was not statistically significant. In other words, the results obtained in the study may not represent a true risk at all. Statistics involve making estimates about a large population—in this case, millions of post-menopausal women—from a much smaller sample—the 16,000 women in the WHI-HRT study. Attempting to study every woman in menopause to answer questions about the benefits and risks of HRT would be a tremendously expensive and time-consuming undertaking. But instead of giving up on finding the answers to these questions, doctors use statistics to try to see if the results obtained from the sample are likely to be an accurate reflection of what is really true for the larger population. If the sample results are statistically significant, it means that the differences in risk found between the women who took HRT versus those who took a placebo are likely to be real—not just a fluke based on the way in which the sample women were brought into the study or the way we calculated the results. When the results of a study are not statistically significant, most statisticians feel they should be ignored or at least interpreted as being highly questionable.

When the WHI-HRT results were announced to the public, the main focus was on risks, but the study also verified some very important benefits. There was a significant reduction in hip fractures from osteoporosis as well as a 34 percent reduction in colon cancer. These were statistically significant benefits of taking HRT. Of course, the important benefit of a reduction in menopause symptoms was not addressed in the study because women with significant symptoms were excluded. And the other "feel better" benefits of HRT/ERT—improved sexual function, increased vaginal lubrication and elasticity, better sleep, and improved bladder control—were not evaluated in either WHI trial.

RESULTS FROM THE WHI-ERT TRIAL

Data released from the WHI-ERT trial that ended in April 2004 showed that women who have had a hysterectomy and therefore take Premarin by itself are not at any great risk of complications from ERT. The following table lists the increases and decreases in relative and absolute risks for the same set of complications found in the WHI-HRT trial:

Complication	Relative Risk	Absolute Risk
Heart attack	9% decrease	None
Stroke	39% increase	1:833 women per year
Blood clots	33% increase	1:1,430 women per year
Breast cancer	23% decrease	None

As you can see, women on estrogen alone incurred no increase in absolute risk of heart disease or breast cancer. This is very good news to the millions of women who take estrogen, particularly those who were mislead into stopping it for fear of developing these two serious complications by the WHI-HRT results. Even though there was actually a decrease in the relative risk of heart attack and breast cancer in the WHI-ERT trial, it was not statistically significant. This means we cannot assume there is a protective benefit from estrogen from these data. Interestingly, the increased risk of breast cancer reported by the press in the WHI-HRT trial wasn't statistically significant either. It should therefore have been disregarded, or at least the finding should have been accompanied by more explanation about why the results were not conclusive. Again, it appears that the media loves bad news about hormones, and in the case of the WHI-HRT trial, didn't report the findings accurately.

When attempting to balance the risks versus the benefits from the two WHI trials, the WHI-HRT trial provides the "worst-case scenario" of the two hormone treatments when it comes to risk. Adding the overall benefits and subtracting the risks in the WHI-HRT trial yields an overall increase in absolute risk of 0.4 percent from taking HRT. This is called the *global risk of therapy*. In other words, if we look at the overall balance of good and bad medical effects of HRT, 4 out of 1,000 (1:250) women who took HRT had more trouble than benefit. Contrast the risk from HRT with the risk of following the common recommendation to take a baby aspirin every day to prevent heart disease. Many experts recommend that healthy people take one baby aspirin (81 milligrams) daily to help reduce the risk of having a heart attack. However, taking aspirin in this fashion carries with it a 2 percent risk of developing gastrointestinal bleeding. Two percent is 2 people out of 100, or 20 out of 1,000. Most experts feel that taking this small dose of aspirin daily is a low-risk therapy compared to the potential benefit or they wouldn't be recommending it. But suffering a complication from taking a baby aspirin every day is actually five times more likely than having all of the problems in the WHI-HRT trial rolled together: 20 complications per 1,000 from daily aspirin versus 4 per 1,000 from HRT. If the risk of 4 complications per 1,000 women is too high for you, then you should avoid HRT (and perhaps ERT as well). But now that you understand risk more fully, you'll probably agree with me that HRT/ERT isn't really so risky after all, particularly if you get a benefit from it. And I think that feeling good is a benefit worth considering.

In the final analysis, you and your doctor must decide the value of the benefits you feel hormone replacement may provide, weigh those benefits against the possible risks involved, and come to a comfortable decision that suits your needs and personal and family history.

PERIMENOPAUSE

Perimenopause is the time of transition between having regular menstrual cycles and menopause. The length of perimenopause is unpredictable and can last anywhere from six months to a few years. Because estrogen levels are fluctuating and ovulation often becomes irregular, perimenopause typically brings some very disconcerting symptoms. Menstrual cycles often become irregular and may get heavier or lighter depending on whether uterine fibroids (benign muscular tumors in the uterus) or endometriosis is also present. Hot flushes and night sweats become more common, although these usually wax and wane at the time of ovulation and with the menstrual periods that do come. Some women don't really experience big changes in their cycle but have other symptoms that sometimes go unnoticed as perimenopause:

- Insomnia, particularly waking up before the alarm goes off

- Moodiness

- Fatigue

- Weight gain

- Low sex drive

- Forgetfulness or a sense of confusion

- Hair thinning (but no bald spots)

These symptoms are also those of Hurried Woman Syndrome and depression. This often produces confusion for women as well as health care providers in determining whether a particular symptom is from a hormone imbalance or an imbalance in brain chemistry. The reason for the confusion is that the two systems are linked; the action of estrogen and progesterone influences the levels of serotonin, dopamine, and norepinephrine in the brain. This is why it's critical to think about perimenopause and menopause in relation to Hurried Woman Syndrome.

The good news is that there is help for these symptoms. If your doctor suspects perimenopause by your history, and your follicle-stimulating hormone (FSH) level shows that you aren't in menopause yet, then you can approach the problems of perimenopause from two directions. First, the hormonal highs and lows can be smoothed out with low-dose birth control pills, patches, or a vaginal ring. Each of these methods will straighten out the irregular periods, provide contraception if you still need and desire it, and help correct the strain on your brain chemistry balance by easing the hormone fluctuations. This approach works for about 4:5 women in perimenopause. It used to be thought unsafe for women over forty to take the pill. However, research now shows that birth control pills are safe for women until menopause begins, usually around age fifty-one. Unfortunately, birth control pills are not suitable for everyone—women who smoke after the age of thirty-five cannot take the pill. Also, women with liver problems, significant high blood pressure, or a history of blood clots will probably be unable to take it either. But for those who can use this type of contraception, it may be the difference between misery and happiness.

Avoiding hysterectomy is another benefit that many women receive from using hormone-based birth control methods. Many women in perimenopause bleed irregularly and may also experience very heavy cycles. However, traditional HRT will not usually control this type of bleeding because the hormones in HRT are too low to stop ovulation when it does occur. Fifteen years ago when a woman reached forty, it was recommended that she no longer take the pill and that's when the trouble began. When menstrual cycles got heavier and more painful, many women had no viable options other than to continue to suffer or have a hysterectomy. Now that newer studies indicate that women can safely take birth control pills into menopause, many are choosing to stay on the pill and thus avoid either suffering through bad cycles and the slings and arrows of perimenopause without help or having to resort to a major operation for relief.

The second approach to treating the symptoms of perimenopause is with antidepressants, which will work for PMS as well. Whereas the symptoms of perimenopause tend to last all month, those of PMS are very predictable and occur only between the time of ovulation (midcycle) and the onset of the next menstrual cycle.

The changes in brain chemistry are very similar; it's the timing that's different. The majority of women in perimenopause, and particularly those with PMS, tend to feel anxious as a major part of their symptoms. This is why I usually recommend a selective serotonin reuptake inhibitor (SSRI), like Zoloft, for these women. Those with perimenopause routinely take the medicine every day. Women with PMS should start the medication about the time of ovulation—two weeks before they would expect their next menstrual period to begin—and stop on the first or second day after their period starts. The strategy behind this approach is to limit potential side effects by allowing patients to take the antidepressant only during the two weeks each month in which they need it.

NATURAL HORMONES, HERBALS, SUPPLEMENTS, AND OTHER OTC PRODUCTS

Many women are experimenting with "natural hormones," herbal products, and supplements in an effort to find a more natural approach to the problems of menopause, perimenopause, and PMS. This quest is sometimes driven by fear that what their doctor or nurse practitioner has to offer is more dangerous or somehow less healthy than the available herbals and supplements, and other times by the fact that what the doctor recommended didn't work very well.

NATURAL HORMONES

The term *natural* can be the cause of much confusion when it comes to hormones. When we say something is natural, are we talking about the hormones that occur in nature—animal, vegetable, or mineral—or the hormones that are naturally found in humans? When people talk about natural hormones, they are usually referring to two very different things. They may be interested in "bio-identical" hormones, which are exactly the same hormones as those found in humans, or they may be referring to hormones or hormone-like substances derived from plants, such as phytoestrogens that principally come from soy.

Bio-identical estrogens are principally estradiol, estrone, and estriol. Estriol is the predominant estrogen in the popular products BI-EST and TRI-EST, two formulations that must be compounded by pharmacists. Consumer literature frequently describes these hormones as the most natural replacements since they contain all three of the most common forms of human estrogen. Estriol is the weakest of the estrogens and comprises 80 percent of both BI-EST and TRI-EST. It is produced in large quantities by the placenta during pregnancy. BI-EST contains 2 milligrams of estriol (80 percent) and 0.5 milligrams of estradiol (20 percent), while TRI-EST has 2 milligrams of estriol (80 percent), 0.25 milligrams of estradiol (10 percent), and 0.25 milligrams of estrone (10 percent). Women who select these products thinking that they are low-dose estrogens should be aware that they do contain significant doses of estradiol and estrone. Estradiol is the most potent of the three estrogens and is the predominant estrogen found in women prior to menopause, whereas estrone is a very weak estrogen found in menopausal women. Because estriol is such a weak estrogen, it causes little breast tenderness and not much endometrial stimulation but does seem to help with hot flushes and night sweats. However, there is no scientific evidence that it protects against osteoporosis or heart disease. Women would also be well-advised to consider using these with a progestin at least every three months to ensure that they don't get endometrial stimulation and possibly uterine cancer.

A number of women use over-the-counter progesterone creams, often to combat what some self-appointed experts call "estrogen dominance." They claim that the natural progesterone supplements will offset the ill effects of estrogen dominance, which they say includes such symptoms as insomnia, obesity, low sex drive, swelling, breast tenderness, mental confusion, depression, and high blood sugar. Many even claim progesterone cream can prevent breast cancer. However, I don't recommend this because there is no compelling scientific evidence that natural progesterone cream can do any of the things claimed except control menopausal symptoms in some women. Interestingly, a lab in California tested OTC progesterone creams a few years ago and found that ten of the creams studied had either no progesterone at all or levels so small as to be of no value. Remember, these products are not regulated by the FDA, which means their contents often vary from jar to jar and from manufacturer to manufacturer, and little is known about how well they are absorbed or even if they work. My advice is to steer clear of the natural progesterone creams until they have been studied further.

There is a natural progesterone product called Prometrium that has undergone scientific study and is also approved by the FDA. It comes as a pill and can be used along with an estrogen to prevent endometrial overstimulation as part of HRT. But don't confuse it with the natural progesterone creams; they are not the same thing.

PHYTOESTROGENS AND SOY

Phytoestrogens are estrogen-like substances found in legumes such as soy, chickpeas, clover, lentils, and beans. Soy is a healthy food and has been found to reduce the risk of heart disease. However, in more than twelve trials of soy or its by-products and their effects on menopausal symptoms, the results have ranged from inconclusive to not effective. Attempting to wade through the mire of different preparations, different dosages, and different potencies makes prescribing these substances very difficult.

BLACK COHOSH

Early studies of black cohosh (*Cimicifuga racemosa*) suggested that it has estrogenic activity. However, more recent studies show that it does not suppress FSH or affect serum estrogen levels. Almost half a century of research in Germany has led to its approval in that country for menstrual cramps (dysmenorrhea), PMS, and the hot flushes and night sweats of menopause. Two long-term studies are underway in the United States to assess the effectiveness and safety of black cohosh. At present, it is recommended that black cohosh be used for no longer than six months at a time because its safety profile is unknown. This product is available over the counter in America as Remifemin.

RED CLOVER

Although red clover (*Trifolium pratense*) appeared promising at first in the treatment of menopausal symptoms, a recent double-blind trial of 225 women randomly given Promensil (82 milligrams isoflavones per day), Rimostil (57 milligrams isoflavones per day), or a daily placebo showed no differences in effectiveness between the red clover products and placebo. Although blended into many OTC supplements, red clover probably offers no real benefit for control of menopausal symptoms.

DONG QUAI

Dong quai (*Angelica sinensis*) is widely used in Asia and is available in the United States and Europe. In a 1997 study, women were randomly given 1,500 milligrams of dong quai three times daily or a placebo daily for twelve weeks. There was no difference in menopausal symptoms in the two groups. These researchers saw no evidence of estrogenic activity in biopsies of the lining of the uterus or in cell samples from the vagina. Dong quai is usually found in combination with other herbals and is felt to be a "balancing herb" to help promote the action of other herbals.

GINSENG

Often promoted to improve mood and energy levels, many preparations of ginseng (*Panax ginseng*) have been adulterated with caffeine and other stimulants through the years. In a sixteen-week study of 384 patients randomly given ginseng extract or a placebo, there was no difference in menopausal symptoms, but those on ginseng did report some improvement in well-being and general health.

Wild Yam

A lot of promotional hype heralded the arrival of wild yam (*Dioscorea villosa*) on the supplement scene a few years ago. Wild yam cream was thought to be the perfect source of natural progesterone. Indeed, Japanese researchers in the 1930s were able to isolate the active compound, diosgenin, from the yam plant and now almost half of all hormones produced in the laboratory come from this compound. Unfortunately, the human body can't convert diosgenin into progesterone. So in spite of all the hype and all the money spent by consumers, wild yam holds no medicinal value. The yam scam provides the perfect example of the near-science many herbalists use to find new products and promote them to an unsuspecting public.

St. John's Wort

Although there have been no clinical trials using St. John's Wort (*Hypericum perforatum*) to treat menopausal symptoms, it is widely used in Germany—often in combination with black cohosh—to treat hot flushes, insomnia, and minor depression. The National Institute of Mental Health is presently conducting a study of 333 patients with minor depression to investigate the effectiveness of St. John's Wort versus Celexa (citalopram) in a placebo-controlled trial. Results from earlier studies of St. John's Wort in treating major depression were not particularly impressive, but it may have some benefit in treating minor depression and Hurried Woman Syndrome. Until there is better scientific support for its use, I don't routinely recommend this herb.

One of the main problems associated with St. John's Wort is that it interferes with the metabolism of several prescription medications and lowers the serum levels of estrogen in birth control pills, leading to breakthrough bleeding and possible pregnancy. It also causes bleeding problems for patients on blood thinners like Coumadin (warfarin) and should be stopped at least two weeks prior to any surgical procedure. The other problem comes from the very nature of the unregulated herbal/supplement market itself. A study of St. John's Wort preparations was undertaken by a California physician who was also a licensed pharmacist. Of the ten preparations she studied, four had no active ingredients whatsoever—none. Of those brands that actually did contain St. John's Wort, there was no consistency in the amount found in pills reported to be the same strength.

Over a century ago, when westerners visited the tropical areas of Africa and Central and South America, malaria was epidemic among the natives and soon became a hazard to foreigners as well. Malaria was the leading cause of death and illness among workers on the Panama Canal more than a century ago. However, visiting doctors noticed that the natives in Peru had learned to chew the bark of the cinchona tree to prevent the recurring attacks of malaria. As the doctors observed the natives chewing the bark, they noticed that sometimes natives who chewed a lot of cinchona bark or got their bark from a particularly "hot" spot of the tree would develop severe headaches, nausea and vomiting, abdominal pain, flushing, deafness, blindness, and, in the worst cases, have a disturbance of their heart rhythm and die. Doctors called this condition cinchonism, realizing that it was coming from an overdose of the active substance in cinchona bark. Eventually, scientists were able to isolate the drug quinine from the bitter bark of the cinchona tree and revolutionize the treatment of malaria. Similarly, some of today's herbals and supplements may one day be studied and proven to be effective in helping certain medical conditions. However, most of them are currently at the urban legend level of effectiveness, many lack any real scientific support of claims about how well they work, and even when they seem to work, they are only at the "chewing the bark of the cinchona tree" phase of isolating the active ingredient that works and studying it for safety and effectiveness.

Medical researchers and pharmaceutical manufacturers are constantly searching out new and better treatments for patients. Let's face it, they can make a lot of money if they find one that works. But scientifically proven effectiveness, patient safety, and uniform product quality are extremely important when trying to choose between a new treatment and an old one that has been effective in the past but could hopefully be improved on.

GETTING SERIOUS ABOUT CHRONIC HEALTH PROBLEMS

Virtually all chronic illnesses—diabetes, high blood pressure, heart disease, allergies, and asthma, just to name a few—tend to drag us down when they are not under good control. If you've been cheating on your diabetic diet, not taking your blood pressure medicine regularly, or ignoring the wheezing you're having because you haven't had time to stop by the pharmacy to refill your inhaler prescription, get back on track. If you don't stay on top of these chronic ailments, they *may* kill you, they *could* hurt you, but they *will* most assuredly lower the quality of your life and how you feel.

It isn't wise to build a house on uneven ground. Similarly, taking steps to maximize your general health will provide the firm foundation necessary for rebuilding your life the way you want it rather than keeping you locked into the way things are now.

7

STEP 2: FIND THE RIGHT CALORIC BALANCE

WHEN MY PATIENTS tell me they are dieting and exercising and can't seem to control their weight, what they are really saying is that the guidelines they used to live by don't apply anymore. Up until now they had kept their weight within a certain range by combining how much they ate with a certain level of activity. They had learned "the rules" of the weight game. Unfortunately for them, the rules have changed—as they do for all of us. And the rules haven't changed for a few months or even a couple of years, but forever. My patients have to learn the new rules and live by them from now on to successfully control their weight.

Diet is a four-letter word. When I say the "d-word" to a patient, I immediately feel negative vibrations. Hearing it invokes an immediate, negative gut-level (no pun intended) emotional response in virtually everyone.

Being on a diet feels like punishment, like being on probation. "Yes, Your Honor, I know I shouldn't have done it [overeaten], and if I promise to be good [diet] for the next six months, can I go free [back to eating like I used to]?" Much of our negative thinking about dieting comes from the fact that few of us have experienced any lasting success with a diet program. Most dieters see a few pounds drop off early, but within a few weeks the weight loss slows, the novelty of the program wears off, and we fall off the diet wagon and gain back the weight we lost (or more).

Another major reason most people have a negative view of dieting probably comes from the way we view food—very positively! We like food. Food tastes good. It takes away hunger. Many of us reward ourselves with a favorite food after a particularly hard day at work or when we need a mood lift. Over the years, through many different experiences, we have crafted a complex perspective on food that influences what we choose to eat, how much we eat, when we eat it, and what it means to us emotionally. I am not proposing that you go through intense psychoanalysis to find out why you make some less-than-ideal choices when it comes to food, but do try to be aware of how you presently use food to fill yourself, not only physically but also emotionally.

The way you view food—what food means to you or does for you on an emotional level—is actually a learned response. In other words, you were "taught" to view food the way you do. Most importantly, you can learn a new way to view food that will help you to successfully manage your weight from now on. This is the cognitive-behavioral aspect of weight management.

STATISTICS

Weight gain is a big problem for many of my patients and for a growing number of people in the United States and other countries. Gaining weight can be one of the cardinal symptoms of Hurried Woman Syndrome, or it can simply be an isolated problem. Either way, being overweight can have serious health consequences, both physical and emotional. According to recently published statistics from the National Health and Nutrition Examination Survey II, approximately 25 percent of American women are classified as "overweight," with a body mass index (BMI) between 25 and 30. Another 25 percent of women are "obese," with a BMI greater than 30. You can look up your BMI on the chart in Figure 7.1. This table provides a range of "ideal" body weights for your height. Through some mystical process, the researchers divined these weights and anointed them as the model to shoot for. In other words, there's a little "wiggle room" in the numbers. Obviously, the ranges are pretty wide, so you will have to decide if you're "small-boned" and pick a number in the lower portion, or if you're "large-boned" and pick a number at the high end of the range that suits you.

Find your height on the left-hand side of the table, then move to the right in that row until you find your weight or the number that is closest to it. Then look at the top of that column to find your body mass index. If your BMI is between 19 and 24, you are within the normal weight range for your height. If your BMI is between 25 and 30, the government considers you overweight. If your BMI is greater than 30, you are considered obese, which carries significantly increased health risks. The following are some weight-related diseases that have been identified and widely publicized:

• **Heart disease.** If your BMI is 29, you are twice as likely to die of a heart attack than if your BMI is less than 22. That risk doubles again if your BMI is 32 and increases steadily as your index rises further.

• **Diabetes.** Women with a BMI of 24 (still considered in the normal range) are three and a half times (350 percent) more likely to develop diabetes than women with a BMI of 22. Even more incredible, women with a BMI of 31 are thirty times (3,000 percent) more likely to develop diabetes!

✿ FIGURE 7.1: BODY MASS INDEX

BMI	Normal						Overweight					Obese																									
	19	20	21	22	23	24	25	26	27	28	29	30	31	32	33	34	35	36	37	38	39	40	41	42	43	44	45	46	47	48	49	50	51	52	53	54
Height (inches)	Body Weight (pounds)																																			
58	91	96	100	105	110	115	119	124	129	134	138	143	148	153	158	162	167	172	177	181	186	191	196	201	205	210	215	220	224	229	234	239	244	248	253	258
59	94	99	104	109	114	119	124	128	133	138	143	148	153	158	163	168	173	178	183	188	193	198	203	208	212	217	222	227	232	237	242	247	252	257	262	267
60	97	102	107	112	118	123	128	133	138	143	148	153	158	163	168	174	179	184	189	194	199	204	209	215	220	225	230	235	240	245	250	255	261	266	271	276
61	100	106	111	116	122	127	132	137	143	148	153	158	164	169	174	180	185	190	195	201	206	211	217	222	227	232	238	243	248	254	259	264	269	275	280	285
62	104	109	115	120	126	131	136	142	147	153	158	164	169	175	180	186	191	196	202	207	213	218	224	229	235	240	246	251	256	262	267	273	278	284	289	295
63	107	113	118	124	130	135	141	146	152	158	163	169	175	180	186	191	197	203	208	214	220	225	231	237	242	248	254	259	265	270	278	282	287	293	299	304
64	110	116	122	128	134	140	145	151	157	163	169	174	180	186	192	197	204	209	215	221	227	232	238	244	250	256	262	267	273	279	285	291	296	302	308	314
65	114	120	126	132	138	144	150	156	162	168	174	180	186	192	198	204	210	216	222	228	234	240	246	252	258	264	270	276	282	288	294	300	306	312	318	324
66	118	124	130	136	142	148	155	161	167	173	179	186	192	198	204	210	216	223	229	235	241	247	253	260	266	272	278	284	291	297	303	309	315	322	328	334
67	121	127	134	140	146	153	159	166	172	178	185	191	198	204	211	217	223	230	236	242	249	255	261	268	274	280	287	293	299	306	312	319	325	331	338	344
68	125	131	138	144	151	158	164	171	177	184	190	197	203	210	216	223	230	236	243	249	256	262	269	276	282	289	295	302	308	315	322	328	335	341	348	354
69	128	135	142	149	155	162	169	176	182	189	196	203	209	216	223	230	236	243	250	257	263	270	277	284	291	297	304	311	318	324	331	338	345	351	358	365
70	132	139	146	153	160	167	174	181	188	195	202	209	216	222	229	236	243	250	257	264	271	278	285	292	299	306	313	320	327	334	341	348	355	362	369	376
71	136	143	150	157	165	172	179	186	193	200	208	215	222	229	236	243	250	257	265	272	279	286	293	301	308	315	322	329	338	343	351	358	365	372	379	386
72	140	147	154	162	169	177	184	191	199	206	213	221	228	235	242	250	258	265	272	279	287	294	302	309	316	324	331	338	346	353	361	368	375	383	390	397
73	144	151	159	166	174	182	189	197	204	212	219	227	235	242	250	257	265	272	280	288	295	302	310	318	325	333	340	348	355	363	371	378	386	393	401	408
74	148	155	163	171	179	186	194	202	210	218	225	233	241	249	256	264	272	280	287	295	303	311	319	326	334	342	350	358	365	373	381	389	396	404	412	420
75	152	160	168	176	184	192	200	208	216	224	232	240	248	256	264	272	279	287	295	303	311	319	327	335	343	351	359	367	375	383	391	399	407	415	423	431
76	156	164	172	180	189	197	205	213	221	230	238	246	254	263	271	279	287	295	304	312	320	328	336	344	353	361	369	377	385	394	402	410	418	426	435	443

Source: Adapted from Clinical Guidelines on the Identification, Evaluation, and Treatment of Overweight and Obesity in Adults: The Evidence Report.

• **Infertility.** Women who are classified as obese (their BMI is greater than 30, or more than 20 percent above their ideal body weight) are two to three times (200–300 percent) more likely to have irregular menstrual cycles and infertility than women who are mildly overweight or in the normal range.

• **Cancer.** Many experts believe that cancers of the breast, cervix, uterus, ovaries, and gallbladder are linked to obesity, as obese women suffer higher death rates from these tumors. It isn't clear whether obesity actually causes the cancers or simply makes them harder to detect early, leading to higher death rates because treatments are usually less effective in more advanced cases. For example, a woman with very large breasts is more likely to die from breast cancer than a woman with small breasts, but this difference is probably because the woman with smaller breasts can usually find her lump easier and earlier than the woman with large breasts who has more trouble with self-examination. Getting started on treatment earlier has a favorable impact on survival.

Whatever the real reason behind these statistics, it is clear that obesity is truly a disease and an epidemic, and it needs to be addressed medically just like chest pain, diabetes, or a butter knife stuck in your forehead.

You may not have a weight problem at the present time, and I hope you never have one. However, I would still encourage you to take the time to read through this information. A more healthful approach to eating helps you maintain your weight as well as lose pounds.

Dr. Barry Sears, in his book *The Zone: A Dietary Road Map to Lose Weight Permanently: Reset Your Genetic Code: Prevent Disease: Achieve Maximum Physical Performance* (Regan Books, 1995), has some interesting insights into what he calls "the fattening of America." I will share some of his ideas with you here and augment them with other more current opinions. One thing that's certain about our scientific understanding of human nutrition is that we really don't understand as much about it as we would like. So use this information to find out what works for you.

NUTRITION: A SCIENCE?

The major problem with studying individual nutrients in isolation is that they never really exist in true isolation in a living animal. Living animals, particularly humans, constantly find themselves in changing circumstances. That's why there are many "facts" about nutrition that seem to be contradictory and why very well-respected nutritionists often disagree. The ongoing conflicts over dietary fiber, cholesterol levels, and what constitutes the "perfect" diet are all recent examples of the problems with getting a firm handle on proper nutrition and weight loss.

Another problem with past scientific research in this field has been the faulty assumption that all humans are created nutritionally equal. In fact, our genes control to a great extent what our individual daily caloric needs are; what we do with excess protein, carbohydrates, and fats if we get too many (which those of us in "developed" countries usually do); and what our biochemical reaction will be to imbalances of the main nutrients. This means that there is no one uniform human response to a high-cholesterol diet; a high-protein, low-carbohydrate diet; or a high-carbohydrate, low-fat diet—although science has conducted much of its past nutritional research with this thought in mind. Little wonder so many similarly designed experiments have come out with conflicting results and thereby caused an almost constant debate among nutritionists about the proper diet for humans and the best technique to use for weight management. Dr. Sears points out in *The Zone* that "in the world of nutrition nobody's really wrong. They just aren't quite correct." And I suspect that this will remain the case for many years. If only God had sent Moses "The Ten Nutritional Commandments" along with the other admittedly more important ten, perhaps we wouldn't be in such a daze about diet and weight control.

One truth that comes out clearly from the available research—and bookstore shelves—is that there are about as many diets recommended by nutrition experts as there are nutrition experts, and most of them actually work to accomplish weight loss, at least in the short run. But short-term success in a weight-loss program is *not* the important part.

The real test of a successful diet effort is in the long term; keeping the weight off is the big challenge. Most fad diets simply cannot do this for you for a variety of reasons we will talk about later. For now, let's discuss the genetic truths about nutrition and weight control, how they affect your efforts to control your weight, and a plan that will work for you—in the long run.

MEDICAL CAUSES OF WEIGHT GAIN

If you've only got twenty pounds to lose, you could probably do it any number of ways, including the method I offer you in this book. If you have more than that to go, I think you should consider consulting your doctor, particularly if you've gained more than ten pounds in the last year. Under these circumstances, you need to be certain there is no underlying medical condition, such as major depression or thyroid disease, that needs treatment.

POLYCYSTIC OVARY SYNDROME

This special condition, estimated to be present in almost 10 percent of women, is associated with obesity in more than half of the women who have it. If you read older information on polycystic ovary syndrome (PCOS), referred to as Stein-Leventhal syndrome when it was first described in 1935, you will get a rather confusing

picture of the condition. I will give you the most current information available, but some new and exciting research will be coming
out soon that will hopefully help those with this condition.

PCOS is diagnosed when a woman of child-bearing age has the
following symptoms:

- Irregular menstrual cycles that are typically five to seven or
  more weeks apart or fewer than eight cycles a year (which
  may sound good at first, but it's more trouble than
  triumph)

- Signs of "male-type" hair growth on the chin or beard area,
  breasts, and the line between the pubic hair and belly
  button (called "hirsutism") and/or significant acne and/or
  abnormal blood levels of male hormone, specifically
  testosterone

- No other medical problems that can resemble PCOS, such
  as tumors that secrete prolactin or produce male hormones,
  thyroid disease, or adrenal gland malfunction

Women with PCOS also tend to gain weight around the waist
and above (making them appear "apple shaped") rather than in the
hips and thighs where most women tend to put on weight ("pear
shaped").

If you think you may have PCOS, you need to discuss it with
your gynecologist or endocrinologist (a specialist in internal medicine who specifically treats hormone and metabolism problems,
most often diabetes and thyroid disease). Unfortunately, most general practitioners don't have a lot of experience with this condition.

The cause of the weight gain associated with PCOS is unknown,
but the best theory at present is that the fat cells somehow become
insulin-resistant in PCOS and therefore don't respond appropriately
to changes in diet and exercise. In other words, women with PCOS
are not only insulin-resistant but also "diet-resistant." This is good
news and bad news. The good news: I can now explain why many

women who diet faithfully and exercise vigorously can't seem to lose weight—they probably have PCOS. The bad news: the only way they're going to lose weight is to eat even less and exercise harder than the average woman—which, of course, you're grandma could have told you. Before you get too discouraged though, there is some additional good news. There is a lot of ongoing research attempting to solve this mystery and I predict that within five years we'll have some better tools to help you control your weight. At present, there is an oral medication for diabetes called glucophage (metformin) that can reverse the insulin-resistance in about 25 percent of women with PCOS. However, I don't use glucophage because it doesn't help 75 percent of PCOS patients, and it must be monitored closely as it can cause hypoglycemia and irritate the liver. For now, balancing diet and exercise is the key to successful weight management and a healthier future for women with PCOS.

GENETICS AND WEIGHT REGULATION

For the most part, we all tend to become like one or both of our parents, in our attitudes and in our physical attributes. Most people who struggle with weight have at least one parent with a weight problem. This certainly points to a genetic basis for weight regulation. Although it is clear that our attitudes about food, our preferences for different styles of foods and spices, and the way we eat our meals are all influenced by the way we were brought up, I think it's important to remember that many of these things change dramatically after we leave home and as we go through life. In other words, our eating style and food selections constantly change from the time we leave our mother's direct culinary influences, yet the trend to be like her physically does not.

Your genetic code determines how you handle the calories you put into your body as well as the efficiency with which exercise burns those calories—in everyday terms, your metabolism. It is important to understand that not everyone responds to food and exercise the same way. When test subjects had a measured amount of carbohydrates added to their diet, about 50 percent gained the amount of weight predicted according to the extra carbs. However, 25 percent gained considerably more weight than predicted, while the other 25 percent did not gain any weight at all. These differences are due to the differences in insulin response to carbohydrates that exist because of the genetic variations among humans. This fact alone explains why a "one-size-fits-all" approach to dieting doesn't work.

Each of us, to a certain extent, has to find the right balance of calorie intake and exercise by trial and error. It might be interesting to know which group of "carbohydrate responders" you fall into, but practically speaking, it really doesn't matter. You cannot change the way your body responds, so you have to learn to cope with it.

If you have always been able to lose weight when you've dieted in the past but have just found it difficult to find a plan you can stay with, you are probably in the "normal response" group—that's about half of all people. If you really can't seem to lose weight in spite of really cutting down on calories, even below the levels of most diets, then you may be in the "overresponder group," which is where one-fourth of Americans find themselves. Unfortunately, you're going to have to do a lot more cutting back on food and a lot more exercising than most people to get control of your weight.

Survival Genes

Actually, people who have trouble losing weight are genetically superior to those who can't seem to gain weight, and even those with what would be called a normal carbohydrate response. Why? Thousands of years ago, our ancestors lived on a pretty harsh diet compared to the one we know today. Experts estimate that the average person five thousand years ago survived on considerably less than a thousand calories per day. During a bad winter or a drought, the calories available for consumption dropped off to starvation levels very quickly. In such harsh times, those people who could "eat anything" and never gain a pound would be dead! In other words, the same genes that confound you now by causing you to struggle with weight gain would have protected you from starvation in harsh nutritional circumstances, so you have superior survival genes.

The only problem is you don't need them now and you can't shut them off when you want. They are constantly there, protecting you from the ill effects of starvation. Most popular diets, particularly the so-called fad diets, are simply that—starvation—swapping one class of nutrients for another. When you start a fad diet, your survival genes see your decreasing nutritional input as starvation— a bad winter or the buffalo herd not coming on time—and begin to turn on metabolic safety mechanisms in your body that prevent you from losing weight. In the early stages of starvation (or any diet), the body causes shifts in its metabolic pathways to keep glucose levels stable. These mechanisms involve mostly water shifts between "compartments" inside the body. Indeed, most of the early weight loss in any diet, particularly the high-protein, very low-carbohydrate diets that are so popular, is from water loss. For most dieters, this is the first five to ten pounds that come off in the first couple of weeks of any diet. This lost water is also the first weight to come back when the diet fails, so it's really false encouragement. Of course, some encouragement beats no encouragement at all, but it's important to realize that this water weight is not the real weight you wanted to get rid of. However, it's a start.

As the diet continues, your survival genes start to realize that this may not just be a bad winter but a bad year (or two), and they begin to crank up some very powerful, long-term changes in metabolism that will protect you from dying under these new harsher circumstances. Theories abound as to what these exact changes are. Dr. Sears reports that high-protein ketosis diets (such as the Atkins diet) make fat cells ten times more efficient at holding on to fat than they were before the diet started. The ability of fat cells to adapt to change probably accounts for the "diet yo-yo effect" that plagues those who attempt to diet frequently. And, although I don't have a lot of scientific proof, I think pregnancy is a metabolic "reprogramming" event for a lot of women. The effects may not be too noticeable after the first baby, but many women don't begin to have weight trouble until after their second or third pregnancy. Of course, it's impossible to factor age out of the equation because everyone is older after their most recent pregnancy than they were after their first. But it is clear that gestational diabetes tends to worsen in each successive pregnancy and more so in pregnancies that are less than a year apart. Regardless of the mechanism, it is absolutely clear that pregnancy creates *children* and having them around sets up a whole set of social and environmental circumstances that can lead to weight gain for women.

In summary, your genes determine for the most part what you look like as well as the way your body handles the calorie equation. You cannot change your genetic make-up but must learn to deal with it effectively to get your weight where you want it *and keep it there*. Understanding how your body's system of weight regulation works can help you avoid common mistakes and learn how to successfully manipulate a diet and exercise plan to fit your physiology, as well as personality and schedule.

It's time to make a choice. Now is the time for you to choose to become committed to a program of weight management *for the rest of your life*. Weight gain is a "forever" issue—one that requires a permanent solution. Not a fad diet or a half-hearted attempt at exercise, but a real commitment to a new way of life. Make a lifelong commitment to manage your weight now and be successful forever. Dodge the commitment now and you will ultimately fail and continue to lose the battle and not the weight. The choice is yours.

CHOOSING A DIET: WHAT REALLY WORKS AND WHY

Dieting is a very popular "sport" today. In fact, over 50 percent of American women have been on a diet this year. Of course, most of them have not stayed on that diet, and only 5 percent of them actually reached their goal weight. Even more disappointing is that of those women who lost weight, over 90 percent gained it all back within twelve months. More proof that being overweight is a forever problem, and that despite all the hype and hoopla, none of the "miracle diets" out there are very effective.

FAD DIETS DON'T WORK—PERIOD!

A quick stroll through the health section of your local bookstore will reveal literally hundreds of books on different diet methods, all touted to be "the best." I am not a biochemist, an exercise physiologist, or a nutritionist. And even though there are some very smart experts out there with fancy titles writing numerous books on dieting, I think it is clear from reading what they say that none of them agree as to the absolute best method to achieve long-term weight control. If you are trying to drop a dress size in two months for your best friend's wedding and really don't care what happens after that, then by all means feel free to choose among these diets. But if you'd like to take a more long-term approach and keep off the weight you lose, you need something different.

Most diets focus only on food and don't include the very important component of exercise. There are also other problems:

- Fad diets are almost always "unbalanced" and will often turn on survival genes that ultimately make the diet ineffective over time; you reach the "plateau phase" and stop losing weight.

- The weight-loss plan doesn't usually allow for flexibility in food selection or match the way you normally eat.

- Once the weight is off, you must change your eating habits again to another diet method for long-term weight control or the weight will come back.

Keeping Your Balance

Many nutrition experts agree that in a healthy diet 40 percent of your calories should come from protein, 30 percent from fats, and 30 percent from carbohydrates. When these ratios become distorted, the imbalance causes complex changes in the body's metabolic systems and can cause malnutrition. In fact, Dr. Sears says that malnutrition is quite common among people on diets. And, more importantly, starvation causes your survival genes to kick in and sabotage the long-term effectiveness of the diet.

I have to admit that keeping this ratio and counting calories—my other big piece of advice—aren't particularly glamorous, sexy, or fun. But it's the most effective method available to include in your lifelong weight management program. Calorie counting has been around for years and it's as boring as "Lassie" reruns, but after years of counseling patients on the subject of weight loss and watching their progress on all kinds of diets, I assure you that calorie counting done properly works well compared to any other diet method I've seen. Besides, in the longest-running full-scale research trial on dieting—some patients were in the study for sixteen years—the most successful method for sustained weight loss was balanced calorie restriction (counting calories).

Balancing calories has several advantages:

- **It's simple.** Once you learn some simple rules and conversions, you will be able to track the calories you eat accurately.

• **It's flexible.** As long as you maintain the proper ratio of carbohydrates, fats, and proteins, you can choose to eat reasonable portions of anything you want at mealtime. You don't have to make or buy special foods unless you want to. This lets you eat the same food as your family and also allows you to eat out without the embarrassment of bringing your own food.

• **It's adaptable.** You can learn to "cheat" without undercutting your weight management program. You can overeat one day and then make up the difference by undereating the next. You can trade exercise for more food. These two facts allow you to individualize your weight management system of diet and exercise to fit your personal needs for the long haul.

• **It's effective.** This system of balanced calorie restriction and exercise is the most effective method I've seen in nineteen years of practice as an ob-gyn to get the weight off and, most importantly, to keep it off. And it works for everyone.

The following chapters summarize the exercise and weight management program I recommend and provide a blueprint to follow in achieving this most important life goal.

8

STEP 3: EXERCISE, NO MATTER WHAT!

THE THIRD STEP to surviving Hurried Woman Syndrome is making regular aerobic activity part of your life. If you already do this, you're way ahead; perhaps this discussion will help you fine-tune your efforts. If you don't, I hope the information here will motivate you to start. The main reasons you need regular exercise are probably already obvious to you. It's common knowledge that exercise will improve your overall stamina, strengthen you muscles (particularly your heart), and help control your weight. But do you really believe all of that? Many Hurried Women "know" that exercise would help them feel and look better, but for a variety of reasons, they just don't ever seem to "believe it"—embrace it—and make exercise enough of a priority for it to become a regular habit.

ENERGY

Regular exercise makes us feel better. Endorphins are small proteins made inside the brain that, when released inside the brain's limbic system, lock onto receptors and make us feel happy. A lot of long-distance runners talk about the "runner's high"—a sense of eupho-ria—they experience when they get past the pain of the first seven or eight miles. When they are on a runner's high, many say they feel they could go on running forever.

Exercise also reenergizes us. Although the exact way it works isn't clear, using energy seems to encourage the body to provide more energy. I guess our physical energy follows the traditional laws of supply and demand. I'm not going to bore you with Keynesian eco-nomic theory; let's talk about breast-feeding instead. It works much the same way. When you deliver a baby, your breasts are preparing to provide breast milk, but as every new mother knows, there isn't much milk produced in the first few days after birth. To get the milk flowing, the baby must nurse regularly; if the baby won't cooperate, Mom is asked to use a breast pump. The act of nursing and/or pumping shows the breast that there is a need for breast milk—a demand. If baby and pump are diligent in demanding milk, over a few days the breast will eventually begin producing it—milk is sup-plied. If, on the other hand, the mother chooses not to breast-feed, her breasts are bound up to avoid any physical stimulation—stop demand. In this case, the breast sees no demand for milk and there-fore won't supply it.

Our body provides us with energy in a similar fashion. If we exercise regularly, we establish a constant demand for energy. But as in the case of breast milk, there is a lag between our demand for energy and when it is supplied. When we first demand extra energy—begin an exercise program—there isn't that much avail-able, because our body is efficient when it comes to meeting its current energy demands. The body provides us with the energy we need based on our prior use; this is our daily energy supply, and it remains pretty constant. The body also maintains a short-term energy reserve in case something bad happens. But there isn't a lot of energy in the reserve tank because it's a backup system and we haven't been dipping into it very often. So when we start a workout program, it wears us out. However, after three to five weeks, the body will adapt to the new situation and as the higher demand for energy continues, the body expands our daily energy supply to meet our increased need. It also increases the size of our reserve tank.

This is when we begin to experience the reenergizing power of regular exercise. Even better, once these new energy levels are established, we don't have to fully empty our energy tanks (daily and reserve) each day to keep the supply of energy coming in. As long as we work out regularly—dip into the reserve tank three or more times a week—both of the newer, bigger tanks will stay full. Of course, investing in exercise pays off not only with a big energy dividend, but also as a powerful tool in managing your weight.

THE CALORIE EQUATION

In its simplest form, the balance of calories going into the body and the use of those calories by the body determines our weight:

$$\text{Calories in} - \text{Calories expended} = \text{Caloric balance}$$

When the calories we take in amount to more than the calories expended, the caloric balance is positive and we gain weight. If we expend more calories than we eat, our caloric balance is negative and we will eventually lose weight. Remember that it takes time for these changes to take place, but for now I want to stress the balance between calories and weight. Simply put, your weight is determined by the balance of calories that go into your body versus the calories your bodily functions use (metabolism) and those you burn up in physical activity. Since on any given day, the calories devoted to metabolic processes are usually constant, we will focus on the expenditure of calories you have control over, namely exercise. (There actually is a way to increase your metabolism a little, but we will come back to this later.)

The central principle of weight management is the calorie equation. If you eat more calories than you burn up, you'll gain weight; if you cut back on the calories you eat or increase the calories you burn through exercise, you'll lose weight. Simple, right? Actually, it is. I think that's what makes it so difficult for many people to accept. But the basic facts are immutable: "You are what you eat" (minus what you can work off through exercise). It is critical to successful weight management to remember that calories in are only half of the story. Calories expended are equally important to successfully controlling your weight, particularly for those over thirty.

Virtually every body function, including reading this book, expends calories. Obviously, the more physically taxing the activity, the more calories you'll use. Some common activities and the amount of calories expended per hour are as follows:

Calories Burned in One Hour of Activity for a 150-Pound Person*

Housework = 100 calories

Light gardening = 150 calories (not just watching the grass grow!)

Golf = 250 calories (walking the course with your bag of clubs)

Tennis (recreational) = 275 calories

Racquetball = 300 to 350 calories

---

*These calorie amounts are estimates based on a middle-of-the-road pace. You may be burning more or fewer calories if you are going faster or slower than average.

> Aerobics = 300 to 400 calories
>
> Walking = 100 calories per mile (assumes a rate of four miles per hour)
>
> Exercise bike = 300 to 600 calories (Most bikes calculate calories burned for you.)
>
> Tennis (competitive) = 425 calories
>
> Swimming = 400 to 600 calories per hour
>
> Running: 100 calories per mile (assumes a rate of seven miles per hour)
>
> Climbing stairs = 1 calorie per five steps (for example, 50 steps = 10 calories)

The more you weigh, the more calories you actually expend with weight-bearing exercise. If you weigh less than 120 pounds or more than 180 pounds, you need to convert the preceding calorie estimates to more accurately reflect what you would burn based on your weight. To calculate your conversion factor, take your weight and divide it by 150, then multiply the number of calories given for a specific activity by your conversion factor. For example, if a woman weighed 200 pounds, her conversion factor would be 1.33 (200 pounds ÷ 150 pounds = 1.33). If this woman walked four miles in an hour, the preceding list says she should burn 400 calories; she multiplies 400 by her conversion factor of 1.33 to calculate her actual calories expended, which would be 532 (400 calories × 1.33 = 532 calories).

You won't be surprised to see that the more vigorous the activity, the more calories are used. Walking up stairs for an hour (1,100 calories) burns almost three times as many calories as walking briskly for the same length of time (400 calories). Exercise that forces you to carry your own weight, as opposed to floating in water or sitting on a bike, expends energy at a much faster rate. An hour of swimming burns about 500 calories, whereas an hour of running burns about 800 calories. However, there are several, very important points about exercise that you won't get from any table. The more important ones are discussed in the following sections.

A MINIMUM AMOUNT OF EXERCISE IS NEEDED TO MAINTAIN WEIGHT

All exercise burns calories and thus has a benefit in helping maintain weight control. However, if you exercise for less than three half-hour sessions each week (considered the minimum aerobic level), you will most likely see your weight creep up slowly or find it very hard to lose weight. Once you regularly reach the minimum weekly level, additional exercise will steadily improve your ability to lose weight because of the calories burned and also because of the positive effect exercise has on your metabolism.

You could lose weight just by eating less, but you would be unlikely to stick with such a diet because the requirements would be so severe. Exercise helps your dieting efforts work better and improves your overall health. And you'll be happier in the process.

THERE IS NO ONE "PRESCRIPTION" FOR EXERCISE

The "kicker" about the minimum level of aerobic exercise is that even though it works for almost everyone, some women will need to do more to get the same effect. It's not fair, but it's reality. I will give you a few guidelines to help you get started, but you may need to go through a trial-and-error process to find the level of activity that's "right" for you.

Most experts recommend starting out at the minimum level of three sessions weekly and adding a session after two to three weeks if your results are less than satisfactory. An alternative to this would be to push up the time in each session by ten minutes each week until you see improvement. A one-hour session would be the maximum I recommend. Besides, going longer than an hour may be impractical and increase your "hurry" if you've got kids to shuffle around or any serious schedule constraints—the heart of Hurried Woman Syndrome.

Also, if you are starting from "couch potato" status, you must build up slowly and progressively so you won't injure yourself or get discouraged and give up. Be patient and build up to your desired level of exercise carefully. This is a lifetime commitment you're making, so if it takes a few more weeks to get your level up where it needs to be—big deal! You've got the rest of your life to work on it.

EXERCISE REPROGRAMS YOUR METABOLISM

Whenever we take in extra calories (those we don't need for immediate use), the body must make a choice about where to store them. Obviously, we all wish our body would let us flush them away, but it doesn't work that way. If the body doesn't see any immediate need for these calories, it puts them into long-term storage, or fat. If, on the other hand, you routinely exercise for half an hour three or four times a week, your body will see the probable need for these calories to provide energy in the near future and place them in short-term storage, or muscle and liver tissue. Although these short-term storage areas also contain some water, it's nowhere near the level associated with fat storage. Fat tissue is 97 percent water and that's where the weight of fat comes from. So encouraging any extra calories to go into short-term storage through regular aerobic exercise rather than fat storage produces less weight gain in the long run. Exercise also makes fat cells less resistant to giving up their stored energy. This allows you to burn fat more easily when you do exercise. The short-term storage areas can quickly convert these "extra" calories into energy; converting fat back into energy takes time.

Marathon runners, high-endurance swimmers, and other "extreme athletes" train to the level of *anaerobic* conditioning, where muscles are trained to work with less-than-normal levels of oxygen. This type of training changes metabolism in such a way as to allow for much more efficient weight loss but in my opinion is not really healthy for most women, particularly those who are interested in childbearing. Anaerobic training often pushes body fat levels too low and disturbs menstrual function as well as bone metabolism and other systems, which could lead to osteoporosis.

A MAJOR PLUS OF EXERCISE: YOU CAN EAT MORE

This fact is what makes exercise so appealing for me. I absolutely hate to diet. Even worse, I love to eat some things that aren't exactly diet foods, like ice cream. In fact, I eat a bowlful of that delicious dessert almost every night. But I have discovered that if I run three miles, three days a week, I can eat my ice cream and not gain any weight. I have also found that if I cut back and eat ice cream every other night, I only have to run two days a week to keep the weight down. (Of course, this strategy costs me about 180 bowls of ice cream each year!)

Knowing my responses to exercise and diet allows me to choose between the two to keep my weight stable. If I want to diet less, I must exercise more. If I don't want to exercise or if I miss running for a week because of the weather or being stuck at the hospital a lot, I can cut back on my calorie intake and keep my weight balanced.

The ability to trade calories in for calories expended through exercise allows you to find the right balance of diet and exercise to develop an effective approach to long-term weight management; one that you can live with. Remember that calories burned is not the only effect of exercise on weight. As exercise levels increase, positive changes occur in metabolism that will further improve the effects of your workout regimen.

REGULAR EXERCISE MAKES YOU FEEL BETTER ABOUT YOURSELF AND IMPROVES ENERGY LEVELS

Getting in shape makes you feel better about yourself. Improving your strength and endurance, shedding flab, and seeing your muscles toning up from working out provides you with a sense of accomplishment. Knowing you look better makes you feel better about yourself. It improves your self-confidence in just about everything you do, including your love life. It makes a woman feel sexy to know that she looks good. Doesn't getting a new hairstyle or a new dress that you *know* looks good on you make you feel better? Absolutely! Exercising regularly and getting in shape will do the same thing for you.

9

GET STARTED
ON THE PROGRAM

I KNOW YOU HAVE READ A LOT, thought about it, and are now charged up and ready to begin your new life as a calorie-balanced, physically fit woman. Actually, if you're like most of us, you're not all that thrilled at the idea of making significant changes. But you need to think of this as a fresh start on an almost guaranteed method to lose weight, improve your energy levels, and live healthier—one that will last the rest of your life. There are a few preparatory steps you need to take during the first week of your new weight management program before you start the eating plan, which will pay big dividends if you invest time in them now.

I. KEEP A FOOD DIARY

During this week of preparation before your diet begins, start keeping a food diary. Appendix B provides a form for your use with instructions. Record the date, time, amount of food eaten by weight or volume, and the estimated calories in, *immediately* after you eat anything—and I mean anything! Even half a cracker or a taste of your child's soda goes on the form. The vast majority of my patients are shocked to see how much they actually consume in a given week. In fact, many women will lose weight simply by using a food diary; when they begin to pay attention to what they eat, they begin to eat less and make better choices about what they do eat. Also, to keep track of your caloric balance, you must learn how to estimate the calories in your food and get in the habit of writing them down, so it's good practice to start now.

For a food diary to be accurate and helpful, you must write down what you eat as soon as you eat it. If you wait until bedtime to record your intake, you will invariably miss things that you ate during the day simply because you forget. You can total up the calories later if it's more convenient for you, but you must record the food you eat when you eat it—otherwise, the diary will lose its effectiveness for your weight management program.

2. GET A GOOD CALORIE COUNTING BOOK AND STUDY IT

Pick up any of the several excellent calorie counting books available, most at a low price. Learn what your favorite foods are made of—carbohydrates, protein, and fat—and the calories associated with each of these components:

1 gram carbohydrate = 4 calories
1 gram protein = 4 calories
1 gram fat = 9 calories

Get a small food scale to help you learn to estimate the size of your portions and be able to account for your calories accurately.

Even though you may already be a "pro" at weighing and estimating food portions, verify that you are doing it correctly during the first two or three weeks of this program simply to make sure that you're on the mark in your calorie counting. Be sure your book lists total calories as well as the portion from carbohydrates, protein, and fat to maintain the proper balance.

Dr. Barry Sears suggests a "quick-and-dirty" way to estimate portions when you are eating out at a nice restaurant and don't feel like enduring the embarrassment of whipping out the old scale in front of everybody. He says that 4 ounces (or 28 grams) of protein will cover the palm of your hand. To maintain the proper ratio of protein to carbohydrates (4:3), you will want to have a slightly smaller portion of carbohydrates on your plate than the portion of protein. This is a valid rough estimate, but the best way to get good at estimating portions is to measure them out at home over and over again until you feel confident that you're doing it right. Let's say you are on a diet of 1,500 calories per day and consistently underestimate your calorie intake by 10 percent. This means you will take in an extra 150 calories each day. That small increase becomes 1,050 extra calories per week and 4,725 calories per month. Since there are 3,500 calories in a pound of fat, being off just 10 percent each day in your calorie estimation will give you an extra 1⅓ pounds to deal with each month or 16 pounds in a year!

3. DETERMINE YOUR MAINTENANCE CALORIE LEVEL AND DESIRED WEIGHT GOAL CALORIE LEVEL

To fully understand the calorie balancing system, it's important to make a few key calculations:

- **Maintenance calories.** This is the number of calories necessary to maintain yourself at any given body weight. This level varies slightly from woman to woman, but a rough approximation can be found by multiplying your weight by 11. For a 170-pound woman, the maintenance calorie level would be 1,870 calories (170 pounds × 11 calories = 1,870 calories). If this woman wants to lose weight, she must drop below 1,870 calories per day by either decreasing the calories she takes in each day or by increasing her calorie expenditure through more exercise. Making this calculation can be an eye-opener for a lot of women, particularly those who are still in denial ("I really don't eat that much"). If you weigh 200 pounds, you must be consuming at least 2,200 calories per day to maintain your present weight. Use the following formula to calculate the maintenance calories for your present weight:

Present weight (in pounds) × 11 calories = Maintenance calories

• **Target or goal weight.** This is the weight you hope to reach and maintain the rest of your life. Your goal needs to be realistic. It is rare to reach your high school weight, particularly after one or more pregnancies, but it is amazing how many people set this particular goal for themselves. If you're unsure what your target should be, look at the BMI chart in Chapter 7. Your goal should be within the normal BMI range for your height but not less.

Here's how to calculate your target weight maintenance calories:

Target weight (in pounds) × 11 calories = Maintenance calories

A reasonable target weight might be what you weighed before your most recent pregnancy or some other point when your weight was in the healthy range. Although for a variety of reasons that weight may be too high, you can still use it as a short-term goal and celebrate when you get there. From that point, add an age adjustment of about half a pound per year over thirty to come up with your target weight.

Let's say that the 170-pound woman from the previous example determines that her ideal or goal weight is 140 pounds. Using the formula, we find that when she gets down to 140 pounds, she will need to keep her daily calorie intake at or below 1,540 calories or she will gain weight again. She can maintain her weight by decreasing her calorie intake, increasing the calories she expends in exercise, or using some combination of the two—that's the flexibility of the calorie balancing system.

What calorie level should you start with to lose weight effectively? For our hypothetical person, I would recommend going to the 1,540 calories per day level and getting started now on the new intake level that she will need to maintain her ideal body weight in the future. If she wants to start out a little lower (say 1,400 calories each day) to lose weight faster, it would be okay, but she has to remember that this is a lifetime commitment to weight management not a "lose the weight and then go back to eating like you used to" diet—which is always unsuccessful.

I do not recommend initially dropping your calorie intake below 1,100 to 1,200 calories per day regardless of your target weight calculation or your desire to lose weight more quickly. This is the maintenance calorie level for a 100- to 109-pound woman. Such a harsh program is unnecessary for success, psychologically looks like a fad diet (deprivation), and may turn on your "survival genes" which will work against you. Besides, you have a built-in "calorie cushion"—we haven't accounted for your exercise calories expended in the three half-hour sessions you're doing for maintenance.

Use your calculated target weight maintenance calories as your new daily calories in when you begin the second week of your weight management program and then monitor your progress.

Congratulations! You've decided on your ultimate weight goal. But take a moment now to set some short-term goals. These will give you a reason to celebrate along the way to your final goal. Calculate 5 percent and 10 percent of your present body weight by multiplying your present weight by 0.05 and 0.10, respectively. When you lose 5 percent of your current weight and again when you lose 10 percent, you should celebrate because you have significantly lowered your risk of death from cardiovascular disease, as well as other medical problems.

Humans are goal-oriented and we all seek approval or praise for what we do. Setting some intermediate goals will make the journey to your final destination not seem so long. I admit that this is a mind game, but it works! Besides, when you reach these goals you will have done something you have not been able to do before—lose weight and kept it off. And you will be able to keep it off this time because you are now on a lifetime weight management program not a diet.

4. START YOUR EXERCISE PROGRAM NOW

I cannot overemphasize the importance of exercise to successful weight management—it is critical! Remember that there is a minimum amount of exercise required for successful weight control, particularly for women over thirty. You have to turn in at least three half-hour sessions of uninterrupted exercise each week. This is a starting point. Some women require more activity than this to maintain their weight at any given level. Also, remember that you can trade exercise for food. If you exercise above your minimum level, you can get "calorie credits" which you can exchange for either faster weight loss—the more calories you burn, the more weight you lose—or more calories in—the more you exercise, the more you can eat.

Start at three half-hour workouts each week. If you walk, that's two miles at a time or about 200 calories each session for a total of 600 calories per week. If you are not used to any real exercise, you will have to start out slowly and work up to this level of activity. Be patient with yourself. It's important to avoid an injury that might prevent you from exercising now or give you trouble in the future. Also, be sure you have the right shoes for your activity. Believe me, they are worth the money.

There is an important phenomenon associated with exercise: a lot of women begin an exercise program and actually gain weight. Why? When you go from a sedentary lifestyle to one that is more active, you build new muscle tissue, often at the expense of fat. But muscle tissue weighs more than fat. So when you replace fat with muscle, you may gain weight initially but still be losing inches. Don't get hung up on what the scale tells you; what's more important is how well your clothes fit. Keep up the exercise and the weight will begin to drop off later. Also, remember that sore muscles are actually injured, although this is generally nothing to worry about. Injured muscles tend to swell a bit with water and other nutrients that help heal and build new and better muscles. Consequently, they will weigh more during this sore phase than they will when the soreness and extra fluid leaves. Common sense tells you that exercise is good for you and will ultimately help you lose weight and, more important, inches. Be persistent!

5. GET YOUR MIND AND HEART FOCUSED ON THE GOAL

This is probably the most important single step toward a successful lifelong commitment to weight management. You have to want to succeed in order to be successful. Sounds trite, but it's true. Many women already feel defeated by their weight, so it is sometimes hard to rekindle that fighting spirit, particularly in an area where they've not tasted success in a while. But if you understand what I have shown you here and believe, contrary to the fad-diet culture, that long-term success is the only success worth having, you can do it!

Understanding the cognitive-behavioral aspects of weight management is critical to your success. Most of us are filled with nega-

tive thoughts, false beliefs, and errors in our logic about food, dieting, exercise, and body image. Many of us aren't even aware that we
have these cognitive distortions because they're just below the surface where we can't "see" them, but we tend to feel them. It's particularly important to expose these distortions because they are often
quite powerful and keep us from achieving our goals.

6. BEGIN THE DIET PHASE OF THE PROGRAM

Cut your calories down to the target weight maintenance level you
calculated earlier. Try to keep the following balance among the different nutritional elements:

Protein 40%
Fat 30%
Carbohydrates 30%

This is the healthy balance that many nutritionists recommend,
and deviating from it may encourage your survival genes to kick in.
Strict adherence to these percentages is not necessary, but don't
deviate too much—no more than 10 percent up or down from the
recommendation for any given group.

7. KEEP TRACK OF YOUR PROGRESS

Write down your calories in and calories expended in your food
diary (see Appendix B). Always write down the food you eat as soon
as you eat it. It's okay to wait and total up your calories at the end
of the day, but write down what you eat right away.

Weigh in weekly, preferably the same day and time of day each
week. For example, weigh in every Sunday evening. Daily weight

fluctuations are quite common, particularly around your menstrual cycle, so don't weigh yourself every day. Record your weekly weight in your food diary. If it doesn't begin to fall within three to four weeks, you may need to reassess your calories in or exercise level.

You should expect to lose about 1 to 2 pounds each week. Trying to shed weight faster doesn't seem to work well for very long—those darned survival genes coming to the rescue again. Slow, steady weight loss is associated with the highest success rates. Realize that if you have 50 or 60 pounds to lose that it will take almost a year to achieve your goal. But don't be discouraged; you have to be patient. Don't let negative thoughts distract you from the prize. Look at it this way instead: if you're forty years old now and it takes you a year to reach your goal, it's no big deal. You'll probably live to be eighty if you get the weight off, and investing one-fortieth of the rest of your life to have thirty-nine years at the right weight is a very good return on your investment. Changing your perspective can turn old defeats into success—today!

If you don't lose weight as planned or you feel that you have reached a plateau weight that you just can't seem to get past (two to three weeks with no progress), consider one of two actions: decrease your food intake (calories in), or increase your aerobic exercise level (calories out).

To adjust your calories, I recommend cutting out 100 calories per day for a start, such as dropping down from 1,800 calories to 1,700 calories. Remember to keep your overall carbohydrate:protein:fat ratios at the recommended levels. If you hit another plateau later or your initial adjustment doesn't work after two weeks, drop another 100 calories from your daily intake (down to 1,600 calories) or increase your exercise level again.

To adjust your calories expended, consider adding one session each week to your program (moving up to four sessions) or pushing to go an additional ten minutes in each of your three half-hour sessions (forty minutes per session). Give this new level of exercise two weeks. If you don't start to see progress again, add another session each week or ten more minutes of exercise per session, up to a maximum of one hour per session. Continue to monitor your progress and whenever you encounter a plateau, adjust your exercise level up by the same method—either add ten minutes to each session or add another session per week. If you add on, it can be a thirty-minute session even if the original three are now each an hour long. The key is to burn more calories each week. Also, be sure that your rate of exercise is high enough to get your heart rate up to between 130 and 155 beats per minute. This is the aerobic level needed to affect the body's metabolism and get the weight control benefits of exercise.

If you have heart disease or diabetes or take blood pressure medication, you should consult with your doctor before beginning an exercise program. Also, don't ignore pain when you exercise. If you suspect you have incurred an injury, let your doctor know immediately. Injuries are the most common (and legitimate) reason women stop exercising.

8. TAKE A GOOD MULTIVITAMIN AND CALCIUM SUPPLEMENT

I recommend over-the-counter (OTC) multivitamins as discussed in Chapter 6. Use one that has been evaluated by the Food and Drug Administration (FDA) for safety and effectiveness and that is known to work. If you're over thirty, also take a calcium supplement. The current recommendation is 1,500 to 2,000 milligrams of calcium each day.

9. DRINK LOTS OF WATER

Water is an essential element for all of the body's metabolic systems. Most of us would survive a fast for several weeks, but without water, we would all die within a few days. Water helps flush out metabolic poisons and draws excess fluid out of your legs and hands. Besides, when you're drinking water you're not drinking less healthy beverages.

10. CUT DOWN ON RESTAURANT MEALS, PARTICULARLY FAST FOOD

This is a big problem if you are a Hurried Woman. It's hard to find time to cook if you're working, taking kids to any number of activities, and trying to keep your home running. Unfortunately, there are no truly low-fat alternatives at any restaurant with a drive-through window. Almost everything on the menu is fried in fat or wrapped in starch. Although some of the fast-food chains are starting to offer salads and grilled chicken alternatives (which can still be high in fat and/or calories, depending on what's included), if you are going to eat out, you will find better food choices at sit-down restaurants. However, you're not totally safe there either, because restaurant owners cook food that is rich in flavor (and calories), and they give you more of it than they think you'll be able to eat so you won't go away hungry.

Try to plan meals in advance as much as possible so that you can control what goes into each dish and how much you serve yourself.

OTHER CONSIDERATIONS

MEDICATIONS

I am not an advocate of diet pills, which are all pretty much amphetamines ("speed") or some combination of caffeine and other "natural stimulants," like the mysterious green tea ("slower speed"). The latter is available over the counter as Dexatrim or Metabo-whatever.

Ephedra, or ephedrine, was a popular stimulant used in many OTC appetite suppressants, but the FDA took it off the market in 2002 after several deaths and adverse events were connected to its use.

Diet pills are the ultimate in short-term strategies. Amphetamines can suppress appetite and help you get a jump-start toward successful weight loss, but they are unsafe when taken for an extended period of time and therefore absolutely not recommended for long-term use. Bontril SR (phendimetrazine), a long-acting version of an old diet pill called Fastin (phentermine), has become popular lately. I have occasionally given selected patients diet pills like Bontril, but only for thirty days and *not a day longer*. I much prefer to stress the long-term approach to weight management through decreasing calorie intake and increasing exercise. It's natural and safe, and it works throughout your life.

Meridia (sibutramine) claims to be an appetite suppressant that works through the serotonin-dopamine-norepinephrine system rather than as a central nervous system stimulant like amphetamines. Some patients experience a significant rise in blood pressure or a rapid pulse rate on the medication, and blood pressure should be monitored regularly. It appears that between 20 and 50 percent of patients respond to treatment with at least a 10 percent loss in weight. Unfortunately, no information is available concerning long-term success with Meridia as no one has data beyond one year of use. Women with a history of heart disease, stroke, high blood pressure, glaucoma, or seizures should not take this drug, nor should anyone taking a selective serotonin reuptake inhibitor (SSRI).

Xenical (orlistat), a fat-blocking drug, holds some promise in helping patients effectively achieve weight loss by blocking the absorption of about 30 percent of dietary fats by the intestine. It causes loose stools and even explosive diarrhea in some patients, particularly if they cheat and have a fatty meal. Most experts believe a 10–15 percent sustained weight loss will be possible with this medication. However, women must take a good multivitamin while on

Xenical to prevent certain vitamin deficiencies caused by the non-absorption of fat-soluble vitamins.

Environment

A lot of us eat when we are bored or stressed out; it's something to do, or maybe eating helps us relax. We see something that grabs our attention—like a double-stuffed Oreo—and we decide to eat it (and perhaps a few of its neighbors) because we know it will make us feel good. But does it? Most of the time after we've downed the contraband item and experienced a brief rush, we feel guilty about it and realize that the additional calories must be compensated for later—we must give up a snack when we are really hungry or add an extra workout to our schedule. Even worse, if we keep making this error, it makes us feel that we will never stay on track to reach the goals of our weight management program (more negative thinking). This is when many people get frustrated and quit their diet. Did eating the cookie make us feel good or not? I think the answer is ultimately no.

In order to avoid temptation, stock your kitchen cupboard with snacks that are low-calorie and nutritionally balanced. Get rid of the stuff that you have trouble saying no to. Instead, stock up on fruit, protein energy bars, and other snacks that are low-cal but will satisfy some of your more intense food cravings. Most fruits are moderate in calories (a medium-sized orange has 100 calories while an apple has about 80); however, some, such as watermelon, are very high in sugar, so you have to eat these in moderation.

What do you think is the average weight of people who watch the Food Network more than two hours each day? Answer: too high! An important part of your weight management program will be clearing your environment of the signals that make you focus on food or stimulate your appetite. There's a reason why snack-food makers always buy airtime for their television ads in the mid-afternoon; that's when people are often hungry and prone to snack. It's okay to look through diet magazines and Weight Watcher's cookbooks for recipes and meal ideas, but don't leave your television on the Food Network all day long. Similarly, don't leave temptation out on the countertop in plain sight. If you feel you must keep certain high-calorie snacks around the house for the kids, put them out of sight if you have a weakness for them.

SNACKS

Snacks are an inevitable part of everyone's diet, especially if you live with small children. This doesn't have to be a problem. Snacks can actually be good for you. Women with true hypoglycemia—and those without it—notice that they often "slump" about one to two hours after a meal. A well-timed snack, like cheese or peanut butter on crackers, an hour and a half after a meal will often keep these symptoms under control. Snacks also help curb hunger and keep you on your weight management program. Since you know you are going to snack, have reasonable alternatives such as the ones described in the last section on hand so you won't use up all of your calorie intake on junk or chronically overeat. I recommend scheduling some of your daily calories for a small snack in the afternoon (maybe a piece of fruit or some crackers), and perhaps even a mid-morning snack if you are an early riser.

Also, be on the lookout for what I call "hidden snacks." These are the little bites and tastes of food that we eat almost automatically. Cooks who sample the food they prepare so often that they're not even hungry at mealtime or parents who take a few bites of their children's food while they eat or finish whatever the kids leave are common examples of people who eat things that go unnoticed until they keep a food diary. If you start writing these hidden snacks down, you will either become aware that they exist and start to account for them accurately or stop snacking as much because you now "see them before you eat them" and choose not to do it anymore.

If you like an afternoon or late-evening snack, you don't necessarily have to deny yourself, you just have to plan for it in advance. Save some calories for the end of the day if you want to have an after-dinner snack, but keep it light and remember that food before bedtime encourages acid reflux disease.

Improve Your Timing

Wide swings in blood sugar cause hunger pangs as well as making you sluggish or jittery. I recommend spreading your calories among three meals—breakfast, lunch, and dinner—as well as a snack in the afternoon and perhaps one midmorning. Keep snacks small and steer away from processed foods. Things wrapped in cellophane from the convenience store or sprinkled with sugar shouldn't be your first choice.

Don't skip meals, particularly breakfast. Virtually all current research points to the importance of "breaking the fast" each morning. Doing so makes you less hungry throughout the day and also encourages your weight-loss efforts. Spreading your calories out keeps your blood sugar from fluctuating widely.

Don't eat anything within two hours of bedtime. Often late-night eating is impulse eating and comes from boredom. As discussed earlier, you can plan for an after-dinner snack if you wish; just don't eat it right before going to bed and don't let it be driven by impulse.

Use a smaller plate. It's a mind game, but it does help some people feel less cheated by smaller portions. Also, slow down while you eat. It takes almost twenty minutes for food to affect blood sugar levels and squelch hunger pains.

When you go out to eat, order a low-cal soup or salad with low-cal dressing. This will give you a head start at curbing your hunger before the entrée comes and also help you stay away from the bread tray or the basket of chips. If you are going to eat the chips and salsa, count your chips out into a little pile and stop when the pile is gone.

CLEAN UP YOUR CARBS

At first glance, all carbohydrates appear to be the same. However, in the early 1980s, Dr. David Jenkins introduced the idea of the glycemic index. He realized that although two foods might have the same weight of carbohydrate molecules, some carbs obviously had a much more rapid effect on blood sugar than others. Pasta and table sugar are both carbohydrates, but table sugar shows up in the bloodstream as glucose much more rapidly than pasta does. Those carbs with a rapid impact on blood sugar have a high glycemic index, while those with less impact have a lower index. The benefit of high glycemic index foods is that they shut off hunger signals more quickly than low glycemic foods do. Yet they also tend to leave us hungry again more quickly as well. This occurs because the rapid rise in blood sugar causes an equally rapid insulin response, which pushes blood sugar back down and stimulates hunger. This is why many experts feel that foods with a high glycemic index tend to cause more cravings in the long run.

Glycemic index isn't the whole story when it comes to the carbs we select and their effect on weight gain. The quantity of the various carbs we eat has a role to play as well. For example, carrots have a fairly high glycemic index, yet you would have to eat several handfuls to have the same effect on your blood sugar as one slice of white bread. This is because carrots have a lot of plant fiber along with the sugar. In other words, carrots contain a "hot" sugar—one with a high glycemic index—but the sugar isn't very concentrated in the food because of the amount of fiber. Fiber isn't absorbed and doesn't have a direct effect on insulin, but it slows down the absorption of the sugar and therefore helps keep the sugar from stimulating insulin secretion.

Most experts agree that you can enhance weight loss by selecting carbs with a low glycemic index over those with a high glycemic index. I recommend selecting at least half of your daily allotment of carbs from foods with a moderate to very low glycemic index. This will allow you to maintain the flexibility in food selection you need to stay with the program without sacrificing the effectiveness of your diet. The glycemic indexes for common foods are listed in the following table.

❀ THE GLYCEMIC INDEX OF POPULAR FOODS

Food	Glycemic Level
Bakery Goods	
Waffles	High–very high
Doughnuts	High–very high
Croissant	High
Angel food cake	High
Flan	High
Muffin	Moderate
Danish	Moderate
Pound cake	Moderate
Sponge cake	Low–moderate
Juices	
Grapefruit	Moderate
Pineapple	Moderate
Grape (unsweetened)	Moderate
Apple (unsweetened)	Low

(continued)

Food	Glycemic Level
Breads	
French baguette	Very high
Wheat (gluten-free)	Very high
Kaiser roll	High
Plain bagel	High
White bread	High
Whole-wheat bread	High
Oat-kernel bread	High
Rye bread	Moderate
Hamburger bun	Moderate
Pizza dough	Moderate
White pita	Moderate
Pumpernickel	Moderate
Mixed-grain bread	Low
Oat-bran bread	Low
Breakfast Cereals	
Rice Chex	Very high
Crispix	Very high
Cornflakes	High
Corn Chex	High
Rice Krispies	High

Food	Glycemic Level
Total	High
Corn Bran	High
Cheerios	High
Golden Grahams	High
Cream of Wheat	High
Shredded Wheat	High
Grape Nuts	High
Life	High
Just Right	Moderate
Bran Chex	Moderate
Mini Wheats	Moderate
Mueselix	Moderate
Oat Bran	Moderate
Special K	Moderate
Oatmeal	Low
All-Bran	Low
Rice Bran	Very low

Candy and Snacks

Dates	Very high
Pretzels	Very high
Jelly beans	Very high

(continued)

Food	Glycemic Level
Corn chips	High
Life-Savers	High
Skittles	High
Mars bar	High
Kudo bar	Moderate
Popcorn	Moderate
Potato chips	Moderate
Jams	Moderate
Chocolate bar (plain)	Moderate
Twix bar	Low
Snickers bar	Low
M&Ms (peanut)	Low
Peanuts	Very low

Grains

Tapioca (w/milk)	Very high
Millet	High
Cornmeal	High
Taco shells	High
Premium white rice	High
Rolled barley	High
Couscous	High

Food	Glycemic Level
White rice	Moderate
Wild rice	Moderate
Brown rice	Moderate
Buckwheat	Moderate
Cracked barley	Moderate
Rice (parboiled)	Low
Bulgur	Low
Instant rice	Low
Wheat kernels	Low
Rye	Low
Pearled barley	Very low

Cookies

Biscotti	High
Vanilla wafers	High
Graham crackers	High
Shortbread	Moderate
Oatmeal cookies	Moderate

Crackers

Saltines	High
Rice cakes	High

(continued)

Food	Glycemic Level
Wheat Thins	High
Breton wheat crackers	High

Dairy Products

Ice cream	Moderate
Low-fat ice cream	Moderate
Low-fat yogurt w/fruit	Low
Fat-free milk	Low
Whole milk	Very low
Soy milk	Very low
Chocolate milk (artificially sweetened)	Very Low
Low-fat yogurt (artificially sweetened)	Very Low

Fruits

Watermelon	Very high
Pineapple	High
Canned apricots (in syrup)	High
Banana	Moderate
Mango	Moderate
Kiwi	Moderate

Food	Glycemic Level
Fruit cocktail (lite)	Moderate
Grapes	Moderate
Raisins	Low
Pear	Low
Apple	Low
Plum	Low
Orange	Low
Peach	Very low
Grapefruit	Very low
Cherries	Very low

Legumes (Beans)

Fava beans	Very high
Green lentils (canned)	Moderate
Kidney beans (canned)	Moderate
Baked beans (canned)	Moderate
Pinto beans	Low
Chickpeas	Low
Black-eyed peas	Low
Baby lima beans	Low
Butter beans (boiled)	Low
Green lentils (boiled)	Very low

(continued)

Food	Glycemic Level
Kidney beans (boiled)	Very low
Red lentils (boiled)	Very low
Soybeans (boiled)	Very low

Pasta

Brown rice pasta	Very high
Macaroni and cheese	High
Linguine	Low
Macaroni	Low
Capellini	Low
White-flour spaghetti	Low
Ravioli	Low
Whole-grain spaghetti	Low
Vermicelli	Low
Fettuccine	Low

Potatoes

Potato (baked)	Very high
Potato (microwave)	High
Potato (instant)	High
Potato (boiled)	High
French fries	High

Food	Glycemic Level
New potato	High
Potato (mashed)	High
Russet potato (boiled)	Moderate
Yam	Moderate
Sweet potato	Low

Sugars

Maltose (beer)	Very high
Glucose	Very high
Sucrose (table sugar)	High
Corn syrup	Moderate
Honey	Moderate
Lactose	Low
Fructose	Low

Vegetables

Pumpkin	Very high
Rutabaga	High
Carrots (cooked)	Moderate
Sweet corn	Moderate
Green peas	Moderate
Artichoke	Very low

(continued)

Food	Glycemic Level
Asparagus	Very low
Beets	Very low
Broccoli	Very low
Brussels sprouts	Very low
Cabbage	Very low
Cauliflower	Very low
Celery	Very low
Collard greens	Very low
Cucumbers	Very low
Dried peas	Very low
Eggplant	Very low
Green beans	Very low
Kale	Very low
Lettuce	Very low
Mushrooms	Very low
Mustard greens	Very low
Okra	Very low
Peanuts	Very low
Peppers	Very low
Snow peas	Very low
Spaghetti squash	Very low
Spinach	Very low

Food	Glycemic Level
Summer squash	Very low
Tomatoes	Very low
Turnip	Very low
Watercress	Very low
Wax beans	Very low
Zucchini	Very low

FREQUENTLY ASKED QUESTIONS

Some topics are better discussed in a question-and-answer format, because the questions other people ask are often the same ones we have. When I present this material to patients or at a lecture, the same queries come up over and over, so I'll share some of them here—along with the answers—to make the daily nuts and bolts of the weight management program easier to understand and comply with.

I don't eat that much and I'm exercising more. Why am I not losing weight?

When patients ask me this question, I immediately ask them two questions: "What diet are you on?" and "How much exercise are you doing?" The answer to the first question is usually one of the following:

> "I'm cutting back" or a variation on the same theme ("I'm doing better").
>
> "Well, I'm taking Metabo-whatever and cutting back on sweets."

"I cut my fats down to 20 percent."
"I have stopped eating beef and switched to chicken."
"No more fried foods."

Certainly, these are all good ideas (except, perhaps the Metabo-whatever), and many of them are incorporated into most diets. However, none of these strategies is an organized plan, and none of them really restrict the amount of food eaten. Yes, "20 percent fat" is a limit, but if you eat 3,000 calories a day, keeping the fat below 20 percent won't really do much to help you lose weight.

Answers to the second question usually require a lot more clarification:

"I'm working out at the gym three days a week."
"I'm walking every evening."
"I do ten minutes on my exercise bike every morning."

By now, you have probably figured out what's wrong with each of these exercise strategies. First, "working out" means different things to different people. Weight lifting is not really aerobic exercise unless you are running from machine to machine. If you do your repetitions very quickly *and* don't rest between stations *and* do this for thirty minutes without interruption, then you are doing aerobic exercise. Anything less than that is "toning," not aerobic exercise, and it will not have the impact on your metabolism that you want. However, I think toning exercises are still good for you—they make you feel better and help you firm up some of the flab you don't like.

As I've pointed out several times, getting the proper weight-loss benefit from exercise requires a minimum of three thirty-minute sessions of uninterrupted aerobic exercise each week. This should be viewed as a maintenance dose; to really achieve weight loss, you will need to do more. Remember that this may not be enough exercise for you to lose weight because everyone is built differently. You will need to experiment to find your maintenance level, but the minimum three sessions a week is a good start.

What if I hate to exercise?

I understand the sentiment, but you must learn to hate being overweight more. I almost guarantee that until you get committed to a weight management program that includes regular exercise, you will not be successful in the long run. Besides, exercise is healthy for you. It improves your energy levels and makes you feel better about yourself. And the last two benefits will help you in your relationships with the people closest to you, particularly your husband.

Although I personally find most types of exercise boring, it doesn't have to be that way. If you enjoy tennis or racquetball, this can be a good way to get your exercise calories expended while enjoying a sport. Aerobics classes are a popular way for women to exercise and enjoy time "off call" from work and family. You can still love your family yet need time away from them. It especially helps women with small children to interact with people who have a vocabulary of more than twenty words and don't routinely have food or snot smeared on their faces. I run between eight and twelve miles each week. And when I run, I like to use it as a time to pray, think through tough problems, and sometimes to just get away and be by myself for a little while. For me, running is cheap therapy.

It can sometimes help to exercise with a friend. If you are able to establish a routine time and place for exercise, your friend may help you be more faithful in your exercise by encouraging you to go when you don't feel like it and vice versa. You know that if you don't go, you'll feel guilty about letting your friend down, and sometimes that is the difference between going and not going. Staying on a regular exercise program is difficult for most of us, so take advantage of any help you can get. Stress the positives and try to ignore or work around the negatives. The payoff from regular exercise is significant.

How can I find time to exercise?

If it's really important to you, you can work a half hour of exercise into your schedule. You've done harder things before—you've had children, been married, worked for a living, right? If you make the commitment to long-term weight control now, the necessity for exercise comes with it. If you keep denying this fact, you will continue to fail at weight control.

If your schedule really is so busy that you cannot work in an hour and a half of exercise each week, then I suggest that you give up on weight loss until you can make the time to exercise or take a long hard look at your priorities and try to reorder them to incorporate routine exercise into your schedule.

What is the best exercise for weight loss?

The one that you'll do! Although it sounds flip, it's true. In general, I feel that walking or swimming (if you have ready access to a pool) are probably the best exercises because they require no special equipment except good shoes, which are very important, or a bathing suit. You walk can almost anywhere—inside, at the mall or on a treadmill if the weather's bad, or outside—and these two activities tend to be associated with relatively few injuries when compared to running or other aerobic activities.

Walking a mile or running a mile burns about the same number of calories (around 100), but most people can run about twice as fast as they can walk, so running burns off calories in about half the time. Therefore, if you're pressed for time—the typical Hurried Woman—then you may prefer running over walking from a time efficiency standpoint. Thirty minutes of running will burn off about 350 to 400 calories; the same time spent walking will burn off about 200 calories. The main thing is to get your heart rate above 130 to 155 for at least thirty minutes without interruption during each exercise session.

I'm on my feet all day at work. Isn't that enough exercise?
I wish it were. When I have a patient in labor at the hospital, I walk over from my office to check on her anywhere from eight to ten times a day. It's about 0.4 miles round-trip from my office to the hospital and back, so that's about 3.2 to 4.0 miles of walking each day, not counting the walking I do in the office seeing patients. But it doesn't count as aerobic exercise. Why not? Because I don't do it all at one time. If I went back and forth to the hospital eight times without interruption, it would be aerobic exercise. But since I go back and forth piecemeal over several hours, all it does is make my feet and ankles sore by the end of the day. Because it's not aerobic, it won't help control my weight or train my heart either.

What if I'm too tired to exercise, particularly after a busy day?
I can really sympathize with this. Some days I come home, as my mother would say, "bone tired." The last thing I want to do after one of those days is hop up on the treadmill and go walking for thirty minutes. But when I do go ahead and work out, I feel much better. Exercise reenergizes me.

If you are absolutely "wasted," you should skip exercise that day and try to make it up the next day after you've rested. The same is true if you are sick or trying to recover from an illness. Remember, you only need to exercise three times a week, so you have a lot of flexibility about when you do it.

What about using sugar substitutes like NutraSweet?
I think sugar substitutes can ease the pain of eating fewer calories and less sugar. But I also think they should be used in moderation. Saccharin works well for most people, particularly in hot drinks like coffee and tea since NutraSweet is not supposed to be heated. Previously, saccharin use had been linked to bladder cancer in animals,

but more recent studies in humans indicate no such problems. However, I still think limiting your use of saccharin to six to eight packets per day makes sense.

Similarly, aspartame (often seen under the brand name Nutra-Sweet) may cause problems if used excessively. I have heard many people say that they have swelling and fluid retention if they drink a lot of diet soda. Some also complain of a great deal of abdominal gas and bloating. This would be particularly true for people with irritable bowel syndrome.

Do I have to follow my calculated daily calories in rigidly, or can I cheat a little?

Of course, everybody cheats on a diet; on average, about three days a week. But cheating on the calorie counting method doesn't derail your weight management program; it simply requires an adjustment over the following few days. I do recommend that for the first four weeks you do the minimum amount of exercise and stick to your daily calorie intake until you get the hang of it and see what this level of exercise and calorie consumption does for you. Remember, each woman is different and must find the calories in and calories expended levels that control her body weight. However, once you establish a daily calorie level at which you will consistently lose weight, I think it's okay to stretch the program out a bit and get the full benefits of its flexibility.

My family won't eat "diet food," and I really don't have time to make two different menus for every meal.

This is a big problem confronting women trying to eat more healthfully—family members just don't want to eat those odd-ball, low-calorie dinners or stick to the food restrictions of a fad diet. The calorie counting program doesn't require you to purchase special food or prepare meals that your family won't eat. You do have to manage how much you eat of what you serve, particularly if you prepare high-fat, high-carbohydrate meals. And you do have to maintain the proper protein:carbohydrate:fat ratios mentioned earlier and stay within your calorie limits. If you opt to make healthier food choices—more vegetables, less red meat and fatty fried foods—you can eat more and feel less hungry after mealtime. It may take some time for your kids to get used to it, but you will be doing them a real favor. If you can help them eat healthier now, they will be more likely to continue good dietary habits when they leave your loving guidance and take off on their own.

I diet and exercise as hard as anyone else, and I still always have to struggle with my weight. It isn't fair!

You're right, it isn't fair. You were dealt a set of genes that, albeit great for survival in bad conditions, forces you to diet more and exercise harder than other people to effectively manage your weight. You can't change your genes, but you can change your attitude about them and learn how to cope with them to achieve the long-term weight control you want through sensible diet and exercise. You will probably have to work harder at it than others, but no one promised us that anything in this life would be easy or fair. Decide that you are going to be a winner, and get started!

Are there other diet programs that you recommend?

I think Weight Watchers packages an excellent weight-loss program that is reasonably affordable. They use a point system to regulate calories in rather than actually counting them, but it is essentially the same method. Additionally, Weight Watchers provides a support group that meets weekly to encourage compliance, and these meetings are very helpful for many people.

You can also consult a dietitian for a personalized weight-loss plan. Your doctor probably knows where to refer you should you choose this route. Sometimes one-on-one discussion and personal attention can help you get a better handle on your unique situation. Certainly if you are diabetic or have other special diet restrictions, or if you have tried calorie counting several times before and never been successful with it, you should consult with a registered dietitian.

What is the metabolic syndrome (Syndrome X) I've heard about that causes weight gain in so many women?

It is estimated that almost fifty million adults in the United States suffer from metabolic syndrome, also called Syndrome X. This condition is characterized by central obesity (weight gain in the trunk and abdomen but not in the arms and legs), high cholesterol, high blood pressure, and insulin resistance. People with this syndrome face an uphill battle when it comes to weight loss—they must diet more and exercise harder to get their weight down. This is the same insulin-resistance seen in PCOS, Cushing's syndrome, and prediabetes. In fact, it's often hard to tell which one of these conditions any given patient has because they look very similar. In any case, the fat cells in all of these circumstances become resistant to the normal triggers that would cause weight loss, namely diet and exercise. Consult your physician if you feel you may have this condition or if you find you just can't succeed with an appropriate balanced diet and exercise program like this one.

I have so much weight to lose, where do I begin?

Confucius said (or maybe it was Elvis) "a journey of a thousand miles begins with just one step." Although it looks like a long way to your goal, you can get there if you will just get started. Take the first step and become committed—not to a diet but to a lifetime weight management program. When you think about it, the rest of your life is a long time, and you've got all that time to work on this problem. Don't be in a hurry. Take it slow and do it right the first time. Remember, the tortoise won the race, not the hare.

It can be very discouraging when you've got a hundred pounds to lose and you remember that you should only expect to lose one to two pounds each week. When you do the math you realize that it may take a year to lose the weight. A whole year! But if you think about it, a year compared to the rest of your life is not very long. Also, this is not a year in "calorie prison" on a starvation fad diet; it is merely the first year that you have begun to eat properly and exercise to begin to maintain your ideal body weight, or at least your target weight. That's why it takes so long for the weight to come off. This is not starvation or total food deprivation but simply changing your eating habits and level of physical activity to fit the weight you want and allowing your body to slowly adjust down to it. There is no gentler way to do it, and besides, this is the way you will need to eat and exercise to stay at your target weight once you get there. These are the facts. There are no shortcuts and no magic bullets to get there successfully. If you understand and believe these facts, the only logical conclusion is to get started now and be patient.

What do you think about the Atkins diet and The Zone?
I don't believe the Atkins diet leads to successful long-term weight loss. Unless you're trying to drop some weight quickly for an event that's coming up in two months and don't care what happens afterward, long-term success is the only success worth having. The Atkins diet remains popular because it gives quick gratification; most people lose several pounds of water weight in the first two weeks. However, it has not been shown to be effective in the long run. Besides, the Atkins diet is difficult to follow because it lacks flexibility in food selection, doesn't allow for cheating, and doesn't fit into a busy woman's lifestyle.

I have to agree with Dr. Arthur Agatston, the cardiologist who wrote *The South Beach Diet*, that the sharp limitations on carbs necessary with the Atkins approach leads to the liberal intake of saturated fats, which we know can lead to blood vessel damage and heart disease. Of course, if your life expectancy is one year or less, this shouldn't worry you. However, if you are planning on being around a little longer, you might wish to reconsider a long-term stint on the Atkins diet.

The Zone, on the other hand, does offer a long-term program for weight management that should prove quite successful. Dr. Barry Sears is a well-respected molecular biologist and bases his recommendations on several scientifically based nutritional studies (which are unfortunately flawed by the inherent limitations on all nutritional studies that were discussed earlier). Much of what he says makes sense though, and I have incorporated that information into this book.

However, I do have two areas of concern with Dr. Sears's concepts. First, he feels that staying in "The Zone" will prevent heart disease, cancer, arthritis, lupus, depression, alcoholism, AIDS, jet lag, PMS, impotence, chronic pain, eczema, psoriasis, and even aging. It is clear from an abundance of research that eating a balanced diet and following a program of regular exercise will lower one's risk of death from heart disease, and The Zone diet certainly offers an acceptable approach to this problem. However, the body of available scientific evidence becomes quite thin in support of Dr. Sears's assertions that his program can ward off the other diseases mentioned.

Second, to stay within The Zone requires an excessive restriction of calories compared to other successful diet programs, including the one I have proposed here.

What do you think of the South Beach Diet?

I think Dr. Agatston should be applauded for pulling together a lot of scientific research on the proper role of diet in the prevention of obesity, diabetes, and heart disease. He also deserves kudos for bucking the American Heart Association's traditional high-carb, low-fat diet recommendations and forging his own program—no mean feat.

Dr. Agatston has obviously produced a very popular diet that appears to be effective for short-term weight loss, and I think will also prove to be effective for long-term weight management for those who can follow it. However, much like The Zone, the South Beach approach is unnecessarily restrictive, and I think this will make it prone to failure for those who simply can't drop "white food"—rice, sugar, and white bread—forever. The South Beach Diet is much more flexible and balanced than Atkins, but it is still much less flexible than the programs presented here or by Weight Watchers. The other shortcoming of South Beach is that it virtually ignores the vital role exercise plays in weight management. Overall, I would not hesitate to recommend it, coupled with an exercise program, for someone interested in pursuing long-term weight management.

What's your opinion of Dr. Phil's approach to weight loss?

As you would expect from a psychologist, Dr. Phil does a superb job of presenting the cognitive-behavioral approach to weight control. He stresses the importance of overcoming our negative thinking about ourselves and dieting, exposes the common false beliefs many of us have about food and what it represents to us, and reverses the errors in logic that tend to fool us into making bad decisions about weight management. He also stresses the importance of regular exercise, which I completely support.

However, his diet program is "confusingly simple." To his credit, Dr. Phil did get advice on his diet recommendations from the American Heart Association, but I think in his effort to simplify the diet plan, he let go of a lot of credibility. In my opinion, the diet is *too* simple. And, as he tells us in Chapter 1 of his book, *The Ultimate Weight Solution: The Seven Keys to Weight Loss Freedom*, the approaches are the same ones he used on patients in his private psychology practice who had 100, 200, and 300-plus pounds to lose. But think about it. A woman with a 150-pound frame who needs to lose 300 pounds weighs 450 pounds and therefore has to be consuming almost 5,000 calories a day at a minimum to maintain herself at this weight. You have to work hard to eat 5,000 calories a day! At this level of obesity, it's obvious that Dr. Phil's clients had some unhealthy psychological attachments to food, and I suspect benefited far more from the cognitive-behavioral aspects of his program than his overly simple diet formula. I don't think Dr. Phil's program will be nearly as effective for the average Hurried Woman who usually has much less weight to lose.

10

STEP 4:
REKINDLE THE FIRE

IT'S NOT REALLY CLEAR WHY, but men and women have struggled
with their different sexual urges for centuries. However, this is not
a trivial issue. A healthy sex life is one of the most critical features
of a fulfilling relationship. In fact, I believe that low sex drive is probably the single most troubling symptom Hurried Women face and
the one problem most likely to damage their relationships permanently. Sexual intimacy is vital because it proves the willingness of
each of you to be vulnerable to the other.

Dr. Phil McGraw, in *Relationship Rescue: A Seven-Step Strategy
for Reconnecting with Your Partner* (Hyperion, 2000), says that sex
has significant symbolic importance as it can represent "the greatest single factor of disappointment in a relationship." It's not that
"sex is everything"; this notion is absurd. But a good sexual relationship with your partner *is* important. In fact, if you and your
partner agree that you have a good sex life, it probably represents
only 10–20 percent of what you feel is important in your relation-

ship. But if you and your partner don't agree that your sexual life is healthy, it can become a dominant issue; one that can overshadow everything else that is good. When sex becomes "an issue," there is an unhealthy tension between partners. Anxiety, rejection, hurt feelings, guilt, inadequacy, and resentment become all too common. Dr. Phil goes on to say that "because sex is so intimate, so personal, feelings of rejection in this particular area are magnified a hundredfold." Rejection in this area is much more painful than being told you don't look good in brown or the joke you just told wasn't funny.

Of course, on a percentage basis, more women have concerns about their weight and energy levels than they do about low sex drive, and many feel that if they could get their weight under control and their energy back that their sex drive would improve, too. This is very likely true, and I encourage women to work on these other issues as well as improving their sex drive because the symptoms of Hurried Woman Syndrome affect one another. This is why it's so important to use an integrated approach to overcome the syndrome. However, low sex drive has a more direct and potentially more damaging long-term effect on relationships than the other symptoms. Even more compelling is that the damage to the relationship can occur very quickly and have devastating results. Finally, low sex drive is a common stand-alone problem for many women, which makes the following information important for them as well.

"NORMAL" SEX DRIVE

When we talk about low sex drive, we are erroneously implying that there is an ideal or normal level of sex drive. As it turns out, no one can agree on a definition of normal sex drive—it doesn't exist. So when a woman is concerned that she has low libido, what she's really saying is that her sex drive is lower now than it used to be (she's noticed a change) or her partner is griping about it (he's noticed a change) or both. For most women, the complaint of low sex drive really means that the difference between her drive and his is causing a problem in their relationship. I have couples in my practice who have sex two or three times a year and are perfectly satisfied, while other couples are having sex daily and continually looking for creative ways to squeeze a few more encounters into each week. I would consider the women in both of these situations normal because their level of sexual desire matches that of their partner. The issue of low sex drive is predominantly one of balance. When both partners have a similar level of interest in sex, there's no issue. But when one partner desires significantly less physical intimacy than the other, "low sex drive" becomes a problem in the relationship. In general, when there is a difference in sex drives, the woman's drive is lower than the man's, although this isn't always the case.

Some women report that they have less drive now than in the past but are still able to satisfy their partner's desire for intimacy. In other words, their desire for intimacy is noticeably lower now than before, but they've been able to keep it from interfering with their relationships. But how long can this go on and be healthy for both partners? If the situation continues over time, several things will usually happen: the woman becomes resentful, feeling that she must have sex when she really isn't interested; the man will come to question the strength of their relationship and her integrity as he begins to sense that she is "faking it"; and intimacy—both emotional and physical—will begin to suffer as both partners become more uncomfortable in situations where physical intimacy might occur, and this lost sense of connection will lead to dissatisfaction in the relationship. Loss of intimacy is one of the most important reasons that relationships fail.

There is little doubt that one of the symptoms of Hurried Woman Syndrome is a lowering of libido, which comes from a decline in dopamine levels in the brain. However, this is usually only one of several factors that contribute to the problem. A woman's level of sexual interest is determined by the complex interaction of many factors, and it is important for us to explore each of these facid how they relate to one another as we try to more fully understand the lack of desire experienced by Hurried Women.

Unfortunately, the medical world has dubbed psychiatrists and ob-gyn physicians as coholders of the title "sex expert." Some would find this title impressive, but I find it frustrating. We have learned much in the last twenty years, but there is still a lot that we don't know about female libido; it is an incredibly complex issue. However, I will share with you what we do and don't know about sex drive—in women as well as men—and, more importantly, how to shrink the differences in drive between the two sexes and make low sex drive less of an issue for your relationship. A woman's sex drive is influenced by several types of factors: physical, situational, and emotional or psychological.

PHYSICAL ASPECTS OF SEX DRIVE IN WOMEN

Humans belong to the animal kingdom. And although we don't like to think of ourselves as animals, it is quite apparent that there are many physical and behavioral similarities between the two. A female mammal will usually not accept the amorous advances of the male unless she is in estrus, or "heat," which occurs at the time of ovulation—the only time pregnancy can occur. Such an attitude encourages efficient reproduction in a species and avoids "wasted" encounters. Interestingly, many women notice that they are more likely to fantasize and have a more positive attitude about sex around the time of ovulation and this decreases when their period nears. A woman's sex drive appears to have an underlying basic rhythm that peaks once a month when her eggs are ready for fertilization.

Similarly, a man's sexual rhythm seems to run parallel to his ability to reproduce. The difference between men and women is that sperm production is a continuous process that occurs every day. No wonder men are ready for sex virtually all the time; they're always ready to procreate. Of course, these underlying sexual currents flow very differently in men and women and may provide an explanation for some of the differences in libido seen between the sexes.

Additional proof for at least some link to our animal roots is found in the seasonal nature of human births. More babies are born in July, August, and September than in any other three consecutive months during the year (not the best timing considering that most new doctors-in-training start on July 1 each year). This seasonal concentration of births would imply at least some cyclic increase in fertility and perhaps sexual frequency among humans. Most women would argue, and rightfully so, that this animal nature isn't the primary factor in deciding whether or not they want to have sex on any given night, but it may provide an underlying rhythm of rising and falling sexual awareness.

Understanding your own sexual rhythms might help explain *why* you feel the way you do *when* you do. Helping your partner understand your sexual rhythm may lead to less frustration and more satisfaction in your love life. Many women notice that they are just not in the mood to make love immediately before and during a menstrual cycle. Sex is often more uncomfortable then. The pelvic organs are congested and swollen with blood, and many women suffer from premenstrual syndrome (PMS) or other mood changes that may make them less likely to want to be intimate during the week or so prior to the menstrual cycle. If you're aware of these cycles, you can tell your partner what's going on so he won't keep making the mistake of approaching you during these natural "down times." Men are trainable.

Also, remember that your partner's natural rhythm is not a couple of beats on a bass drum each month but more like a drumroll. Try to be more patient with him; don't necessarily read his almost constant readiness as "pressure to perform" but rather as a natural consequence of his underlying physical rhythms.

Illness

Illness can have a significant impact on sexual function in women as well as in men. Women who are debilitated by chronic disease or are often in pain are likely to have much less sex drive. Patients worn down by advanced cancer, severe anemia, low thyroid function, and chronic infections all report lower levels of sexual desire. In fact, fatigue from any cause lowers a woman's normal interest in sex.

Women who suffer from chronic vaginitis (yeast infections, bacterial vaginosis, and trichomoniasis), endometriosis, or uterine prolapse often experience painful intercourse and begin to have less desire for sex. Uterine prolapse is a condition where the uterus drops down into the lower pelvis. It occurs in about 20 percent of women who have delivered a baby vaginally and may also be associated with backaches, a sensation of pressure in the vagina after standing for extended periods of time, and sometimes a loss of urine when coughing, laughing, or sneezing. Let's face it, if it hurts to have sex, why would you want to? Many men say they will have sex while in pain, but women tend to feel differently.

Painful intercourse is always a sign of illness. If you're experiencing pain during sex, see your doctor. Trying to force the issue over time is not a good idea because it may lead to a condition called vaginismus, as well as a lot of resentment. Vaginismus is an involuntary spasm of the powerful pelvic muscles that close off the vagina, making sex extremely difficult if not impossible. This condition can absolutely wreck your sex life until it is treated. Don't let pain of this kind go undiagnosed and untreated—see your gynecologist immediately.

If you suffer from a chronic medical condition, try to comply with the treatment program suggested by your doctor and get your medical problems under control as much as possible. This will make you feel better overall and maximize your chances for a happy sex life.

Testosterone

Testosterone has received a lot of attention in the popular press as well as in scientific journals over the past few years. Testosterone is the most active male hormone in both men and women. It generally has similar effects in both sexes but can have the opposite effect in certain areas. Testosterone encourages libido in both men and women, but it would be too simple to say, "He's got too much and I have too little." In some cases, it may be the truth, but not in all or even the majority. Several celebrities and sexologists have made the talk-show circuit touting that testosterone was the answer to curing a woman's low libido. They told women to rub testosterone cream on their forearms thirty minutes before sex and it would transform them into "sex goddesses." Then they came back on the afternoon and late-night television shows about six months later saying that testosterone cream was still better than sliced bread, but to get the maximum effect, you have to rub it right on your clitoris. Well, if you massage your clitoris for thirty minutes with or without testosterone cream, you'll most likely be ready for sex. When you're in the right frame of mind, this technique almost always works. And you can put anything you want on the clitoris —KY Jelly, Karo Syrup— it all works the same in generating the desired physiological response. In a recent survey of ob-gyns from across the country, only about 20 percent of our patients with low libido respond to testosterone replacement. Unfortunately, for the majority of women, using extra testosterone just isn't that effective.

That said, if you have a low sex drive, you should have your testosterone levels checked and consider testosterone replacement only if they are low. We replace estrogen in menopause and should also consider replacing testosterone if symptoms and blood work verify the need. However, I don't recommend taking male hormone "just to see if it helps." You might start singing bass in the choir or need to shave every morning if you take extra testosterone and don't need it. If your levels are already normal, adding a little more won't help anything and may wind up leading to an overdose. Overdose symptoms include extra hair growth, acne, moodiness, channel surfing, and declaring war for no apparent reason.

Besides improving sex drive for some women, testosterone is anabolic. In other words, testosterone tends to build muscle rather than fat by modifying your metabolism. It also appears to build bone and blood cells that help prevent osteoporosis and anemia. Other areas of current testosterone research include prevention of hair loss, Alzheimer's disease, depression, and connective tissue diseases such as lupus.

If your testosterone level is low, I think you should consider a trial of replacement therapy. I usually recommend Estratest (a combination of estrogen and testosterone in pill form) or transdermal testosterone cream preparations compounded by a pharmacist. The skin absorbs certain hormones and other medications very efficiently. You don't need to worry about growing a patch of hair where you rub it on—I usually recommend the forearm, but you're welcome to put it elsewhere if you like—and it's not much more expensive than pills. Once you begin hormone replacement, you should have your testosterone level rechecked in about two months, because none of the testosterone preparations gives predictable blood levels. Remember, not too much and not too little. Take the medicine faithfully and get your hormone level rechecked to be sure it's in the proper range.

MENOPAUSE AND ESTROGEN

Testosterone is not the end of the hormone story. Other hormones are important as well in supporting a normal sex drive. Women in menopause still report a desire for sexual activity, but they tend to be much more satisfied with sex if they are on estrogen. Estrogen primes the female sex organs for intercourse and allows for vaginal lubrication as well as elasticity. Menopausal women will often complain of vaginal dryness and even painful intercourse if their estrogen levels are too low. Estrogen has also been shown to improve sexual sensitivity and heighten a women's ability to achieve orgasm. Several studies have documented that women in menopause report more satisfaction with their sex lives if they receive estrogen. Moreover, the levels of satisfaction improve even further if testosterone replacement is given as well, but only in women whose testosterone levels are low. Achieving the appropriate balance of estrogen and testosterone can allow most women to enjoy a healthy sex life far into menopause. Recent studies have revealed that hormones aren't for everyone, particularly women who have been in menopause for several years without them. The risks, benefits, and alternatives to taking estrogen, testosterone, and progestin are discussed in Chapter 6.

SITUATIONAL FACTORS

Even though physical factors influence libido, situational factors are probably the most important cause of low sex drive in women. When the pressure's on, sex becomes a low or "no" priority item for most women. Research has shown that women who feel stressed are much less likely to fantasize about sex than men under similar pressure. Indeed, this is one of the more important ways in which men and women differ in their reaction to stress. Big deadlines, hectic schedules at work and home, troubled teenagers, and money problems all produce stressors that decrease a woman's desire for sex. Living at your mother-in-law's house for a month, preparing for your daughter's wedding, or bringing a new baby home are all examples of stressful situations that decrease sex drive. Fortunately, most situations like these are temporary and their effects are easily recognized.

But what about situations that are not so temporary—an extremely stressful job, a chronically sick parent or child, or precarious financial circumstances? These situations may last a lot longer.

Sometimes when the immediate effects of the initial stress die down, we forget that the chronic stress left behind can take its toll on our energy levels and our desire to enjoy many aspects of life in which we once found pleasure, including sex. After one of these situations has dragged on for a while, many of my patients tell me that they are used to the stress and that it no longer affects them. At this point, they are clearly suffering from denial and perhaps even depression or the predepression of Hurried Woman Syndrome. Sadly, these conditions are often unrecognized, but they nonetheless are having a significant impact on a woman's life and the people around her.

Most people would eventually recognize the situations I've described as stressful. It might take some time to appreciate the full impact of the stress on their health and attitudes, but they would at least agree that they *might* be stressed. What about the little things that stress us, such as our kids' sports activities—Little League, Little Dribblers (basketball), gymnastics, cheerleading, dance lessons, or (dare I say it) soccer? Don't these events weigh on your schedule and therefore your mind as well? Could the stresses from all these "little things," when combined with the big things in your life like work, husband, family, religious activities, school, and so on, produce a very hectic schedule and higher levels of stress? Of course they can and do for most women. Trying to manage your busy life and the busy lives of your children and spouse takes its toll on your mental and physical energy. Sure, no one of these things will make or break you by itself, but don't underestimate the overall effect that juggling each of these "little things" in your life has on your stress levels. They are very significant. Most of the Hurried Women I see day in and day out are desperately searching for the "one big thing" they can get rid of to lower their stress levels. But my patients are very intelligent people, and if there were only one big thing causing all the trouble, they would have already identified and gotten rid of it by the time they see me. For most of them, there is no one big thing but rather a lot of little things that, when added together, have caused Hurried Woman Syndrome. Fixing some of the little things in their lives is where the answer to surviving the syndrome lies.

Even when a woman understands the situational stress she is under, she often feels that changing the circumstances is beyond her control. Sometimes it is, but for many there's another problem:

"My husband's work is too important." (. . . *and I'm not*)

"No one else can take care of my mother." (. . . *the way I want it done*)

"My job is very demanding and I can't cut back my hours." (. . . *because I like to feel important and needed, even though it's killing me*)

"My kids just can't give up soccer this season." (. . . *but I guess they can give up my happiness without too much trouble*)

Through almost twenty years of medical practice, I've seen countless women who have used similar explanations as to why their particular situation is "unfixable." When I confront them with the hidden message you see in parentheses, they often look at me as if I'm from another planet and say, "You obviously don't understand, doctor." For these women, everyone else's needs must be met first. Then and only then will they really take any time out for themselves: time to unwind, time to think, time to relax, time to just be themselves. They've simply placed themselves too low on their own priority list.

So many of the women I encounter are willing (too willing) to sacrifice themselves for the benefit of their families. And I do appreciate that this comes from a strong sense of duty and love. It is this trait that makes my wife a hero in my eyes—she constantly denies herself to serve her family in so very many ways—but at what cost? You may be one of the many women who suffer under the horrendous workload of trying to run the kids to gymnastics, swimming lessons, baseball practice, soccer games, playdates, music lessons, school programs, church programs, and on and on. All of these are worthwhile endeavors. Who could argue that playing sports or taking music lessons are, by themselves, bad for your child? But what is it costing *you* in terms of physical and emotional energy (much less your budget) to meet all of their schedules, project deadlines, practices, and performances? Do you ever sit back and calculate how much all of this stuff costs? Humorist Erma Bombeck once said that raising kids was "like being pecked to death by chickens." It's not that any one "peck" is going to kill you, but after dealing with this kind of nagging stress over several weeks, months, or years, you're going to start feeling its effects. The hurry in your life simply drains the sex drive out of you.

And don't expect the people around you to fix the situation for you. They don't realize how much you're hurting because you don't tell them. Remember, your kids are too young to realize what anything really costs, and your husband doesn't view all of this from the same perspective as you (yet), so he's unlikely to figure it out by himself. You are going to have to take the bull by the horns and change things to make your life better. Otherwise, these stresses will continue to peck away at you until you experience a meltdown or the circumstances change by themselves (your kids move away or your relationship suffers).

It's certainly not that your children, boss, husband, and friends hate you. On the contrary, they love you and also love all the things you do for them, but they don't realize (and maybe you don't either) how much all the little things they ask of you—and you ask of yourself on their behalf—affect you and how your body and mind reacts to them. The first step to fixing this problem is recognizing the importance of "the little things" and how they affect you and your attitudes toward sex and life in general.

We discussed this in some detail in Chapter 2. I bring it up again here because it is critical to your understanding of Hurried Woman Syndrome and why it makes you feel this way. In the final three chapters, we will discuss how to fix the problems of the Hurried

Woman—"unhurry" yourself, so to speak. At this point, it is important for you to understand that situational stress lowers your sex drive and can do so quite dramatically. Indeed, it may be one of the major reasons why you are where you are—unhappy. The good news is that situational stress is something you actually can exert some control over.

MEN AND WOMEN APPROACH SEX DIFFERENTLY

Unless you've been marooned on a desert island, I'm sure that you've read or heard about this subject before. There are several interesting books on the topic, including the popular *Men Are from Mars and Women Are from Venus: A Practical Guide for Improving Communication and Getting What You Want in Your Relationships* by John Gray (HarperCollins, 1992) and Dr. Phil McGraw's *Relationship Rescue.* If you've read any of these books, some of what I say here will probably be repetitive for you. But it's important for you to have at least a basic understanding of how the sexes differ in their approach to sex or you will continually be frustrated in your marriage for one very important but simple reason—your husband or partner will *never* be like you. Wishing won't make it so! And if he did become just like you, you probably wouldn't like him anymore anyway. Sure, it would improve your relationship in some ways, but he will never think and act as you do because men and women are not only built different physically, they also approach life and their relationships very differently.

Much of the information in this chapter is based on observed behavior. In other words, scientists have studied the habits and opinions of male and female subjects, both children and adults, and observed differences in how the sexes act and say they feel. This type of information is held to be pretty reliable because it is based on scientific observation. However, the underlying reasons that men and women behave differently are still a mystery in many areas. We're not really sure how much is nurture and how much is nature. And of course each individual is unique. This type of information is therefore speculative. We don't really know that much about it for certain, but reasonably intelligent people are giving us their best guess as to why the sexes approach certain tasks differently, don't act the same in specific situations, or express differing emotions when challenged.

The other problem with this type of discussion is that it leads to stereotyping. Everybody knows that all men are not the same—some are more athletic, others more scholarly, some aggressive, and others gentle. Just as you can't pigeonhole all women into two or three tidy slots, most men are a blend of several traits rather than one stereotype. So don't be surprised when you find that some of the examples given don't exactly fit your situation. This section may be a review for you, but it will still help you focus your thoughts on the subject.

Gender Identity and Its Effect on Relationships

In general, men relate to each other through activities such as sports or work. They gather with their friends to go golfing, hunting, fishing, watch a ball game, play poker, or swap tall stock market tales with each other. Men often obtain their identities through competition and goal-oriented activities. How often do you see your partner chatting with his buddies? You know, "guy talk." Men are much more likely to gather for an event or activity than to simply talk. It should be no mystery why men find work and sports rewarding—it's the way they receive gratification. Competing and accumulating "prizes" such as money, a fancy car, a nice house, an attractive wife and family, or a promotion at work all contribute to a man's self-esteem. Unfortunately, losing the race can sometimes take it away, too.

Women, on the other hand, often call each other just to find out what's going on, how the kids are doing, or what happened over the weekend. Now don't think that men don't gossip, because they do. Yet gossip is not the primary reason for male interaction, it's the event that counts—gossip just *occurs* at the event. Women tend to show affection for each other through talking, sharing emotions, gathering opinions, and touching—relating. Establishing and nurturing relationships with the important people in their lives gives women much of their identity and purpose. With more women entering the workforce, this male/female paradigm has become somewhat blurred. However, studies of professional men and women demonstrate that these differences are still very much present. Male executives place more emphasis on achieving work-related goals than their female counterparts, while female executives stress relationship building at work more than their male colleagues do.

Differing Perspectives and Priorities

Gender differences can also be seen in how men and women view the same event from different perspectives. A few months ago, two friends told my wife and me about a car accident they had been involved in over the weekend. Once we realized they weren't hurt badly, I asked the husband about the particulars of the accident—how much damage was done, what it was going to cost to fix their car, how the accident occurred. My wife asked if anyone else was hurt and whether they were still shaken up by what had happened. I was more interested in the action and the "prizes" at risk in the accident, while my wife was more concerned about the people and relationships at risk. Men and women approach life from different perspectives and with different priorities. These general differences also lead to some very specific attitudes regarding sex.

Timing. If you ask a man how much time he needs to have a fulfilling sexual encounter, he'll say, "Seven minutes. In fact, three

ould do in a pinch." Men can start right after the weather—I'm
rry, the sports—and be through before Letterman gets cranked
p. No problem. But women are different. They don't need time for
x, they need time for sex to *happen*. Making love needs to be an
teresting idea, a notion. And if it's been a bad week, this might take
ree or four days to develop. In general, guys are always ready for
x, whereas women need time to get ready for it. Although a lot of
ouples enjoy "a quickie" now and then, men usually get much more
ut of brief, impromptu encounters than do women.

EX AS A PRIORITY. If a man and woman get up in the morning and
ach one makes up a "Top Ten List" of things they'd like to do today,
ex will be number one, two, or three on his list unless he's had open
eart surgery that week. If the surgery was last week, sex will be back
ıp there again. But for most women, if sex is on the list at all, it will
)e number nine or ten, and it will be there because she feels guilty
ıbout sex not having been on the list for a while. For men, sex is like
[ell-O; there's always room for more. Not so for most women. A fel-
ow gynecologist told me after attending a lecture on Hurried
Woman Syndrome that sex requires energy, and since women who
are struggling with fatigue don't have enough energy to get everything done, they tend to allocate energy to their high-priority items
first. These are often the things that are "in their face," or the squeak-
iest wheels. Unfortunately for most of her patients, there just isn't
enough energy left over at the end of most days to include sex on
the schedule. It becomes a low priority that tends to get pushed
down on the to-do list when things get hurried.

This is why if decreased libido is troubling you, it is important
to schedule time to allow sex to happen—without feeling that it is
being forced on you. If you decide it's going to be a priority, clear
unimportant or less important things off your list, take time to relax,
time to exercise, get some of the stress and pressure out of your life,
and save some time in the schedule, at least a few times each week,

to reflect on "physical matters." Otherwise, unpressured sex simply won't happen.

How the Sexes View Sex Differently

Men are physically oriented when it comes to sex. If you touch a man in the right spot, he'll probably be ready to have sex (sometimes with the wrong person, which can get him into trouble). However, if a man touches a woman in the right spot without her permission, he'll probably get slapped—even if he's been married to her for years. The same stimulus produces a very different response.

Women tend to be much more cerebral about sex. Most women must be courted properly—or "in the mood"—before they will become aroused, and this requires a few more things to line up properly. The proper mood includes being happy with your partner. If you're angry with him, you probably won't want to have sex with him. This anger could be from recent or past events. If you haven't forgiven him for an affair he had five years ago, or if you're upset by his not helping out with the kids enough or siding with his mother too often, you may not want to make love with him. Many times, these attitudes are not conscious efforts to punish him but travel just under the surface of your awareness, flaring up briefly and then subsiding. In fact, when I have asked women who complain about decreased libido whether any of these situations applied to them they often vehemently denied it. Yet when I see them back in the office a few years later for their annual visit (a perennial favorite), I am sometimes surprised to learn that their sex life has improved dramatically. What's different? They have a new husband. Now they will tell me that they were having trouble at home for the past several years. Their ex-husband was abusive or an alcoholic or had a girlfriend, or they were angry with him over some issue. So if you're complaining of low sex drive, it's important to ask yourself the following questions:

- Am I happy in my relationship with my husband?

- Are there problem areas we need to work on (other than low sex drive)?

- Do we need counseling?

If you have asked yourself the last question more than once, you probably do need counseling. Virtually all marriages have room to improve, but if you and your spouse communicate well and the problems aren't very serious, then counseling may not be needed. However, if you find yourself butting your head up against the same wall over and over again, or if the problems involve substance (or any other kind of) abuse, counseling can be a lifesaver. I recommend starting with your pastor, rabbi, or priest if you are part of a religious community. These people are sworn to secrecy and usually have experience in dealing with couples having problems. It is highly doubtful that they will help much with specific sexual problems, but they usually understand the underlying problems in a marriage. If your clergy doesn't seem to be the right person, then he or she can usually recommend someone. If you are not religious or simply prefer another route, ask your doctor for a recommendation.

Opinion research shows that the most common areas of disagreement in marriage are as follows:

- **Raising the kids.** Often one parent takes on the role of disciplinarian while the other parent disagrees with the first one's methods and therefore doesn't help enforce the rules. They often disagree in front of the children who then lose respect for the authoritarian parent. This undermining of authority aggravates the disciplinarian who retaliates by attacking the more passive parent, which further undermines each parent's authority. This produces a vicious circle with the kids caught in the middle.

- **Money.** Who makes it, controls it, spends it, saves it, invests it, and allocates it are all issues surrounding money and finances that can cause problems for couples. Money is the second most common subject over which couples argue.

- **Work.** Should both spouses work? Whose job is more important, or which career will take precedence over the other when tough decisions need to be made? Who pays for each of the various household expenses? What are each person's expectations of his or her own role and the role of the spouse for child care and household duties? When does "working hard for the family" become "hard work for the family"?

If you've tried many times and failed to resolve these types of conflicts, I recommend you seek professional help. A neutral third party can often help you sort out these issues and reach some common ground. But do it now, before too much water passes under the bridge.

SEX IS LOVE—NOT! For most men, sex *is* love ("If you love me, you will want to have sex with me"). A lot of women don't like it, but this is a very "male" notion. Many men feel that sex is a necessary expression of love and perhaps the most important one in a marriage. Women are more "process oriented"; how they get to the sex is usually more important than the act of making love itself. For a woman, sex isn't love; it is a by-product of a loving relationship. Therefore, most women don't necessarily need to make love as often to feel loved, whereas most men equate the two. This is why having sex is often a much higher priority item for men than for women.

NO SUBSTITUTIONS ALLOWED

Most couples get married because they love each other—*really*. When a man and woman fall in love and get married, they establish a primary love relationship; a lifelong bond between two people "to love, honor, and cherish till death do you part" as the traditional wording goes. But as the years go by, two unhealthy substitutions frequently occur in this primary love relationship: (1) a man will substitute his work for the relationship with his wife, and (2) a woman will substitute her relationship with their children for the one with her husband. Since in most families the man is still viewed as the primary breadwinner (the wife works at home or holds a job that both view as secondary to that of the husband), we will first look at the dynamics of this traditional situation and then analyze relationships under other conditions that are becoming more common as the nature of work and the workforce change.

It is a natural consequence of reproduction that the husband will have to stand back somewhat and allow his wife to raise and nurture their children, breast-feeding being an obvious example. However, a mother's bond with her children should be viewed as a secondary love relationship, because without the primary love relationship, the secondary one would generally not have occurred. Nurturing infants and small children requires virtually all of her time and energy at first, but then the center of her affection should turn back toward her husband because he is the focus of her primary love relationship. Obviously, she now must share her affection between all the members of her family, and the primary relationship between husband and wife will never be quite the same again. However, a strong and unique relationship must be carefully maintained between Mom and Dad to prevent a critical substitution from occurring that could injure the primary love relationship.

Many couples wake up when the kids are gone to discover that they are each married to a stranger. They've both changed through the years but have not tended to their primary love relationship and have therefore grown distant, somehow unfamiliar. In the old days, this led to lives of "quiet desperation." Nowadays, it leads to depression, alcoholism, extramarital affairs, and divorce. Let me make it very clear that this phenomenon is not the woman's fault. In nature, it is very common for a female to guard her offspring and even shun the father to protect them. However, it is equally as natural for the shunned male to go off and impregnate other females once his reproductive work is done at one location. I find neither of these scenarios very adaptive for humans since both behaviors can lead to marriage failures. So let me encourage you to rise above your natural instincts and not push your husband away once you have children, just as I would encourage your husband not to be offended by your temporary loss of interest in his reproductive power once children arrive. He needs to be patient and supportive of you and your role as mother to his children.

Equally important to preserving your primary love relationship is for your husband to not allow work to dominate his life. Corporate America is beginning to see the value of including spouses in the careers of its workers, both male and female—bringing family to corporate events, encouraging paternity as well as maternity leave, and providing more financial security for the family through insurance and retirement plans. Yet substituting career for home is a classic "man thing" to do and must be constantly guarded against. Interestingly, as more women have entered the workforce, they are also experiencing the same pressures as men to substitute work for home but with a twist to be discussed later.

For most men, this substitution is not necessarily a conscious effort to withdraw from the family but a natural consequence of the male need for gratification through competition and winning "prizes." Work is where most men choose to compete because it provides constant prizes such as a paycheck; social interaction; potential promotions; and other perks like a car, meals, entertainment opportunities, and vacations. Winning the prizes at work, but also sharing them with his family, are the tools a man uses to build his self-esteem. Most men link their identity to their job—it defines them. This is not necessarily the healthiest way to define oneself, as evidenced by the high death rate among men immediately after retirement, but it is certainly common.

Of course, *work* is a four-letter word for a reason, and as such it has its unpleasant side. Long hours, deadlines, tough travel schedules, and ultimately the fear of failure may make your husband feel he has to turn away from you and your family at times to "get the job done." It's helpful if you and your husband are able to communicate with each other so you know when these tough times arrive, and you can be supportive rather than critical of his efforts. However, it's important at these times to gently remind him that the home "prizes" he's already won—your love and the love of your children—are always going to be there for him and are the most important ones to keep. Did you catch the paradox in that statement? On the one hand, he needs to know that you and the kids love him and support him in his efforts away from home and that he can be confident that your love will always be there for him. On the other hand, he has to acknowledge that if he takes you for granted or if he turns away too far and ignores you and his family, he could lose your affection. There's a fine line between working hard for the family and working too hard for the family to survive. There's an equally fine line between reminding him that his family needs him and criticizing him for working too hard, which will tear down his self-esteem. This can be a very sensitive area for some couples and one in which they both feel inadequate at times. My best advice to wives, particularly those who have left the paid workforce to work at home, is to always make the prizes at home appear as attractive and important as the prizes at work.

If you both work outside the home, this becomes a much more difficult issue. Twice as many women with school-age children work today as did in the 1960s. And as more women enter the professions and corporate boardrooms, both stress levels and pay levels are rising. In many families, the decision about whose career will dominate is becoming much less clear. You must sit down together and discuss the goals each of you hope to achieve in your respective career paths and find the areas where these goals merge (common ground) and where they clash (trouble spots). Enjoy the common ground areas first, then tackle the trouble spots one by one. Counseling can be helpful here, particularly if you just can't seem to come to an agreement. It's important for you to let your husband know when deadlines are looming at work or when you're dealing with extra pressure, so he can give you some extra space when it comes to physical intimacy.

A couple of interesting twists to the traditional dual substitution model described earlier have occurred as women have entered the higher end of the employment scale en masse. First, many working women not only make the traditional substitution of placing their children ahead of their partner but are often pressured to place their career above him as well. Under these circumstances, the husband finds that he has been displaced not only by his children but also by his wife's career. The first substitution is hard enough on the relationship without compounding the problem with the second one. It is critical for women who work to guard against making either of these common substitutions and—even more important—to not allow both of them to occur, just as the man must not make the common mistake of putting his work ahead of his primary relationship with his wife.

The other wrinkle in the traditional model that occurs more frequently as women achieve higher levels of pay and prestige in the workplace is to let Dad stay at home while Mom goes to work. I couldn't find an accurate statistic on this phenomenon, but I have several friends who are now stay-at-home dads, and although I am sure that some naysayers will protest that this is not the ideal situation, most of the men I know who are doing it actually love it as much as any woman does—which means much of the time it's great, and much of the time it's the most frustrating job in the world.

Stereotyping the various roles we play as parents by gender can be just as problematic as stereotyping careers the same way. Women can be superlative physicians, lawyers, astronauts, and politicians. So too can men be excellent caregivers, babysitters, nurturers, confidants, and teachers for their children. In my opinion, it is the responsibility of each couple to determine for themselves the roles ach parent will play in the process of raising their family and also o decide on the proper balance of work and home for each part- ier. Interestingly, I have received many e-mails from stay-at-home dads who complain that they have "Hurried Man Syndrome," suf- ering many of the same symptoms as women do, particularly fatigue. The difference is that their sex drive has gone up, while that of their working spouse has gone down. No one said it would be easy, guys.

ONE MORE THING

Change is scary. Even people who feel locked into a bad situation sometimes prefer to keep slugging away at it in the same old unsuc- cessful ways rather than face the specter of change. But change can also be rewarding. If you're unhappy with the way your relationship is going now, change makes a lot of sense even though it won't nec- essarily be easy at first. One commonly used definition of insanity is to keep doing something the same way over and over again and to expect a different outcome. But sometimes your relationship is simply too far off course for you to turn it around without profes- sional help. If you read through this chapter and don't feel hopeful that these changes will help, or if you can't seem to find any com- mon ground from which to work, consider going to a counselor. It's not that you're stupid or not trying, but you may need more help than a self-help book can provide.

LOW SEX DRIVE: SUGGESTIONS FOR WOMEN

Okay, now it's time to get down to the nitty-gritty. You understand that men and women are different in many ways and particularly in how they approach sex. But rather than trying to make women out of men or vice versa, both sexes need to agree to be different and learn how to make these differences work to their advantage.

Analyze Your Health

If you suffer from a medical condition that is out of control and needs treatment, go to your doctor for help. If you have painful intercourse, have never been able to achieve a climax, or think there may be some other physical problem keeping you from being satisfied sexually, consult your gynecologist. If you scored 65 or higher on the Attitude and Mood Self-Assessment Quiz in Chapter 3 and you haven't seen your family doctor or gynecologist for evaluation yet, I would urge you to do so now.

Some primary care doctors don't like to give antidepressants or hormones to their patients. They may feel that another doctor who has a special interest or extra training in this area will do a better job of monitoring and adjusting the medications. So don't be shocked or offended if your doctor refers you to a psychiatrist. You have to be crazy to see a purple cow, but you don't have to be crazy to see a psychiatrist. They are the doctors with the most expertise in prescribing antidepressants and other medications in this area. And often just as important, they are usually better able to hook you up with a counselor or other stress management programs than your regular doctor, gynecologist, or nurse practitioner would be.

Analyze Your Primary Love Relationship

Are there other problems in the relationship that must be solved first? If you are married to an alcoholic or an abusive husband, nothing I recommend here will work for you until you get these problems resolved. Go for counseling now. If there is any hint that he may become violent, you must get out of the house with your children immediately. You can locate a safe place to stay by calling the National Domestic Violence Hotline at 1-800-SAFE (7233) or search or help online at the National Coalition Against Domestic Violence website (ncadv.org).

Are you angry with him over something that might be interfering with your normal level of affection? This might be something that isn't necessarily obvious to you at first glance. Does he have a bad attitude about one of your relatives? Is he stingy when it comes to money? Do you feel neglected because he spends too much time at work or "out with the boys"? Although you may be aware that there is something bothering you, the real depth of these conflicts isn't always apparent on the surface. As stated earlier, you need to find and fix the problems in your marriage first, otherwise a happy love life is difficult at best.

Dr. Annette Smick, a psychiatrist with the Mayo Health System, says that one of the major areas that causes conflict in relationships is a mismatch in priorities between partners: "When priorities are not aligned in the relationship, it's like two people paddling a canoe in different directions; they fight and fight to get to shore but never go anywhere." This leads to fatigue, frustration, and all too often, relationship failure. Dr. Smick recommends sitting down with your partner and making a quick priority checklist to see where you agree and where you differ. I think it's wise for each of you to make two separate priority lists: first a "time" list for where you think you should be spending your time as a family and second a "money" list for where you should spend your money. This will be a great exercise for one of your date nights or weekends away alone together (discussed later). Several options for the time list include: work/career, friends, family, church, fixing up the house/yard, travel, education, sports, hobbies, exercise, and volunteer work. Likely choices on the money list might be fixing up the house/yard, new furniture or appliances, getting out of debt, saving for a rainy day, investing, saving for retirement (possibly early retirement), saving for college, helping family members with needs, updating your wardrobe, charitable giving, travel, leisure time and equipment (boats, jet skis, RV, ATV), and vacation property.

Pick at least five, preferably seven, of what you feel are your top priorities on each list, then pare it down to your top three. Now compare lists with your partner and discuss as clearly and unemotionally as you can why you ordered the priorities the way you did and what specific goals you had in mind for each one. This discussion may astonish you. Many couples report how surprised they were that their individual priorities were so radically different. No wonder they feel they are paddling in different directions. After discussing your separate lists, try to merge them into joint lists—one for time and another for money. This may take some time, but it will certainly give you something to talk about during your time alone as well as think about at other times. Do this exercise again from scratch, at least every three months, until your individual lists start looking similar. If you don't seem to be making progress within six months, or if the discussions seem to be getting too heated or going nowhere, consider counseling. Having a successful meeting of the minds on priorities can be a huge boost to turning your relationship into a true partnership again.

Unhurry Your Life

Recall that stress, particularly the chronic stress that accompanies a busy lifestyle, can disturb the normal balance of your brain chemistry and cause your sex drive to fall as part of Hurried Woman Syndrome. Antidepressants are very effective at correcting this imbalance, and many women benefit from this therapy. But what I find incredibly exciting is that you don't have to take medication to get well. Lowering stress levels is just as effective as taking antidepressants in treating this problem. For most of my patients, the majority of stress they deal with comes from a hurried lifestyle—juggling work, spouse, children's activities, going back to school, church activities, parents with needs, and so forth. The solution to the problem: choose to change your lifestyle in ways that will lower your stress levels and allow you to be more interested in sex. This olution may sound too simple to be effective. Actually, it is a simple solution to understand, yet it will not be simple to accomplish. However, no matter how hard the task may seem, it is critical for you to realize that this is probably the most important aspect of olving the problems of a low sex drive and a subsequently unhappy ex life.

Ob-gyn physicians in a recent survey reported that the main auses of low libido in more than 80 percent of their patients are (1) ack of time, and (2) problems in their primary love relationship—ur patients and their partners are simply not communicating the "I ove you" message effectively. Doctors further reported that in most cases a woman's low sex drive is not caused by a lack of testosterone or because of her partner's poor lovemaking technique but rather by high stress levels from a hectic schedule and the loss of an emotional connection with her partner. To properly address this problem you must (1) unclutter your schedule with the things that in the long run don't really matter so that healthy sex will have time to happen and (2) reconnect emotionally with your partner. Chapters 11 through 13 focus on how to analyze, prioritize, simplify, and organize your life so you can get your happiness back. Many women don't believe me when I tell them that this is probably the single most important move they can make to improve how they feel as well as to restore their passion. Make the choice to change things now.

Schedule Quality Time Together Away from the Kids

Many couples routinely schedule a date night, perhaps twice a month. This is a night that the two of you can go out to a movie or dancing or dinner and just talk (relate). Most couples having problems in their love life have trouble communicating in other areas, too. Spending time together as a couple is very healthy for your primary love relationship and helps build better communication. Relive some of your favorite experiences from dating or gossip about your crazy relatives. In addition to developing your time and money priority lists, talk about the kids, your future together, and the good times you've had in the past. It may be a little awkward at first, but anything worth having is worth working for. Most couples tell me that this technique really helps strengthen their relationship.

Try to schedule a weekend or overnight trip away from home with just the two of you. Couples retreats at church are sometimes good because the speaker at these events can give you ideas about improving your relationship. However, when it's time for activities, many times the men go one direction and the women go another. This is not quality time with your spouse. You need to have time to play, talk, rest, and go places together. The other reason I encourage time away with each other is that it helps reverse the common substitutions that occur in marriage.

Finally, this is not a "once-every-decade" event. Make these times away a priority and schedule them as frequently as you can blackmail Grandma or another relative into keeping the kids. For those who don't have family close by, many couples support one another in this effort by keeping each other's kids for the weekend—not the *same* weekend, of course. Swapping kids for a weekend isn't going to help your marriage that much unless your kids are a lot worse than theirs, but you get the idea.

ADD A LITTLE SPICE TO YOUR LOVE LIFE

Sometimes a woman becomes so bored with the way her husband approaches making love that she just really isn't interested anymore. I have heard patients complain about this on occasion, and I believe that it comes after years of frustration and lack of communication. Even couples with a healthy sex life complain about it some, but how many pairs of boxer shorts covered with hearts or skimpy silk panties does it take to reach the saturation point?

Try to put a little romance back into your love life. Leave each other little notes—perhaps in the underwear drawer. Surprise him one night when he comes home from work by greeting him at the front door wearing something alluring and with the kids tucked away at Grandma's house for the evening. Call him at work and tell him you're thinking about him. Remember those little things you did when you were dating to make him want to be with you? Even though they may seem silly now, most men will appreciate your thoughtfulness in doing them again. Besides, it will give you something to talk about if you're having trouble getting conversation started on your date nights. The whole point of these suggestions is to refocus both of you on having fun together and to help you remember the things about each other that made you fall in love in the first place.

LET HIM KNOW THAT YOU LOVE HIM

I often get in trouble when I suggest this one. "Oh, come on, doctor! He knows that I love him—I wash his clothes, keep a clean house, cook for him, and do most of the child rearing around here." You're right, those are important things that show your love, but if you think about it, none of those are necessarily personal to *him*. In fact, these things are probably more important to you than they are to him. He probably wouldn't care if the house were a little less neat or if you ate out another meal or two each week if you were more responsive physically. The point is that the things you think show your love don't necessarily mean the same thing to him. Each of us sends and receives the "I love you" message differently.

If you want to make him feel loved in ways other than sex, try appealing to the little boy that's inside all men. You've probably heard the adage "The only difference between men and boys is the price of the toys." How do you show your children you love them? Yes—you cook, and clean and so on. But until your kids move away from home and have to do these things for themselves, they will never fully appreciate that kind of sacrifice. If you want to show love to a child, you encourage him, you cuddle her, you make a special effort to tell them "I love you." And you don't mumble it in passing as you walk by them in the hallway; you stop what you're doing and tell them how you feel eye to eye. Try it on your husband. He may not know how to react at first, so give him time to digest what's happened. But I almost guarantee that you will find he is more likely to begin responding in a similar way, not in anticipation of sex, but because you love each other independent of your physical relationship. Then you both win.

Let Your "No" Mean "Later"

The average guy will jump at the chance to let off steam or bring himself out of a bad mood by having sex; it's a release or an escape for him. But when most women are anxious, tired, angry, or sad, making love just isn't desirable for them. Believe it or not, most men actually know this about women, and your partner will likely respect your feelings on this point if you will do three simple things: (1) gently tell him why you don't want to make love right now, (2) make it clear that your "no" means "later" instead of "no and who knows when," and, (3) make time in your schedule for "later" to happen soon.

Sex is an important aspect of a healthy marriage, as is good communication. Interestingly, when couples go for counseling, most men complain about not having enough sex and most women complain about not having enough communication. So imagine how angry you'd be if you asked your husband to talk to you and he said "no" without an explanation. It would be particularly aggravating if he kept refusing to talk to you, even after you had made several heartfelt requests for his attention. His actions would be not only rude but also disrespectful of you as a person. If you are just not in the mood when your husband asks for your physical attention, try not to react to his request as if it is unreasonable because, quite frankly, it isn't unreasonable from his perspective. He may not know why you are tired or angry. Remember, men are not good at subtleties and even worse at reading minds. Let him know you appreciate that he loves you, then tell him you love him and why now is not a good time to get physical. Although some relationship experts say you should never withhold sex from your partner, I would never tell any woman that she should just go ahead and have sex to please her husband when she really doesn't feel like it. That only breeds resentment and isn't fair to you. Besides, making love is much more intimate and personal than loaning someone your hairbrush. The important point here is to not use sex as a tool to manipulate your partner.

This brings you to the second step: as soon as feasible, tell him that you want to get together "soon" for an intimate rendezvous. This will both excite and please him, as he knows you've been thinking about his request, that you are anxious to be intimate, and that you listened to him. Think about the week ahead and be realistic, but try to honestly set a target date for time alone within the next couple of days. This is often best done the next day after you've had time to think about it, but don't wait later than the next evening— before bedtime—in case he has already set his sights on that night. Setting the date ahead of time also allows you to get ready for sex emotionally. You may be surprised to find that you get excited too as you both count down the time till "lift off."

Of course, this technique will fall flat if you don't do step three: carve time out of your schedule so you can follow through on your promise. What frustrates men about being turned down for sex is not that it happens—they know it's going to happen—but that it occurs frequently with little explanation as to why and with no hope in sight as to when it might occur in the future. You can solve all three of these complaints by following this simple approach. The first step can happen today, but the other two will take some time and effort on your part. Again, the most critical feature of fixing the problems of low sex drive in a relationship is putting time back into your schedules to allow stress levels to fall and for intimacy to be unhurried and fulfilling for both of you. Spontaneous would be even better, but unhurried will rekindle the fire in your relationship.

ENCOURAGE HIM

We all need encouragement, particularly when we are young and unsure of ourselves. Although we sometimes forget it, grown men are included in this need. This is because at the heart of every man is an insecure little boy who needs to be affirmed, to know that he is still your hero, your knight in shining armor, that you still find him attractive sexually, and that you respect him as a man. The fear of failure hangs like the sword of Damocles over the heads of most men. These are the areas in which men fear failure most:

- Work—having a second-rate job; being passed up for promotion; not getting respect at work; and, particularly, being fired

- Home—losing the respect of his spouse and kids, and not providing adequately for the family (for example, nice house, cars, vacations, clothes, school, gifts)

- Personal—losing his hair, appearing older, gaining weight, and losing his physical strength

- Very personal—impotence and his partner's lack of interest in sex

Affirming your man in these areas will go a long way toward building his self-esteem, and it will also cause him to respond to you differently in other areas of your relationship. Encouragement can come in the form of a compliment or a word of thanks:

"Nice tie."
"I really appreciated you washing dishes tonight."
"I'm proud of you." (particularly after a hard day at work)

"I love our home."

"Last night was fun." (after sex, perhaps)

These lines are all best delivered with a hug, by the way. A man likes sex because the physical release it provides allows him to relieve tension and lower stress levels. But much more important than the physical aspects of sex is having a loving partner who responds to him sexually; this both affirms him as a man and reassures him that the relationship is strong. When you respond to your partner's desire for physical intimacy, you have affirmed your love for him; he knows you love him. Unfortunately, the reverse message is much more powerful—if you shun his advances, he will perceive this as a signal that there's something wrong. Most men are smart enough to know that an occasional "no" is to be expected, but a pattern of frequent denials—or even several half-hearted physical encounters—will be read by most men as trouble in the relationship.

A lot of men who complain about not having enough sex are really complaining about not feeling affirmed. In other words, when your partner feels insecure and underappreciated, this causes him to desire sex as a way to confirm that everything's all right—he's okay personally and in his relationship with you. But this also means you can fulfill your partner's need for affirmation not only through making love but by affirming him in other areas as well. If your sex drive and his are too far apart, try affirming him in the other areas discussed in this section. Remember that the problem of low sex drive is really a mismatch in the level of sexual interest between partners. You can close this gap in two ways: (1) increasing your level of interest by lowering your stress levels and making physical intimacy a priority, and (2) lowering his need for sex by affirming your love and respect for him in other ways.

Encouraging also means to not discourage. A man's self-esteem is a fragile thing, particularly when the one person in the world who means the most to him—you—is criticizing him. Solomon, who prayed that the one thing God would give him was wisdom, said, "The tongue has the power of life and death." Use this power wisely.

Don't Try to Change Him

Men are not women and women are not men. And most of us know that. There is a popular e-mail that gets amended and recirculated every few months called "The Rules for Men." It comes in about twenty flavors, but the gist of it is always the same:

The female always makes The Rules.
The Rules are subject to change at any time.
The female is never wrong.
The male is expected to read her mind at all times.
The female can change her mind at any given point.

There's also a "Rules for Women" e-mail (surely written in retaliation) which includes some of the following:

Ask for what you want. Subtle hints don't work.
If you ask a question you don't want an answer to, expect an answer you don't want to hear.
Sometimes he's not thinking about you; live with it.
Anything you wear is fine. Really.
Christopher Columbus didn't need directions and neither do we.
Anything we said six or eight months ago is inadmissible in an argument.
You can either ask us to do something *or* tell us how you want it done—not both!

Both of these sets of rules are obviously meant to be jokes, but the reason they are funny and why these e-mails keep coming back around is because there's a fair amount of truth in them. Men are different from women and they always will be. Learning to deal with these differences is how you can improve your relationship. If you keep fighting to change your husband, you'll probably find yourself changing husbands instead.

USE DIRECT COMMUNICATION

Men are not fond of mind games and don't play them very well. If you want your man to do something, speak to him directly. Dropping hints and waiting to see if he figures it out usually will not work and will simply frustrate both of you. This also includes saying what you really mean. Women often replay in their head what someone said earlier in conversation and think, "I wonder what she really meant by that?" Guys tend to take most conversations at face value. Think about sports. If the coach tells him to play third base, he doesn't stand on the bag and think, "I wonder what he meant by that?" It's not that men are incapable of complex thoughts and emotions; they just appreciate being given a straightforward message. To them, anything else smacks of manipulation.

BE RESPECTFUL, ESPECIALLY IN FRONT OF THE CHILDREN

Respect is important to both men and women. From a guy's perspective, if his partner—the woman he has supposedly bared his soul to and who knows all his faults and weaknesses—doesn't respect him, who will? Most women don't say things outright to their man like "you idiot" or "moron," but they sometimes unwittingly imply them by giving too many complex instructions when they leave the kids with him for the day or attempt to micromanage the project they asked him to do. Remember the rules above: you can either ask us to do something *or* tell us how you want it done— not both! I find it amazing how many men carry out very intricate and complex tasks at work every day and yet, when they arrive home, are considered to be unable to manage even simple things. In most cases, this is an innocent mistake. In women's defense, the woman has probably already carefully considered all of the options and decided on "the very best way" for something to be done, but he starts working on it from another direction. Criticizing is heard as a direct affront to his personhood, particularly if you frame your suggestions in critical terms: "Don't do that. This is the right way to do it!" or "Stop. Let me show you . . ."

Another big area for remembering to show respect for each other is in raising and disciplining children. Always come to an agreement on how to approach important issues where the kids can't hear you. There are many instances where you will disagree. This is perfectly okay. However, if there is any other way possible, never disagree on punishments in front of the kids—ever. Talk together in private, come to an agreement on as much as you can agree on, and then approach the kids with a united front. Often a parent will undo a punishment the other parent has set up because he or she thinks it's unduly harsh, but this sends the child a clear message that your spouse's opinions no longer matter. Don't take away each other's effectiveness by undermining each other's authority.

Avoid Nagging

Sometimes we don't realize that our "helpful reminders" are really nagging. And nagging is not nearly as effective at achieving results as positive reinforcement is. If you have to continually remind him to do whatever it is you want done, it's usually not because he doesn't know that you want it done (you've told him several times) or necessarily that he doesn't want to do it (he may want the project completed as much as you do). It may be that some big projects require a lot of time and energy. If it's one of these chores, he may be mentally working out the details while only appearing to be stubborn. But in many cases he may not be doing what you want done because he's trying to make a point—you are not his parent.

Nagging is an attempt to punish someone verbally, just like a parent would a child for not following commands. Not only is this detrimental to a strong relationship, it doesn't work. I suggest you sit down and discuss the situation as sincerely and as nicely as possible: "I'm sorry I've been nagging you about cleaning out the garage. I know it's 'your area' but I just wanted our home to look nice, and you know how much trouble you have finding your tools at times. I was just trying to be helpful. You do it when you're ready." And don't mention it again. This may be hard, but it's the right approach for a positive relationship as well as getting the garage cleaned out. Once it's no longer "an issue," he's much more likely to do it. Imagine how you'd feel if your husband came home and told you how to do your daily tasks, such as the best way to organize your desk at work or rearrange your closet, over and over until you gave in. Consider a different approach.

A note about health-related problems and men. Men are notoriously bad about having health complaints—such as chest pain, a sore hip, or symptoms of depression—and ignoring them until there is a crisis. Many couples in midlife find themselves arguing over these issues. However, nagging him about it usually won't get him to the doctor. Instead, try to convince him that you want him to go to the doctor because you care about him, that the problem can most likely be fixed more readily if approached earlier, and that he's not the only man who's had this type of problem. It may help to find an article in a popular magazine or a website that addresses the problem he's experiencing. This might encourage him to look into it. Terry Bradshaw's recent revelation about his struggle with depression is a good example of one such resource.

ACCENTUATE THE POSITIVE THINGS

If you want more help around the house, compliment your spouse when he does something helpful. Make a point of thanking him for making dinner, doing the dishes, or staying home with the kids while you go out. We usually treat family worse than we would a stranger. If you hired someone to wash dishes, even though you paid him or her, wouldn't you say "thank you" at the end of the evening? Of course you would. Yet so many of us don't show our spouses the same courtesy. If you make a point of complimenting your spouse for doing something you want done, you will find more and more things getting accomplished to receive those compliments. This is a fact of human nature. (Many women stop me at this point and tell me about how their husbands take them for granted and don't show them the proper amount of consideration for what they do. They're right; men shouldn't take their partners for granted either. But if you set the tone by acknowledging his efforts, he's more likely to begin to do the same. And I'm going to give him the same advice in the section on suggestions for men.) I know this works because my wife used this technique to get me to make the bed in the morning.

For the first twenty-three years of our marriage, I was up and gone to the hospital every morning by 5:30 A.M. while she was still sleeping. Consequently, she always made the bed. But during the last few years, she has been getting up at 4:30 A.M. three days a week to exercise. On those mornings, since I'm the last one out of bed and she makes the bed the other four days each week, she told me that on exercise mornings I should make the bed. Well, I must admit that I have never really cared whether the bed was made or not, so I gave it a half-hearted effort. Some days I forgot to do it; some days I *really* forgot to do it. Either way, I probably did manage to make the bed one or two days a week. At first, my wife, being the perfectionist that she is, reminded me on the days I didn't make the bed that she had to do it ("I had to make the bed *again* this morning"). After a few weeks, it sounded more like "I had to make the bed again this morning (*you uncaring oaf*)!" So making the bed had become an issue for us—I was forgetting on purpose more often and she was becoming angrier with me about not cooperating. Before you take sides, remember that making the bed was one of her goals and not mine.

After a few months of this, something changed. One evening, on a day when I had actually made the bed, she came up to me after dinner and gave me a hug and said very sincerely, "Thanks for making the bed this morning, Brent. It made the bedroom look so much nicer." Things started to change for me. I began to remember to make the bed. When I did, she would tell me again how she appreciated it. Soon I actually began to think about making the bed when I got up so that I would be certain not to forget to do it. Her change in attitude totally changed my attitude. At first glance, this would appear to be an insignificant event. But it highlights the power of rewards to reinforce and encourage the positive behavior you want. This doesn't mean men are simple, stupid creatures that need to be trained like puppies to perform. Rather, it demonstrates the importance of mutually agreeing to adopt common goals (making the bed) and reinforcing the right behavior with a reward (saying "thank you") until it becomes a habit. Stated simply, discuss with him what you want done and reward him for doing it. This approach can have a positive spillover effect into other areas as well.

If you can genuinely compliment him when he "gets it right," he will try harder in other tasks, too. Your change in attitude toward him will change his attitude toward you. But it must be a genuine change. Faint praise and half-hearted compliments tainted with sarcasm won't work. "It's about time you washed the dishes" is not the same as "Thanks for doing the dishes, honey. You saved my day—I was just worn out." When you focus your attention on the things your spouse does that annoy or disappoint you, you are giving in to negative thinking. Dwelling on the negative aspects of your relationship, and particularly your partner, poisons your perspective on both.

A good way to turn your negative thinking around is to stop and make out a list of the good things your partner does for you and your family. When I ask women to do this, they often tell me, "I can't think of anything." This means that they are deep in the habit of negative thinking. After a little prompting, most women start to see that their partner actually is carrying a fair amount of responsibility for them and the family. Here are some of the more commonly listed "good things" partners do:

- He rarely misses work. He works hard.

- He pays the mortgage each month.

- He takes care of the yard or pays someone to do it.

- He keeps the cars maintained or pays for it.

- He gives up a lot of his salary to cover the family's need for food and clothing.

- He provides money for Christmas presents for the family.

- He provides us with a vacation regularly.

- He helps with housework sometimes.

When I find myself saying "poor me" over some disappointment or failure, it helps me to count my blessings—to realize that in spite of the recent unhappiness, I've got things pretty good overall. This shift in thinking helps me get over the disappointment and move ahead. The same strategy can help turn your relationship around as well. Focus on his strong points, what he brings to the relationship, and the ways he pitches in. Deciding to change your perspective can turn a pessimistic view of your relationship into one of optimism and hope for renewal and growth. Get rid of your negative thinking and see the good things that start to happen.

LOW SEX DRIVE: SUGGESTIONS FOR MEN

Okay, this section is for the guys. It's time for you to learn why your partner has a low sex drive. These are the facts as we know them: it's all your fault. No, I'm just kidding. You're actually both at fault and not at fault. Some of the reasons her sex drive is lower are the result of ruts you've both gotten into in the relationship—how you have learned to approach each other—but these can be overcome if you both choose to make this relationship work in a better way, even when the going gets tough.

Some of the other reasons why she hasn't been as responsive to you are built into the way we do business as a society, how we define success, the goals we choose to work for and what our priorities will be. Some of the things that will need to be done to make things better between you will require careful reflection, some candid discussion between the two of you, and some decisions about your future. But there are some things that you can do right now to improve the situation.

My advice would be to go back and read this entire chapter for background information. This will help you understand that it usually isn't a hormone problem that's causing your partner's sex drive to fall, but a combination of stress, no time in a hectic schedule, and not feeling the emotional connection she needs with you to relight her pilot light. If you'll take the time necessary to do this, you'll be able to apply the nuts-and-bolts approach to improving your love life that is discussed in this section. Then look carefully at the seven major suggestions that follow. Spend some time by yourself thinking and, if it helps you, praying about them to see which ones pertain to you and how you might adapt the suggestions to fit your particular situation. For you to be successful in this planning phase, you'll have to take a candid look at yourself and rethink your goals and priorities for yourself, your marriage, and your family. This is no easy task, particularly since none of us is very good at predicting the future. It's possible that you might need to let go of something you think is important so you can hang on to the things that really are important. A wise man once said, "The most important things in this life aren't *things*." This is an important concept to remember as you try to focus on reordering your priorities.

Before you think this is another one of those "blame-it-on-the-guys" books and you've got to go through more changes than a caterpillar to fix things, look at all the advice your partner got earlier in this chapter. Low sex drive is a "couples" problem that requires a "couples" solution. You've both got to have a meeting of the minds if you want to have a meeting in the bedroom.

Stop Feeling Sorry for Yourself

Doing this one thing will probably help you more than anything else. Take a look at your spouse's situation through her eyes and then help her by gently discussing how she can cut her stress level. As it turns out, she's most likely not undersexed, she's overworked! But you can help her fix it by offering to help *her* fix it. When I discovered that my wife had Hurried Woman Syndrome, I made the mistake of rushing in and trying to fix her problems for her. This is not what she wanted and I'd bet neither does your wife. Instead, be supportive and make yourself and adequate resources available to her so she can fix the problem. There is a difference.

Pitch In

Support her efforts to prioritize, simplify, and reorganize her schedule. Offer your time and energy to help her get the work at home done. Remember that you are a team. Help with the chores; offer to barbeque or go out to eat more often; make an extra effort to help with the kids; and let her know that she's still an A-1 mom even if she doesn't volunteer to be homeroom mother or Cub Scout den leader this year. In fact, she may be more of a great mom for feeling less stressed. This support is particularly helpful and I think even more necessary if she works outside the home. In that case, you need to pitch in even more.

Approaching the family chores as a team encourages esprit de corps, a sense of belonging and togetherness. I have never been closer to my wife than in the times we have had to struggle together to get a job done. In men's defense, a lot of us grew up in a traditional household where Mom stayed at home and took care of the house and kids while Dad went off to work every day and took care of the cars and lawn on weekends. It seemed fairly equitable and worked pretty well for several generations. But with more women entering the workforce and spending the same time away from home as their men do, men have to take on a bigger share of the household responsibilities. It's only fair, particularly if her salary is being used to help pay for the family's financial responsibilities. And while it can be a burden, many couples find that they feel more like true partners if they are sharing that burden more equally. Men can find it particularly rewarding to spend some time really caring for their children, rather than seeing them as the woman's chief responsibility.

LEARN TO RELATE TO HER

I really hate the term *relate*, but it is so commonly used that I find myself saying it, too. It's a cliché, but it's what you need to do. Learn to give her a hug and say "I love you" without any hint that sex is on your mind. Or to paraphrase Garth Brooks, she needs to hear you love her somewhere other than in the bedroom.

Call her at work (whether that's in or out of your home) and tell her that you're thinking about her. Try to remember how you used to sit on the phone and talk to each other when you were dating. It's not easy to do at first and probably not a good idea to "force it," but a quick call can mean a lot. A word of warning: there is a right and a wrong time to call. Don't get mad when she tells you it's a bad time to talk, just make a mental note of it and try again another day at a different time.

TELL HER YOU APPRECIATE HER

This is powerful medicine. Everyone needs encouragement, particularly people who work at home. The workplace has its encouragements—a paycheck, a job title, a pension plan, a bonus, employee evaluations, service awards, and so on. What encouragement does a stay-at-home mom get? The kids probably thumb their noses at half the food she spends hours preparing; everyone probably leaves the house a wreck four out of seven days each week; there is an endless amount of dirty laundry available at any given time; and the only recognition she gets is when someone's favorite thing isn't available or ready when he or she wants it. If I worked at a job like that, I would have quit a long time ago. Realize what she does for you and your family and recognize her for her efforts. If you don't understand how difficult her job is, try doing it for a while. No, one Saturday is not enough. You have to take it on for a good week before you realize that it's very tough. You can also help by organizing the older children into a workforce to help get the chores done.

Send her a card once in a while. You can go to the card store and pick up three or four "Thinking of You" greeting cards and leave them at work. Every few weeks—put it on your calendar or day planner if you need help remembering—write a note about whatever is going on in your lives and mail one to her. Flowers are also nice, as is a little box of her favorite candy. Of course, if she's dieting, you'll need to limit the latter. There's no need to spend lots of time and money, though, particularly if those are limited. A phone call or note is inexpensive and can mean a lot.

Adjust Your Timing

When it comes to getting in the mood for sex, men have been compared to microwaves and women to Crock-Pots. In other words, it takes women a lot longer to go from the idea of making love to the stage where they're ready to participate. This is why you may find yourself being turned down if you give her short notice, particularly if she's had a rough day. For many couples, foreplay needs to be slower and less rushed so that you can both be ready at the same time.

At seminars I jokingly tell listeners that foreplay starts on Monday for sex on Thursday. Foreplay isn't necessarily kissing and caressing but more often consists of doing the dishes, staying home with the kids one night so she can go out with her girlfriends, or telling her that your mother is wrong (occasionally). You will find this type of foreplay much more effective than what you used to use earlier in the relationship.

BE RESPECTFUL

I don't think chivalry is dead; it's just taking a breather. Open doors for her and hold her chair in a restaurant, if she likes those gestures. Obviously don't if you know she finds them condescending. Helping around the house seems to be welcome to every person ever born, so doing that sends a very clear message that she and your home life are important to you. I am amazed at how many of us treat our family with less respect than we would a stranger. Our emotions sometimes bring out the worst in us, but do your best to never yell at your wife, particularly in front of the children. It is disrespectful, and as your volume goes up, your ability to think clearly goes down, so a discussion between adults deteriorates into dueling. I am not asking you to hide the fact that you have disagreements from your children, but I don't think it's a good idea to give them all the dirty details either.

A special note to fathers of teenagers, particularly teenage boys. When sex hormones first hit the human brain, they wreck havoc on our emotions and our ability to reason. This is why teenagers say and do some pretty goofy things. They will also tend to dislike and disregard your parental advice and try to exert more control over their lives by challenging your authority and acting in a rebellious manor. This will often include talking back to you and your wife in a disrespectful fashion. My advice is to not let this get out of hand. Teenage boys, who often tower over their mother physically, may be tempted to exert themselves inappropriately when she attempts to discipline them. Take the lead in enforcing discipline so that your wife doesn't have to do this by herself.

TRY A LITTLE ROMANCE

Your love life is lackluster not only because she's overworked, but also because she's underromanced. You can work on this from two different directions: (1) you can help her unhurry her schedule by pitching in and helping out to keep sex from being pushed off her list of things to do today; and (2) you can make her feel so special, important, and sexy that she wants to push sex up on the priority list. We've already talked about the first option, but the second is just as important.

Taking time out to talk to her, letting her know you are thinking about her, and showing her you appreciate her are all good ways of encouraging a change in her priorities regarding making love. But it is also important that you let her know that she is special to you and that you still find her attractive. Compliment her looks, the way she does her hair, an outfit you find particularly appealing. She wants to know that you still find her desirable; not in a lewd sense, but in the way you first looked at her—when she caught your eye the first time. If you can make her feel this special again, she is much more likely to respond to you.

One final word of warning, most women are very sensitive in this area and they can smell a fake a mile away. Faint praise may do more harm than good. Don't be patronizing or make the mistake of coming off as insincere in your compliments or your strategy may well backfire. Be sincere and honest. It will pay off in the end.

Set aside time for just the two of you. Many couples find a "date night" very effective. Perhaps two nights a month, go out to eat or catch a movie together. You may find conversation awkward at first, but after a few dates, you'll find more and more to talk about. Talk about your past, the kids, and your shared dreams for the future. It sounds hokey, but it really helps couples reestablish meaningful communication. As you get into it, you may want to sometimes share a night out with other couples. That can be fun, but don't do it without discussing it together first. I also recommend setting these nights up on a regular schedule so you can keep the evenings free from other commitments. Give it the importance it deserves by making an effort to preserve it for each other.

Schedule a weekend away all by yourselves. It doesn't necessarily have to be a fancy hotel or a romantic location, but these are both ideal. Be careful not to assume that sex is part of the plans. Many women get put off if they think they are expected to perform. You have to allow time and opportunity for sex to "happen," not force the issue by putting pressure on her. Don't pout or get angry if it doesn't happen on the first night or even the first trip away. Give her room and time to come up with the idea herself. This vacation is a gift to her, not merely an opportunity for you to make up for lost time. Do this because you love her and want to give her a weekend away from work, kids, and stress. Good things come to those who wait.

Enlist your parents, in-laws, or friends to keep the kids. Some couples trade weekends and watch each other's children. If you are really sporting, you can surprise her with a night away from home, with all arrangements for the children and the getaway made in advance.

Sadly, your wife has read all about our strategy to improve your love life, so the element of surprise may be gone. The good news is that you will be starting to work together better as a team to improve your relationship and bring her energy levels back to normal. The bad news is that if you follow my recipe like a cookbook, the Russian judge (your beloved) will take points off for originality, which might mean the difference in you taking home the gold versus the silver medal. With any luck, you've gained some insight into the underlying problems and how to fix them. Hint: either come up with your own creative ideas or wait about two weeks after she knows you have read the book before you implement any of my suggestions. After about ten days with nothing changing, she'll think you haven't learned a thing. Then right before she gives up and declares you a hopeless case, you can start to "shine." Maybe she'll think you came up with some of it on your own. Good luck!

FREQUENTLY ASKED QUESTIONS

Can birth control pills lower my sex drive?

They certainly can and do for about 10–15 percent of my patients. Most authorities think that birth control pills tend to lower the amount of testosterone in your bloodstream, which can in turn lower libido. Pills that have a relatively lower dose of progestin (such as Ovcon 35) will be less likely to cause this side effect. Ask your doctor about changing pills if you have this problem. If you are still having problems after three months on the new pill, you should consider checking your testosterone level and starting replacement if it's low, or getting off birth control pills for about three months to see if the symptom goes away. If your libido doesn't improve after three months off the pill, you should definitely check your testosterone level if you have not already done so. If it's normal, you need to look for another cause.

Birth control pills, the contraceptive patch, and the vaginal ring can actually improve sex drive for some patients, particularly those with severe PMS, endometriosis, painful periods, or excessive fear of pregnancy. One of the main consequences of these conditions is decreased libido. Helping the other symptoms go away will often improve sex drive, too.

Will taking estrogen make me gain weight?

There are different levels of estrogen therapy. Birth control pills contain estrogen and progestin, but both are in much higher dosage than those used in menopausal hormone replacement therapy

(HRT) and estrogen replacement therapy (ERT). Most women will gain about 5 to 7 pounds when they start taking birth control pills. However, this weight gain can be avoided. Recent studies indicate that the increase in weight when starting birth control pills generally comes from an increase in appetite—what some would call "the munchies." Women in these studies who watched their food intake when they began taking the pill did not gain more than 5 pounds, and the pill's effect on appetite went away after two months. Therefore, the weight gain from birth control pills can be anticipated and controlled by diet.

Most studies on the initiation of HRT and ERT don't show any significant weight effects because much lower doses of estrogen and progesterone are used. I know that many of you are shaking your heads and saying, "I didn't gain all of this weight until I had my hysterectomy and started taking estrogen." And you're right, many women do gain weight after this surgery, but so do most women by the time they reach their late forties and early fifties, whether they've had a hysterectomy or not. The truth is that most women tend to gain a pound each year after the age of thirty. Of course, they don't actually gain one pound each birthday, but when they wake up on the morning after their fiftieth birthday, they generally weigh about twenty pounds more than they did when they went to bed on the night before their thirtieth. In fact, most women maintain the same weight for several years, then suddenly gain seven pounds at age thirty-five or so and wonder what happened. That's when they come in and discuss it with me. We've all heard about "middle-age spread," and trust me, it's a real phenomenon. Fairly good scientific studies have followed groups of women through these middle years, one group with hysterectomy on estrogen replacement and another group without estrogen replacement: the weight gain is the same in both groups. As we discussed in the section on weight gain, the rules on weight control change sometime after thirty, making it difficult for most women to keep the weight off as long as they continue to eat at the same level, unless they can compensate by increasing their level of activity through exercise. I know it's not fair, but this is life.

Does it actually hurt my husband not to have sex regularly?

Emotionally, yes; physically, probably not. Most experts agree that men have a more basic physical need for sex than women, but proof that physical harm occurs from avoiding intercourse is lacking. A man who has been aroused for a prolonged period of time may experience some pelvic and even scrotal discomfort if he does not ejaculate afterward, but this is not quite the same thing. Prolonged abstinence, particularly if it's forced on one partner by the other one, damages intimacy and the relationship.

Is there a medication or an herb I can take to make me want to have sex?

Another way to ask this question would be "Are there any true aphrodisiacs?" Either way you say it, the answer is "no." Although many chemicals, herbs, and foods have been touted off and on as sex stimulants, nothing has yet passed double-blind tests against a placebo. This is the only way to factor out the power of suggestion from a study of this nature. However, if you find certain foods put you in the mood, feel free to share them over a nice dinner.

Will I grow a beard if I take testosterone?

Not if you have your blood levels tested to be sure they are within the normal range. Of course, you may suddenly be unable to ask for directions, begin scratching yourself in public, and start letting out embarrassing gaseous eruptions, but otherwise there are very few side effects to testosterone therapy.

Unfortunately, the long-term results of testosterone supplementation in women complaining of low sex drive have not been that impressive. In fact, only about 30 percent of my patients with this complaint actually have a low testosterone level. I only give testosterone to women with a documented deficiency and replace it with doses that bring them into the normal range. Most patients see some improvement initially, but after about six months, a large portion of women take themselves off the medication because they don't think it's working anymore. Our present knowledge of testosterone and its role in promoting sex drive in women is still in its infancy. Hopefully, more information and better treatment options will be forthcoming.

Does having infertility affect your sex drive?

It certainly can. Many couples get tired of the emotional roller coaster they experience in trying to get pregnant each month. Instead of just letting sex happen, it must be timed to match ovulation. This is usually accomplished with basal body temperature charts or an ovulation predictor kit, both of which require daily monitoring around the time of suspected ovulation and forcing sex to hit the right day for pregnancy to occur. This turns making love into a home science experiment, which takes a lot of the fun and spontaneity out of it.

Additionally, each month has its own emotional cycle that matches the ovulation cycle. Ovulation occurs and there's a lot of artificially timed sex, which sounds good at first but loses its novelty and becomes more desperate as several months go by without success. Ovulation is then followed by two weeks of hopeful anticipation (and sometimes a lot of worry), which go by slowly along with imagined symptoms of early pregnancy or impending menstruation until either success is achieved, or more commonly, failure is announced when the period comes. After a few days to a week of despair, the final days before the next attempted impregnation drag by until the excitement of ovulation is predicted again and more forced sex occurs, starting the cycle all over again. The emotional ups and downs that accompany this cyclic ritual, as well as the loss of sexual spontaneity that goes with it, make the infertile couple (both the woman and her man) a prime target for loss of sex drive.

Do you ever recommend divorce for your patients?

Although I am often forced to be a "gynechiatrist" (gynecologist and psychiatrist), I refuse to be a marriage counselor; I don't make recommendations like this. If a patient tells me that her husband is physically abusive or that she and her children are in immediate danger at home, I recommend that she leave and go to a safe shelter or stay with family or friends immediately. She can then contact a lawyer and perhaps the police to sort out the details once she's safe. I think that divorce is all too common in America today. In fact, more than half of the marriages in this country end in divorce. To me, this is a startling and troublesome statistic. I think that one of the major reasons divorce has become so popular is that it has become so easy and socially acceptable to get one.

When a couple hits a rough spot in their marriage—and even the most happily married couple will hit rough spots along the way—they often try counseling for a while, then perhaps a trial separation. If things don't work out pretty quickly, they get divorced. One, two, three—it's just that simple. Of course, it's really not that simple for the kids and the rest of the family or for the new families formed by remarriage. But when things are at their worst in the marriage, divorce may appear to be the easiest way out at the time.

I have often pondered why people who were so in love with each other at the beginning of a marriage are so out of love at the end of it. What happened? Did they grow apart? Did they change so dramatically through the years that they have nothing left in common? I can't solve this mystery in the short course of two or three paragraphs, but most of what I hear from women (of course, as a gynecologist, I usually hear only her side of the story) relates to a lack of agreement on priorities between husband and wife and, more often than not, low sex drive (which at the end of the marriage is really more a symptom of the failed relationship than a medical problem). Major areas for mismatched priorities include raising the kids, money, sex, work, friends, other family, and leisure activities. Finally, either the man or woman (or both) will decide that the other one is "wrong" and acting selfishly, at which time they choose to stop working on the relationship. This is when hurt feelings get worse, resentment and anger build, and relationships are ultimately torn apart. In most instances, no matter who started it, both spouses have contributed to the problem.

All that being said, I think the most important thing to realize is that love is a choice. We choose whom we love and whom we don't love. We may make the decision unconsciously and sometimes for the wrong reasons, but we are in control of the choice. I remember back in high school, a good-looking guy named Dave was head over heels in love with a nice girl named Sally. He brought her candy at school (she gave it away), wrote her love notes (she threw them away), tried to sit by her at lunch (unsuccessful), offered to carry her books to class (she refused), and even sent her flowers a couple of times. None of us had much money back then, so this was an all-out effort for a teenage boy in 1975. But in spite of all he did, Sally never gave Dave the time of day, much less agreed to go out with him. From Sally's perspective, it didn't matter that Dave had pushed all of her "I love you" buttons; it was in her power to decide whether or not to respond, and she chose to not love him. But look at it from Dave's perspective: in spite of being rejected in every way imaginable—ignored, snubbed, publicly embarrassed, and humiliated—he still chose to love her. He chose to love her at all costs. No matter what it took, he was going to do his best to make her feel loved and hope she would reciprocate.

I honestly believe that in virtually every divorce situation, the two people involved got married because they each made an individual choice to commit themselves to the marriage. They chose to love each other and that's why they got married. Then life came along and threw a lot of problems and changes their way—jobs, children, obligations, pressure, temptations, and disappointments— and some of these things began to drive a wedge between them. The wedge was driven deeper by fatigue, stress, misunderstandings, tragedies, illness, and even other people who sought to disrupt the relationship. Then when things just seemed too hard to fix, one or both of them changed their minds and chose to not love the other anymore. This is the point at which the marriage ended. The divorce may not have occurred for another two or three or twenty years, but when one of them chose to not love anymore, that's when it was over.

If you are considering divorce as an option, think about this. When a team has a bad game, the coach always tells the sportscaster, "We're going to get back to the basics," meaning they're going to work on the fundamentals to get back to top form. The same strategy works for a marriage. Try to recall why you got together in the first place. Pull out your old picture albums and home movies, and remember the good and bad times you've shared. You have a history—review it together and perhaps you can catch a glimpse of the things that made you fall in love in the first place. Meditate on those memories and feelings to help you make a very important decision, probably the most important decision of your life. You must decide whether you are still committed to this relationship or if you've already moved on. If you both choose to make it work like Dave did—at all costs—it will surely work. If even one of you chooses to make this marriage last, it might still work because the difference between your situation and Dave's is that you and your spouse once had a loving relationship. If neither of you is willing to choose to continue, then it's a sure bet your marriage won't last. It simply can't unless you decide that it will. The repercussions of divorce can be devastating on a family, so I hope you'll choose to stick it out and make it work. But the decision is yours. Good luck.

Are there any other books you recommend to help couples improve their relationship?

In his book *The Five Love Languages: How to Express Heartfelt Commitment to Your Mate* (Northfield, 1995), Dr. Gary Chapman explains that there are five basic ways that we express love and receive love. He calls these "love languages." Each of us has a primary love language—the language that speaks to us most effectively. Many of us also have a secondary love language, but the primary language is always the one through which we receive the "I love you" message most effectively. We also tend to send our love messages in a particular language. However, the love language we "speak" may not necessarily be the same one we "hear" most effectively. The five love languages according to Dr. Chapman are as follows:

1. Words of affirmation—verbal compliments, words of encouragement or congratulations, requests (rather than ultimatums)

2. Quality time—a sense of togetherness, genuine conversation (relating), listening as well as talking, sharing feelings and emotions, playing together

3. Gifts—both giving and receiving physical gifts and money, gifts of time and attention, and gifts of yourself (just being there)

4. Acts of service—doing chores, helping each other, acts of chivalry, watching the kids so the other person can have a night out

5. Physical touch—holding hands, kissing, giving back rubs, brushing against each other in the hallway, sitting close to each other in the car or on a couch, sexual intercourse

Dr. Chapman feels you must learn to speak your spouse's primary love language in order to make him or her feel loved. Your mate's primary love language is probably different from yours and may be difficult for you to "speak" naturally, but if you don't learn how to express your love in a way that you can each understand, your attempts to communicate love to one another will be much like American and Chinese business colleagues attempting to negotiate a contract without an interpreter—utter chaos and frustration.

Dr. Chapman explains in great detail how to determine your primary love language, as well as that of your spouse, and how to use this information to improve your marriage. I simplified his approach in my explanation about how men and women view sex differently, as well as in the chapters on ways to improve your marriage. I included recommendations that allow you to "speak" in all of the five love languages. That way, no matter what your spouse's primary love language is, you will be able to communicate your love effectively. When a couple knows how to communicate love in a way that provides fulfillment for both partners, the end result is a happy marriage. I highly recommend Dr. Chapman's book to couples who find that they are feeling unloved and struggling to communicate.

Another book to consider is Dr. Phil McGraw's *Relationship Rescue*. It's chockful of quizzes and worksheets to help you sort out your own feelings and find the hot spots in your marriage. It will take a concerted effort to get through the workbook, but your marriage is certainly worth it.

I recently caught my husband on the Internet looking at pornography. He said it helps him "get by" when I'm not in the mood for sex. Is this okay, or am I being a prude?

I'm sure many of my colleagues would call me old-fashioned, but I think pornography can be very damaging to a relationship. Whether it's the soft-core pornography of a magazine like *Playboy* or the hard-core porn of numerous websites, women are portrayed as sex objects rather than people with feelings and emotions. Pornography, particularly the hard-core type, gives men several unrealistic expectations about women, relationships, and making love: a distorted perception of what beauty is (it's hard for the average wife to look as "hot" as the posed, silicone-implanted, airbrushed women presented there); the proper circumstances for sex to occur (as part of a loving relationship, not as an affair at the office or with the wife of a friend who is out of town); and what the physical act of sex should represent emotionally (an expression of love rather than simply friction and ejaculation). Pornography takes the love out of sex and makes it look attractive and exciting. Many men transfer these misconceptions about sex from the cyberworld to the real world with devastating results.

The dirty little secret about men and their porn is that most of them view it and then masturbate to relieve the self-inflicted sexual tension it causes. Pornography is not a good substitute for making love with someone you love and care about, although many men think it helps them get by when they find themselves in a sexual "dry spell" at home. Pornography is not the answer to this problem because it fills a man's mind with sexually stimulating pictures. Men are very visually oriented, which is one reason many of them like to make love with the lights on. Pictures from this internal pornographic photo gallery pop into a man's mind all day long, filling him with a desire for sex. This recurring and potent stimulation only increases the differences in sex drive between the man and his partner, which was already causing trouble in the relationship. If he requests sex and is turned down, he goes back to the pornography, gets aroused by more new images of sex, masturbates for short-term relief, and the cycle starts all over again. This type of behavior can become compulsive, and like gambling or drinking alcohol in excess, can also become addictive.

If you find your husband is visiting adult websites regularly, let him know that you know what he's up to and share the above information with him. Try not to be judgmental. Masturbation is a common activity for men—even married men—but one that most of them are embarrassed to discuss, particularly with their partner so don't get into a lot of detail about what happens after he signs off the Internet. You may be surprised to find that he's relieved that his "secret life" is no longer a secret and that you are interested in helping him get away from his habit. A good book on how pornography and masturbation can undermine a couple's sex life is *Every Man's Battle* (Waterbrook Press, 2000) by Stephen Arterburn, Fred Stoeker, and Mike Yorkey. If you think he may actually be addicted to pornography, consider seeing a counselor about the best approach or visit no-porn.com or enough.com for more information and links to other resources. One move that can really help once you agree that Internet pornography is a problem is to install an Internet content filter on your computer such as Cybersitter, Net Nanny, or Covenant Eyes. These will help your husband stay honest with his commitment to quit surfing porn sites and keep your children away from them as well.

What about Viagra (sildenafil) for men and for women?

Being unable to achieve an erection or sustain one is a common complaint in men during midlife and beyond. Women also notice that orgasms are harder to achieve and may be less intense at this time in life. Viagra and other medicines like it, which improve blood flow to the sexual organs and make them more sensitive to stimulation, have allowed many couples to resume sexual activity when it appeared to be fleeting or even gone for good. However, this is not always a desirable goal. Many of my menopausal patients have complained that after several years of no sexual activity, their partner suddenly discovered Viagra and, like a kid with a new toy, wanted to use it—a lot. Unfortunately, many years of sexual dormancy, often coupled with a lack of estrogen support, cause the vagina to lose its natural moisture, shrink in caliber and depth, and become less pliable, making sexual relations very uncomfortable, even impossible in some cases. Reinstituting estrogen replacement (and frequently using vaginal estrogen), stretching exercises, and patience can usually revitalize the tissues and make intercourse comfortable again, if the woman desires this.

In addition to the physical aspects of your partner's use of Viagra, several emotional issues can arise as well. Many women feel threatened by "the little blue pill," thinking that they are no longer able or needed to provide sexual arousal. Some couples find that what was once impossible—having sexual intercourse—is now a lot of work because the Viagra produces an erection, but it is sometimes weak and must be vigorously maintained for sex to be "successful." Dr. Alan Altman and Laurie Ashner, in their book *Making Love the Way We Used to ... or Better* (Contemporary Books, 2001), provide a thorough discussion of the pros and cons of Viagra. This book is also a great reference for those interested in learning more about female sexuality.

Preliminary studies of Viagra for women have been somewhat disappointing. Because it increases blood flow to the clitoris and vagina, Viagra can enhance orgasm and vaginal lubrication in women. However, it appears to have limited ability to stimulate the desire for sexual intimacy. Hopefully, future studies will determine whether Viagra and the other medicines in this group have any real value for women with low sex drive.

11

STEP 5: IDENTIFY YOUR PRIORITIES AND SET REASONABLE LIMITS

STRESS—PARTICULARLY the chronic, persistent stress that comes with work, kids, a spouse, extended family, and friends, as well as the constant strain of trying to juggle all their needs and schedules—is the most common cause of Hurried Woman Syndrome. Research has verified that antidepressants are very effective in treating the syndrome. In fact, more than 80 percent of women treated with antidepressants can get back to feeling normal again. However, if these women don't also take positive steps to lower their stress levels they will either (1) find that the medications don't work as well as they should, or (2) be stuck taking antidepressants until the stresses in their lives lower themselves—the kids grow up, the husband moves out, the sick parent passes away, they lose the high-stress job, and so on. Although they are very helpful at times, I feel that antidepressants are a short-term solution to the long-term problem. Besides, lowering stress levels is equally effective as medication, a whole lot cheaper, and has no negative physical side effects.

I do have several patients in my practice who have overcome the syndrome without outside help. Some of them figured it out by themselves; however, for most of them, it required several years of suffering—for them and the people around them—and often involved major life changes. My hope is that providing insight into Hurried Woman Syndrome will help you see that this is an important problem and that you need to consider your options seriously. I certainly don't mean to push medication as an answer for everyone. You may not need to take antidepressants if you can make the decision to devote yourself to making changes that lower your stress levels now. On the other hand, you may find that antidepressants can help you get back to a point of strength from which you can make some important decisions to lower stress levels and ultimately stay well without medication. Each of us has only one life. Why live it stressed out, tired, overweight, and unfulfilled?

The last three steps to surviving Hurried Woman Syndrome are designed to help you in this quest for less stress, better health, and more happiness. Some women find them the most challenging, not because they are difficult to understand but because they require you to change some things—the way you view yourself, the people around you, your priorities, your possessions, your activities (in other words, your life).

Hurried Women have often lost track of who they really are and where they wish to go because they have given up on meeting their own needs, feeling that they must first meet those of everyone else. Many women honestly believe that once everyone else's needs are fulfilled, they will finally get around to meeting some of their own.

"When the kids grow up, I'll work on my marriage."
"Once my youngest child is in school, I'll start exercising and get on a diet."
"After baseball season is over, we'll focus more on family time."

The flaw in this logic is that you will never be able to meet everyone else's wants and needs because they are unlimited. Once a need has been met, it will immediately be replaced with a new one. This is a fact of human nature. So if you're waiting until everything else gets done before you take time for yourself, it will never happen—never. It's time you realized that taking time out for you is essential to your health, not only your physical health, but your emotional health as well.

ESTABLISHING YOUR NUMBER ONE PRIORITY: YOU

It may sound trite, but the first priority in your life has to be you. I don't mean this to be a selfish, "me-first" attitude—I doubt you'd do this anyway—but one of self-preservation. You can be generous and give yourself to others. This desire to give is what separates us from the animal world and can actually be therapeutic, but how can you give away something you no longer own? It's okay to sacrifice for others, but you can't be the sacrifice! It's unhealthy. Believe me, your family would rather have 75 percent of your time when you're 100 percent yourself than have 100 percent of your time when you're at only 75 percent of your capacity. They sound comparable, but they're not the same. The quality of your interaction with family is far more important than the quantity.

If the plane on which you're traveling loses cabin pressure, oxygen masks will drop from the overhead compartment. The safety manual recommends that you put your mask on first, then assist others who need help. This is because if you're unconscious or incapacitated, you can't help other people. Likewise, you must take care of yourself first—not just because you are important—but to do otherwise will lessen your ability to help others effectively.

The first step in establishing your new priorities is to find time for you. Carve it out of your schedule now. Block out one afternoon or evening each week or a full day each week if you can. Mark it on the calendar. Many women find it beneficial to get a new calendar at this point and start over on a brand-new schedule. Accept that this may require taking time away from others. You might have to miss one or two of your child's ball games. It may mean giving up some business if you're self-employed. It will also require saying "no" more often—to the new assignment at the office, to going on the field trip at school, to helping a friend with a project. Be nice, but stand firm. If you feel you can't leave the business with someone else for the day or you can't afford to be out of the office like this, you obviously have a problem. You can spend the time however you like. Sit in the bookstore and read, get a pedicure or massage, start walking or swimming regularly, or just sit in the backyard and watch the grass grow. The biggest benefit you will receive from this gift to yourself is a new sense of who you are. It will also start your reenergizing process and help you focus on the task ahead.

FILL IN THE REST OF YOUR NEW PRIORITY LIST

Now it's time to reorder your other priorities, but first it's important to have what psychologists call a reality check. There is only one you. And at times, there's really only a piece of you trying to do all of the things you currently do. Forcing one person to do everything is killing that one person—you! If you are a single parent, the problem is compounded exponentially because even the least helpful of husbands probably helps sometimes. Single moms don't even get this kind of help. Whatever your situation, you must realize that there is simply not enough of you to go around at present, and the way you feel is proof that this is true. You are mortal, flesh and blood.

It's time to prioritize the things in your life so you can be certain to get the most important things done first. You have to establish your priorities and be sure that the things that matter most don't get swept away as the busyness of the day unravels.

Stephen Covey uses a great example in motivational lectures to illustrate this point. He sets a big glass jar on a table and puts three or four brick-sized rocks in the jar. With the last one sticking out over the top, he asks the audience members if the jar is full. They generally think so. He pulls some gravel out from underneath the podium and pours it into the jar. The gravel filters into the small spaces around the big rocks, and he asks the crowd again if the jar is full. Sensing that he has more to show them, they usually answer "no." He then pulls a bag of sand from underneath the podium and pours that into the jar as well. The sand filters down into the smaller spaces between the big rocks and the gravel, and Covey again asks if the jar is full. The audience is really into it by now and answers "no" loudly. Covey interrupts them and says, "Of course the jar is full! But what can we learn from this demonstration?" There's always a guy in the front row wearing a three-piece suit who will say, "You can always do more if you just plan ahead." Covey shakes his head and replies, "No, you have to put the big rocks in first. If you don't, you can't get one in later. It's too late." If our lives are like the glass jar and the big rocks are our priorities, if we don't put the big rocks in first, the world will fill our jars with sand and gravel—the stuff we didn't want. Once that happens, it's too late to fit a big rock in. In fact, many women come to see me when they attempt to put a big rock into their jar and they hear it cracking. Now is the time to establish your priorities so you can get what you want in your jar.

It's time to create your priority list. Where do you want to spend your time? With whom do you wish to spend it? Many of us feel trapped into spending our time with people and in situations not of our choosing. We may feel trapped by our previous decisions: our past haunts us, we're stuck in relationships that have soured, we're stuck playing the role we've always played. Most often, we are trapped by our own fears of no longer being accepted by others. These traps are actually lies that many of us have accepted as fact.

Realistically, there are very few situations over which we have no control. We may have given up control or assumed that we lost it, but this can be remedied. We can decide to take control.

Get out a piece of paper and write down a list of the top ten areas in which you'd like to invest your time, talents, and money. List the area or concern and also jot down a couple of practical suggestions that you can do right now to work toward that goal. It's okay to be philosophical, but you're not in the Miss America pageant. World peace is a worthy goal, but it's unlikely any of us will be able to accomplish it by ourselves. Keep it practical. Also, nebulous goals like "prepare for retirement" are not as helpful as "retire by age fifty-seven" or "get out of debt within five years." These are the key areas to think about:

- Emotional and physical health

- Relationships

- Your spiritual well-being

- Work

- Service to others

- Fun, adventure, and leisure

- Finances and future goals

Reflect on what used to bring you joy—music, travel, reading, time with friends, a hobby—as well as what you think might be fun—photography, learning how to fly, or going back to school. This is a time to dream about the way you'd like things to be rather than how they appear—stuck in the present. You need to make your own list, but here are some suggestions:

- **Emotional and physical health:** start walking two miles, three times a week; catch up on fun reading by knocking out a bestseller each month; stop eating fast food; start eating a light breakfast each day; start a weight management program.

- **Relationships:** devote last hour before going to bed spending time with partner—talk, games, sex; schedule date night every other week and weekend away together every other month; get homework out of the way on arriving home to free up evening for fun; start family game night once a week (TV off and play games); start reading to kids at bedtime each night; limit kids' activities to one extracurricular activity at a time; limit children's computer/TV/phone time each evening to two hours.

- **Spiritual well-being:** set aside ten minutes of "quiet time" each morning for meditation, prayer, or inspirational reading (such as the Bible or a self-help book).

- **Work:** focus on resolving conflict with coworker; try to cut back hours to three days a week (or move up to a full-time job); look for a better job; get up fifteen minutes earlier each morning so getting everyone ready for the day won't be so rushed; let work go when arriving home and avoid bringing work home; bring lunch from home to have quiet time during lunch break and save money; cut back from two night classes to one each semester; start shopping for groceries using prepared shopping list; assign chores to kids and post the list; look into getting a house cleaner; cook simpler meals.

- **Service to others:** volunteer two evenings each month at the hospital; work one Saturday morning at the homeless shelter; help more at school, church, Scouts, and so on.

- **Fun, adventure, and leisure:** schedule next summer's vacation and start dreaming about it; take music lessons; schedule more time with friends—one girl's night out each month, hobby club (cooking, investing, crafts), regular night out with other couples; get a boat (or sell the boat).

- **Finances and future goals:** set up a family budget and live by it; start maximum withholding in 401k plan at work; get wills made out; talk with financial planner about funds for college, retirement, and so forth; look at moving into a bigger (or smaller) house.

Once you've made out a top ten list, select the top five and then the top three. Keep the top five, but be sure the top three are the first items listed. This list now represents your top five priorities and also includes a few short-term goals for each one. Think about how to best use your resources to meet these goals and about obstacles that may interfere with achieving them (people, lack of money, or time commitments) and think about ways to eliminate these obstacles.

It is impossible for me to tell you what your limits are and what your priorities should be—only you can make these decisions. But be sure you are the one who decides. Don't let other people tell you what you should do. You are not trapped by your history; choose to change the way you've done things in the past. The role you've always played in a relationship isn't cast in stone; if in the give-and-take of a friendship, you always give and she always takes, decide to change that. If she won't accept you in the new role you've chosen, let the relationship go; it's not a healthy one for you. Don't let your fear of not being accepted by others force you into doing things that sacrifice your goals to meet theirs. It doesn't make sense.

Let's look at some of the most common problem areas that confront women and how many of them have resolved these issues. Sharing these examples may help you find solutions you can live with.

CHILDREN

Children are truly a blessing, but no one will deny that they are also a challenge. The issue of how to raise children is the second most common reason couples in America fight. Kids wear us down to some extent, because they are "anti-adults." Like matter and anti-matter—they can't exist together without an explosion. How are kids anti-adults? Look at all of the things that we as adults would love to do and our kids hate to do: clean your plate, take a nap, stay

in your room (and read a book or just hang c
early. They hate all of these things; we would lc
probably as often as we could get away with it.

In my family, we have four children between th.. ages of twenty-one and thirteen. My daughter is the oldest, followed by three teenage boys. With four children, things can get hectic around our house pretty quickly. But through the years, we have noticed something very interesting about the anxiety levels in our home when it comes to our children. When one of them is gone, the level of commotion drops by 50 percent. At first glance, it doesn't make sense that decreasing the number of kids by only 25 percent (one out of four children) would decrease the household angst by 50 percent, but it does. And it's not as though one is a real troublemaker. It really doesn't seem to matter which one is absent. Why this dramatic change? I'm not certain, but the best reason I can come up with is that the number of possible combinations for conflicts between children and their schedules drop exponentially when one of them is out of the picture.

In a group of four people, there are nine total potential interactions between the people in the group. But when only three individuals are involved, the total possible interactions drops to four, less than half the original number. If you think about it mathematically, it actually makes sense that having one less child around will significantly decrease the amount of conflict in your home and the accompanying noise, emotion, and anxiety. But I didn't make this point to encourage you to get rid of one of your children. Sending one child off each day to the neighbors' or Grandma's house isn't really practical. Nor did I mention it to discourage you from having more children (as an obstetrician, that kind of talk could put me out of business). I want to show you how much children complicate your life exponentially. Don't make the mistake of underestimating the amount of hurry they add to your day and how adding only small amounts of hurry results in much higher stress levels.

hildren's Activities

Children choose their activities like they pick out food in a cafeteria line. If left to their own devices, kids would grab more items than a truck driver with a tapeworm, particularly if dessert and fries are available. They would never eat all the treats they took, but they'd let you pay for them. This is because they haven't learned that the decisions they make going through the line must be paid for at the end.

Actually, they really only wanted a taste of each of the things they picked out, but you have to buy a full serving instead. Aren't your kids' activities pretty much the same? The activities look good when they're signing up to participate, but when it comes time to make all of the practices and play to the end of the season, they lose their desire to keep playing.

Like most children, mine had a big appetite for starting activities. When homework was added in on top of the sports, Scouts meetings, music lessons, and church activities, our family schedule got dreadfully busy very quickly. On most days, there were at least two kids away from home, usually heading in opposite directions at conflicting times. My work schedule often kept me from helping out with shuttling the children around, so this difficult task fell almost completely to my wife LaNell. I realize that having four children is a self-inflicted wound to some extent and that I shouldn't expect a lot of sympathy, but even couples with only two kids experience the same, almost insane, scheduling problems at times. The hurried schedule was very hard on my wife and our marriage. After one particularly difficult baseball season, I finally noticed how tired and grumpy my wife and I were both becoming. At that point, we both agreed that something needed to be done.

After a lot of prayerful thought, we realized that as parents, we had to set limits on the activities our children could be involved in and not leave it up to them. Children don't come into the world knowing what's best for them; they have to be taught. Children, particularly young children, have no concept of time or the future—

they see things only in terms of now, particularly *right* now. They don't understand the long-term consequences of their decisions. Have you ever made the mistake of telling a four-year-old that you were going to take her to the fair the following week? What happened? You most likely spent the next seven days in pure torment, counting down the days one by one and telling your child over and over again, "No, not tomorrow. We are going *next* Tuesday. That's six days from now." Not only are children locked into the present, they see themselves at the center of the universe, meaning they are incredibly selfish. Of course, we are all selfish at times, but in their defense, they are often unaware of their selfishness, whereas most adults should recognize their own. Kids simply don't think that what they do could possibly have an impact on anyone else; they never stop to consider it. Before you allow your child to participate in any activity, ask yourself three very important questions.

WHAT GOAL OR GOALS DOES THE ACTIVITY SERVE? The conflict will usually be between family and individual goals, and long-term and short-term goals.

• **Family and individual goals.** Does the activity benefit other family members or just the individual who participates? Another way of looking at this question is to assess who really pays for the activity in terms of time and effort—the child involved or the other kids and parents who sit on the sidelines and watch the games, perhaps missing other opportunities for growth or fun themselves. For most families, a day at the park or the beach is better overall than a day at the ballpark watching Janie play soccer. The former activities build relationships among family members and create common memories, which are really all we have left when the kids grow up and leave home (besides each other). Common memories are a substantial part of the glue that binds family members together.

• **Long-term and short-term goals.** Is the activity something that will benefit your child later in life, or does it simply entertain him or her today without any clear future benefit? Learning team-work and cooperation are important goals for any child and are probably the most commonly cited reasons for children to partici-pate in team sports and group activities. But are there other, less expensive (in terms of time spent and anxiety produced) ways to get the same benefits now and later? It's okay to participate in an activ-ity that is purely for the purpose of entertainment, but don't be quick to pay too high a price for entertainment alone. If letting your child participate costs the family too much relative to the joy received by the individual, then I don't recommend sacrificing the rest of the family's happiness. Besides, doesn't participating in chores as a family and helping neighbors and extended family with their needs teach your child teamwork, responsibility, and cooper-ation? I think they can if they're properly structured. It may sound trite, but the family is actually a team, or an organization, with spe-cific roles and duties for its members. The members must interact and cooperate with each other to achieve a goal. Children need to have chores and be expected to participate in the work of the fam-ily, because it gives them a sense of belonging and self-worth. Allow-ances in exchange for chores are a family choice, but a child should be expected to contribute something just because he or she is part of the family.

Meaningful individual goals should certainly not be squelched. Some of these goals can be quite important to your child's devel-opment. After all, we are not all alike. We each have different talents, needs, interests, and abilities, which often change as we mature or our circumstances change. But other family members should not be asked to sacrifice unreasonably for any one person to achieve their individual goals; it should be give-and-take. Life doesn't allow any of us to always be a taker, so teach your children how to cope with this fact by denying them occasionally. They will be happier in the long run, and you might live longer!

Learning to play a musical instrument would clearly be a per-sonal goal and could be very beneficial to the individual. It may provide a lifetime of entertainment for the musician as well as his or her family, help promote a sense of self-worth and confidence, and inspire creativity in other areas of the participant's life. As such, it represents a long-term goal. Another example of an activity that fulfills long-term goals might be a summer reading program. Improving a child's ability to read may make doing homework easier, improve writing skills and vocabulary, and encourage a love of reading and knowledge in general that inspires the child to reach for higher goals. This type of activity is much more likely to be useful in the future than learning how to dribble a basketball, do a cartwheel, or pitch a tent in less than two minutes.

It is important that you establish the family's long-term goals as well as the individual goals you feel are important for each of your children to achieve. Although I think your children should have more input into these decisions as they get old enough to make logical choices, you shouldn't necessarily expect them to be able to see the differences in these different types of goals at first. They may not be willing to hold out for long-term goals when the short-term ones look good at first glance. You must teach them how to weigh their options. In fact, we all need help in this area.

WHAT ARE THE BENEFITS VERSUS THE COSTS OF THE ACTIVITY? How much does participating in the activity cost in terms of time, money, energy, and emotion? Who pays these costs? What other opportunities were given up by the participant and the family to allow participation? Economists call these opportunity costs. Who ultimately benefits from the child's participation and how much? For example, when you compare costs and benefits, will Johnny's (age eleven) benefits from playing Little League baseball through June and July, because he made the all-star team, compare favorably with the weeklong vacation at the beach the family (Mom, Dad, and his brother Tom, age eight) will lose because there isn't enough time left in the summer to go since his sister, Sue (age sixteen), starts drill team practice in late July? These are tough questions to decide sometimes. Ask yourself what the costs are to Johnny if he chooses to play. There will be at least two practices a week and two or three games each week in June and July—that's four nights and a Saturday each week for nine weeks. Since there are really only about ten to eleven weeks of summer vacation, you've got to make a mental effort to plan long before summer arrives if you want to preserve time for a family vacation. Besides practices and games, your evening meal plans will need to be altered somewhat to accommodate baseball four nights each week. You'll either have to fix a second meal for Johnny or do what most busy moms do—eat out at the ballpark or grab something fast on the way, making your healthy eating plan that much harder. Certainly some or all of the rest of the family will (be forced to) come to most of the games to show their support and will have to fit these outings into their schedules, which will add a little more stress here and there. These are all opportunity costs that should be factored into the decision about whether Johnny plays, but the most important opportunity cost in this scenario is the loss of the family vacation. This one will hurt everyone involved, including Johnny.

To paraphrase a popular thought, the family that plays together, stays together. Families go on vacations together for a reason. Working parents get away from work, which is always helpful, and parents and children can interact with each other away from the distractions of work, friends, telephones, computer games, and television. Vacations are a great opportunity to improve the relationships among members of the family. Many people say that they find these situations stressful, probably because they are not used to communicating with each other so directly over an extended period of time—it's like being forced to sit beside someone on a waiting room couch or talking to somebody in an elevator. Once things get rolling though, these interactions can often be quite pleasant and build better family relationships.

My wife and I went to Vermont one October weekend a few years ago to see the fall foliage. (We both agreed that we had obviously gotten older because we thought it would be exciting to see leaves change colors.) My week at work prior to leaving town had been particularly grueling with several evenings away from home, and LaNell had also been very busy with school projects and activities. As we drove to the airport, the conversation was a little awkward. I was thinking, as I'm sure she was, that we would have a bad time, not only because we were crossways with each other, but that we were going a little early in the season and the leaves might not even be turning yet. True to form, I had scheduled us there about three weeks too early. We drove all over the state of Vermont that weekend looking in vain for trees turning colors and the quaint little wooden bridges that are the sine qua non of the Green Mountain State. But instead of being miserable, we had one of the best weekends together that I can remember. By the end of the trip, she was even laughing at my silly puns.

That weekend together in Vermont taught me three important things. First, vacations with family encourage time together, which helps build relationships through better communication and creating common experiences. Second, married couples need time away from work and children to simply have fun together, which keeps the fire burning that brought them together in the first place. Third, that I loved my wife very much and even though work and our busy family schedule were pulling us apart, there was something between us that was and still is very special and worth holding on to.

That trip also helped me make an important decision about our relationship, probably one of the most important decisions I have ever made—I chose her and I chose us. I decided that I would do whatever it took to keep our marriage strong. I made the decision that no matter how bad things looked, how lost or unloved I felt, and what troubles came our way, I was committed to her and our marriage for the rest of my life. I thought I had made that decision when we got married many years earlier, but we were both immature, untested, starry-eyed kids at our wedding. Now, after almost twenty years of marriage, career, and children, we were seasoned, battle-weary veterans who had fought side by side, and sometimes against each other, in many conflicts. This new commitment was tempered with the full knowledge that marriage wasn't a one-hour ceremony but a lifetime project, one we would have to constantly work on to keep it strong and see it grow. LaNell shared with me a few years later that she had come to a similar decision, and this renewed commitment to each other has strengthened our marriage immeasurably.

Make the effort to plan meaningful family vacations and arrange regular opportunities for quality time alone with your spouse. These are important to developing and sustaining a healthy primary love relationship.

Returning to the example of Johnny's extra baseball season, the loss or serious curtailment of a family vacation in my opinion would be a critical mistake for most families. This is a good time for Mom and Dad, and even Johnny, to take a reality check: the odds that Johnny will be a major league baseball player are almost a million to one, so why should the entire family trash their vacation to allow one family member to meet a short-term, individual goal? None of the activities most of our kids want to participate in are bad. In fact, many of them are very good things for our children to do, but you must look at the overall situation and evaluate the costs versus the benefits to everyone involved before deciding whether or not to allow your child to participate in the activity. If baseball is the only activity Johnny will participate in all year, or if you think Johnny really is good enough to play at the college or professional level someday, it might be worth sacrificing the family vacation to allow him to play ball. Under these circumstances, playing ball this summer looks like it meets more long-term than short-term goals. But for most kids, this all-star season would be the second dessert at the end of the cafeteria line; their tray is already full of more food than they can, or even want to, eat. Why let them put it on their plate? And more important, why should you and the rest of the family have to pay for it?

CAN WE REALISTICALLY TAKE ON THIS EXTRA COMMITMENT? Most of us don't set out to make ourselves miserable by becoming over-burdened with hurry; it creeps up on us slowly. We usually make the mistake of adding things to our schedule like we add charges to a credit card. In the past, when I was at the mall and I saw an item I wanted—sometimes premeditated, but often on impulse—I would charge it. I didn't feel an electric shock go up my arm or hear an alarm going off when I did it. I was unaware of any negative impact that would come from charging the item at this point, because I wasn't really keeping track of what I'd charged so far during the month. It seemed to me that I could afford it, so I got it. When I received my credit card statement though, I was often awestruck to see how much stuff I had charged throughout the month. After receiving several shocking credit card statements, I have come to the realization that I can't "eyeball it" and accurately keep track of my spending on a credit card. I think most of us, to a varying extent, feel that as long as there's room on the card, we can buy more stuff. As if the credit card company wouldn't grant us more credit than we could handle. Of course, what we forget when we think this way is that we are going to have to eventually pay for all the stuff we've charged. This is the harsh reality of the situation. And to add insult to injury, we are going to have to pay a lot of interest charges if we don't pay off the balance quickly.

The Hurried Woman often adds activities to her schedule in the same fashion. If there's room in her schedule and the activity appears to have merit (Johnny wants to play, and baseball is good), she'll add it to her load. Even if she realizes it's going to be a squeeze to fit it into her already busy schedule, a mother will often do it any-way because:

"He really wants to play."
"The season lasts for only ten weeks."
"Surely it won't be that bad."
"All of his friends are doing it."

But remember, just like the credit card, you do eventually have to pay for all the activities you've let yourself get involved in—and with interest. This situation reminds me of the "Ed Sullivan Show." When I was a kid, we would always try to watch Ed Sullivan on Sunday night. It was live TV back then, so you got to see the "bloopers" right away; they weren't edited out. I remember seeing a juggler one night. This guy juggled everything—bowling pins, plates, baseballs, knives. At one point in his act, he started juggling two pins and had his lovely assistant (they always had a lovely assistant) toss him another pin every few seconds. He juggled three pins, then four, and then five. He had a little trouble with five pins, but he kept them going. But when she threw him the sixth pin, he dropped them all. How embarrassing for him. He had finally found his limit and when he attempted to go past it, he fell apart.

The message from this story is that we all have limits, and the Hurried Woman tends to let her kids, her husband, and even herself toss her more pins until she is juggling at her capacity. Some women try to push past their limit and in doing so, begin to really struggle. Life loses its flavor. Easy things become hard. It is valuable to periodically rethink each activity you and your family are already involved in to see if your goal priorities, the costs and benefits of participating, or schedule commitments have changed. If so, you will want to consider dropping activities that don't fit in anymore. You, and your partner if you're not a single parent, must establish the priorities for your family; a very important part of that process is setting reasonable limits on your children's activities.

This is a very tough area for a lot of parents today. For any number of reasons, children's activities have left the neighborhood and become very organized, very competitive, and available in many venues virtually year-round. Children are presented with a number of opportunities for extracurricular participation in athletics, music, gymnastics, and educational experiences. It's probably good that kids have more opportunities available to them today, but it's bad when these activities lose their primary focus—fun or mastering important skills—and become a burden to parents and children alike. It almost seems as if mass hysteria (or mass hypnosis) has produced a drive in our culture to participate and compete in everything we can—as long as we can, in as many different areas as we can, and as frequently as we can—often to the detriment of the family. Identifying priorities and setting goals is important for the Hurried Woman, but it's also important for parents to teach these skills to their children.

YOUR ACTIVITIES

You should ask the same three important questions when attempting to assess the value of your own activities:

- What goals does it serve?

- Is the benefit received greater than the costs involved?

- Can I realistically fit this into my schedule?

If the activity measures up, then try it and reassess the situation periodically—maybe twice a year. However, there are a couple of key differences to remember when assessing your activities versus those of your children.

First, you deserve to have a life also. Really! Don't be willing to sacrifice all of yourself for the sake of your family. Think twice before you accept new responsibilities. Moms who stay home are particularly subject to abuse because they are the first person other people think of when they need a room mother at school, or a Cub Scout leader, or a volunteer for the book fair at church. Of course, none of these are bad things to volunteer for, but they can be bad for you and your family if you don't have room in your life for the extra hurry and stress these activities produce. You may feel that you need to "take your turn" at these chores occasionally and rightfully so. But don't feel prodded into doing it by other parents, teachers, or your children, particularly if you are already feeling the pressure from a busy schedule.

There were several years when my wife was the room mother for at least three of our four children. Those were some very hectic times. Not only was it hard to get all of the stuff needed for the parties and activities throughout the year, she often had to run back and forth between parties because she needed to be in more than one place at the same time. I'm sure she felt rewarded to have provided the kids with a good party, but she had several evenings of hard work getting ready. She felt she had to get party favors and balloons, bake cookies and cupcakes, and get party bags together for every child. Many of these evenings were not particularly joyful for her or the rest of us.

Of course, this is only a minor example of the hurry that many moms heap on themselves, but I want to stress that you must try to balance the amount of effort (cost) you put into an activity with the benefit you'll receive and always be aware of the long-term effects of your choices. Volunteer work, whether through school, church, Junior League, or other charitable organizations, is a good place to spend time helping others and is certainly not bad in and of itself. But you have to place it in its proper perspective with the rest of your obligations—to yourself, your spouse, and your family. You have to put the big rocks in first, then you can add the gravel and sand in later if you want. In her book *Take Time for Your Life* (Broadway Books, 1998), Cheryl Richardson suggests that you say "no" unless your answer is an "absolute yes." This will not only get rid of unnecessary commitments that wear you down and steal time away from your high-priority activities, but also puts you back in control of your schedule.

Earlier in this chapter, I explained the importance of family time to play together, specifically the family vacation. Begin to think about your family vacation for next summer—even if it's a year in advance. Think about what you want to do, how long to take off, and what it will cost. If cost is difficult, try to be creative—arrange to visit family or friends by car or bus rather than flying to some fancy resort. Just try to get away from your usual surroundings and distractions. After making a few inquiries, come up with a tentative decision, but leave it on the back burner until around Christmas-time. Put *vacation* on your calendar in red letters on December 10 of this year to remind you to think seriously about next summer. Then, right after New Year's, make a final decision and start to schedule it. It's a good idea to think about alternative dates in case the opportunity to do something you really want presents itself at the last minute but would interfere with your original plans. Decide early so that the vacation is set and becomes one of the big rocks. Keep in mind that some vacation spots require reservations far in advance—even a year ahead of time—so if you're thinking about one of these places, you'll have to move your timetable up.

I also recommend scheduling family events, like reunions and graduation parties, as soon as you can set a date and posting them on the family calendar where everyone can see them. This avoids confusion and conflict later. Also, let it be known that no one can put an event on the calendar except Mom and Dad. This keeps the calendar neat and easy to read and allows you to decide what is important for the family and what is fluff.

SAVING TIME FOR YOURSELF

You must save time for yourself. If you don't think to do it, no one else will. People are inherently selfish, and they will continue to ask you to do more and more for them unless you let them know that you need time for you. They don't necessarily mean to harm you by their selfishness, but it will harm you just the same. You need time away from work and family to relax and have fun. Until you begin to schedule time for yourself, you are likely to continue to feel out of control of your life.

I recommend that one of the first things you do with your private time is exercise. I'm sure you're thinking, "What a silly (*male*) idea! Exercise is not relaxing." But it can be. When I'm running, I have time to think, pray, and sometimes just clear my head of the thoughts that are troubling me. I don't have to answer the phone, wear a beeper, or answer questions. Time for exercise is my time for me. Plus, it gives me energy later and helps keep my weight under control. It's important to schedule your time for exercise just like you would schedule a doctor's appointment—and be faithful. Time for exercise is a critical element to surviving Hurried Woman Syndrome.

In addition to exercise, I recommend setting aside time to be alone—time to think and pray if you have a spiritual connection. Everyone needs time to think through problems. Complicated issues are difficult to resolve with kids screaming or while being constantly asked important questions like "What are we having for dinner?"

Wherever you are, make the commitment now to reserve some quiet time each day for yourself. Even though it may be just ten minutes, it will help you stay focused on your priorities and goals. Regular quiet time allows you to check your bearings to stay focused on your goals.

IS THERE LIFE AFTER CHILDREN?

Yes, I've heard about it. Not for us yet, of course, but others have told us it exists. Actually, this is a serious area of concern because many women make raising children the center of their lives. Virtually everything they do is focused on the kids—their happiness, their activities, and their lives. Of course, if raising her children has been the primary focus of a woman's life for more than twenty years, what happens when the last child leaves home? Her world collapses. Often called the empty nest syndrome, it's really a form of depression. Much of what gave the woman who suffers with this problem her sense of worth or self-esteem has been removed from her day-to-day existence. Phone calls and even frequent visits help, but these are no substitute for the constant interaction with a child living in her home. If she has failed to maintain a close relationship with her partner or doesn't have one, has not established firm social contacts with other adults, and has no significant activities to occupy her emotional energy and time—like a hobby or work—when her "baby" leaves home, she has lost everything in her world that gave her a sense of purpose. This is a devastating loss.

I am not suggesting that you should distance yourself from your children to avoid this problem, but you do need to spend some of your energy now investing in your relationships with your spouse and other adults, as well as developing interests other than "child ranching," as my wife calls it. You may think that this couldn't possibly happen to you, and I hope you're right. But I have seen it occur over and over to women who I thought really "had it all together." And when it hits, it can bust up a marriage, wreak havoc on the lives of everyone involved, and lead to other serious problems.

Avoiding the empty nest syndrome is yet another reason that it is imperative to make time for your spouse. Certainly, you should spend quality time together with the kids, but spend it without them as well. You also need to keep and nurture your relationships with other adults. They may also have children, which is the main reason most of us have our current circle of friends—our kids are involved in the same activities or go to the same church or school. It's important to nurture these adult relationships, and not just the women, but also the men if you're compatible. When the kids are gone, these people will become very important to your emotional health. Have friends over to eat or play games, sometimes with the kids and sometimes without. Setting your priorities and being able to value one against the other is probably the most difficult task any of us has to master. Most of us still have trouble keeping our priorities ordered correctly and staying focused on our goals. This is an area of my life that requires almost constant attention.

CONSIDER YOUR SPIRITUAL SIDE

In a society that focuses so much attention on being politically correct, it may seem odd or even dangerous to discuss spirituality. But as Cheryl Richardson writes in *Take Time for Your Life*, "At one point or another, most of us long for more meaning in our lives—a sense of purpose, a connection to something greater than ourselves." I think the silent majority of humans actually do believe that there is more to our world than what we can see and touch and that there is more to our existence than the fourscore or so years we spend alive on this planet. The fact that as of June 2004, Rick Warren's book *The Purpose Driven Life* (Zondervan, 2002) had spent seventy-one weeks on the *New York Times'* Bestseller List speaks to the truth of this statement. People are spiritual beings. Why do we cry when others hurt? Why do we reach out to those in need? Why do we feel an overwhelming sense of awe when we look up into the clear night sky or down into the Grand Canyon? It is because we sense a connection between ourselves, other people, and a greater power—one that is larger than ourselves.

For me, spirituality and religion are the same thing. I connect to my spiritual side through my relationship with God. But this is not the case for everyone. There are more organized religions than Baskin-Robbins has ice cream flavors. And although many beliefs separate them, they all share some common ground. Almost all of them recognize a supreme being or force that is worthy of praise and worship and that has powers that we mortals don't possess. One of these powers is usually the ability to foresee future events or at least have wisdom about the future. Most organized religions also provide a way to access this power through meditation, ritual, or prayer. If you have a religious affiliation, why not use it to access this power when you are trying to sort out your priorities and goals? If you believe what your religion teaches to be true, then to ignore this resource would be foolish.

I use much of my personal time to ask God for help. I pray that God will guide me through the tough decisions about making personal commitments, planning for the future, raising my kids, and even the day-to-day events in my life. I am continually surprised at how things—surgical procedures, one or more women in labor, and an office full of patients needing help with various problems—seem impossible to sort out in the morning; in fact, it appears unlikely that I will be able to accomplish it all. But by the end of the day, the surgeries have been done, the babies delivered safely, and the office hours ended without too much wailing and gnashing of teeth. It all miraculously worked out somehow. Some people would say this phenomenon is just luck or skill or some combination of the two, but I firmly believe it's more than that.

I find that my relationship with God helps me most with keeping my priorities straight and staying focused on the big picture. Once you have a handle on your priorities, you won't let the little things that often masquerade as big things throw you off target. Prayer also brings me comfort and direction when times seem hard—something we all need. Reading the Bible is also a source of inspiration for me. In fact, in Luke 10:38–41 (NIV, 1984), Luke—who also was a physician—wrote about an incident during the life of Jesus that demonstrates the importance of keeping our priorities straight and not neglecting our spiritual nature. Two sisters, Mary and Martha, lived together in a town where Jesus was teaching and had invited him and his entourage to visit for the evening. Mary was "sitting at Jesus' feet listening to what he said. But Martha was distracted by all the preparations that had to be made." Martha got upset by this and asked, "Lord, don't you care that my sister has left me to do the work myself?" To which Jesus replied, "Martha, Martha . . . you are worried and upset about many things, but only *one* thing is needed [emphasis added]. Mary has chosen what is better, and it will not be taken away from her." Jesus recognized that much of the busyness that accompanied his visit was really unnecessary and that Martha was "worried and upset" by those many little things. However, what was most important for Mary was not being the best host but attending to the spiritual matters at hand. In this case, hearing what Jesus had to say.

We often get distracted by the busyness in our lives and the many things we feel obliged to worry about and spend our energy on because we feel that these things are expected of us. They represent what we think others will think it's important for us to do. However, if we get hung up in the details and let the busyness distract us from the spiritual side of life, we will often miss out on the more important things in our lives, just like Martha was doing.

Believe it or not, medical evidence is mounting that spirituality and religion can play an important role in disease prevention and healing. More than seventy studies have examined the role of religion in medical conditions like arthritis, cancer, diabetes, heart disease, lung disease, HIV/AIDS, sickle-cell anemia, amyotrophic lateral sclerosis (ALS), and chronic pain. The majority of these studies show that patients who have religious ties, but more importantly who regularly practice their religion, have much better coping skills and feel better overall than those who don't embrace such practices. Several prospective studies have also shown that people who are more religious or spiritual have lower blood pressure, fewer heart attacks, recover better from open heart surgery, and live longer in general. Why would a greater focus on spirituality and religion help us stay healthier?

Recall that the brain won the title of master gland for a reason. Our thoughts and emotions clearly affect our physiology, particularly through the effects of cortisol and norepinephrine—the two stress hormones that have been implicated in the many stress-related illnesses discussed in Chapter 2. It is logical that religious beliefs and prayer could help lower stress levels, resulting in lower levels of cortisol and norepinephrine and thus counteracting the stress-induced physiologic changes that would slow healing or even cause disease in the first place. Indeed, there is preliminary evidence suggesting that religious involvement may result in a stronger immune system and lower cortisol levels. Those who practice a religion will say these changes are proof that prayer works; others will continue to doubt its effectiveness. You will have to decide for yourself. As for me, I believe in miracles; I just can't predict when and where they will happen.

The best way to nurture your spiritual side is to allow time for spiritual things. It's very hard to feel spiritual when you are constantly being bombarded by the busyness of life. Commit some of your quiet time each day to prayer, meditation, yoga, or just sitting quietly and allowing yourself to relax and reflect. If you are a member of a religious community, spend more of your time focusing on your beliefs and religious practices, particularly those designed to provide insight into problem solving and to produce peace and comfort for yourself and those around you—if for no other reason than to lower stress levels. Another simple way to encourage your spiritual side is to get out of your day-to-day surroundings and into nature. The apostle Paul wrote in the book of Romans that God reveals himself to us through nature. It's interesting how small our problems can become when we get away from our desk and the struggles we face at home and wander out into open spaces. Cheryl Richardson says, "Some of the best 'soul food' is just outside your window—a spectacular sunset or sunrise, a hike up a mountain [to look at the horizon and the valley below], a full moon, or the chance to lie on your back and look at the stars." Try it and see what happens.

You can also nurture your spirituality by giving back to others outside your family, particularly as you take time away from the things you used to do but felt trapped into doing. As you begin to recover from Hurried Woman Syndrome, consider doing a project at a homeless shelter or soup kitchen. This is not a long-term commitment but rather the chance to test on a less-than-one-day basis that what I'm saying is true: giving to others is actually giving to yourself. Be careful to maintain a proper balance with your other activities and goals, but developing your spiritual nature can have a powerful positive effect on how you handle stress and your physical health as well.

12

STEP 6: GET THE BEST OF STRESS

THE STRESS IN OUR LIVES comes to us from three basic sources: (1) things we can't control and have to learn to deal with as they are, (2) people and circumstances that we may be able to modify but not avoid entirely, and (3) situations and people we can eliminate from our lives completely. Some of these sources fill us with a lot of negative energy that causes us to feel anxious or moody, while others drain us of our energy, making us unhappy and withdrawn. Think of your energy and sense of wellness—your attitudes, emotions, interests, and mood—like a pot of "life water." When your life water level is high, you feel great. When the level drops too low, you feel bad. Some stressors are like turning up the burner on the stove; they can inject you with enough anxiety that your pot boils over and the water spills out, thus lowering your water level. Other stressors cause little cracks to form in your pot, allowing the life water to drip out the bottom. Ultimately, both types of stress lead to the same problem—too little life water in your pot. In a way, Hurried Woman Syndrome can be viewed as having too little life water in your pot. To bring your water levels back up to normal, you need to turn down the burner, seal up the cracks in your pot, or preferably both.

SITUATIONS YOU CAN'T CONTROL

We will all eventually have to deal with sources of stress that we can't control. When a parent is diagnosed with a terminal illness, a child is injured in a major accident and requires months of medical treatment, or a spouse dies unexpectedly, stress levels will run high for an extended period of time with no immediate relief in sight. These are situations we cannot change. Fortunately, many of these situations will resolve over time or progress to a point where stress levels are more manageable, but in many cases, we must learn to deal with them to avoid letting them overtake us.

To experience relief from stress in these circumstances usually requires a change in perspective. Taking a step back emotionally to reflect on the big picture often helps in these times of tragedy. Try not to allow yourself to feel guilty; you didn't cause the problem. More importantly, you cannot fix the problem. Try not to waste your emotional energy worrying and fretting about things over which you have no control. Rather, in approaching these tough situations, keep two things in mind:

• Don't try to take on too much responsibility by yourself. For example, you can't sit up with your parent every night at the hospital and work the following day for the next two weeks. Marshal your resources and use them wisely. It's okay to ask siblings, friends, and church members to help with this responsibility. It's frustrating that you can't drop everything else in your life and focus all of your attention on the sick person. But the fact that you still have people in your life that need, love, and care about you will provide the emotional support you need to get through this situation and help comfort you.

- You can't take care of all the things that you normally do because of the circumstances, but you can't disregard them completely either. When you find yourself in a situation where you cannot change the outcome, the best way to lower stress is to adopt the proper perspective.

SOURCES OF STRESS THAT CAN BE ELIMINATED COMPLETELY

Few people believe that a significant amount of the stress they experience can actually be removed entirely, but it often can. This requires changing your viewpoint about what you do every day, what you work for, and what you "own." We'll come back to this concept as we discuss the common areas of stress and the practical approaches to lessen their effect on your brain chemistry and overall health.

Don't Put it Off

Some stressors that could be eliminated instead linger on your to-do list. These are the pesky projects that make up what Cheryl Richardson calls your "procrastination list" in her book *Take Time for Your Life*. Tasks like cleaning out your closet, visiting a relative in a nursing home in another city, or catching up on your reading often hang like dark clouds over your head. They cast a shadow over you and all you do because in the back of your mind you keep thinking, "I can't relax because I still need to . . ." but you never get around to doing it. Putting these things off just gives them more power over you. Make a list of these "clouds," and realistically plan out how to get rid of at least four of them in the next month—that's one cloud per week. Set time aside in your schedule to do these things yourself, hire someone to do them, or ask friends and family to help. Throw things out, fix what's broken, have a garage sale, give stuff to charity—whatever it takes, just do it! Don't put it off any longer; let the sunshine back in.

JUST SAY NO

Another way to eliminate stress is to not allow it to enter your schedule in the first place. Refuse to take on any new commitments for, at a minimum, the next twelve months—I call this "The Year of Saying No." It doesn't matter who asks you, how important a cause it serves, or who it will disappoint—just say "no." Say it at the office (as long as it won't get you fired), at church, and to your relatives when they ask you to host Christmas dinner. Say it to everyone outside your immediate family. You'll have to say "no" to them sometimes as well, but you'll need to be more selective when it comes to their activities. This will slowly but surely free up more and more time in your schedule, and you will begin to see real results from this technique if you have the discipline to turn people down. Many of my patients find it especially hard to say "no" to church activities and volunteer organizations such as the Junior League and the Red Cross, particularly if you feel your social standing depends on participating in these groups. My suggestion is to type out the following statement and keep it by the telephone or in your purse. When a volunteer group calls, tell them, "I'd love to help you with [name of project]; it's such an important and worthy cause. But my plate is too full right now for me to do it well. I don't want to disappoint people, so I'll have to turn this one down."

After the twelve months are up and you feel good again (sometimes it takes only six months but can often require more than a year), you can slowly begin to say "yes" to the groups that serve the more important goals on your new priority list and fit into your more appropriate schedule. Believe me, these groups won't forget that you're a capable leader or bear a grudge that you have been out of the loop for a year. If they don't respect your decision to bow out for a while, choose to serve with better people.

Turn Off the Worry Projector

Just as it's important to stop worrying about things you can't control, you'll lower your stress levels if you can quit wasting your energy worrying about things that may never happen. Many women tell me how they often lay in bed at night worrying about activities that will happen later in the week. They find themselves thinking about things like "What if my mother can't pick up the girls from school for me Thursday afternoon so I can make my dental appointment? Who can I get as backup [and sometimes backup for the backup]?"

Instead of putting yourself through this, try this experiment: This Sunday evening, jot down the things that are coming up during the next week that you've caught yourself worrying about over the past few days and seal them in an envelope with the date on it. Ten days later, open the envelope, and think about how these problems resolved themselves. It's a sure bet that most or all of them worked out just fine—not necessarily the way you'd planned, but okay nonetheless. Do this exercise again if you need to convince yourself that many of the things we worry about are just what-ifs that rarely come true. My editor, Judith McCarthy, tells me that she keeps a pad of paper and a pen on her nightstand, and if something seems to be keeping her awake, she writes it down so she knows she won't forget it in the morning. This allows her to stop worrying and get to sleep.

SOURCES OF STRESS THAT CAN BE MODIFIED BUT NOT ELIMINATED

The vast majority of stress in our lives comes from sources we can control somewhat but not entirely. Many of us don't realize how much control we really have over our stressors until we analyze them from a different perspective. We also tend not to fully appreciate the impact small stressors have on our overall stress level. Many of these "little things" pass beneath our stress radar yet add up to affect us over time. Most of my patients who've overcome Hurried Woman Syndrome didn't do it by getting rid of one big thing but by lowering stress levels in small increments from several areas of their lives.

Hurried Women are typically intelligent, motivated, and highly adaptive people. If they have one big thing that is causing the majority of their stress, they will find it and resolve it quickly—if it is within their power to do so. For most women with the syndrome, getting better is a matter of degrees, realizing 2 and 3 percent reductions in stress from several different areas that ultimately add up to a significant overall drop. This is also the more practical and less painful approach for many women; small changes aren't as hard to implement as a wholesale shift in the way you live your life. We'll evaluate both strategies as we discuss the common areas from which our stresses come.

GENERAL CONSIDERATIONS ABOUT STRESS

One general principle that will guide you in your efforts to lower stress is simplification. Henry David Thoreau's words "Simplify! Simplify! Simplify!" are as important now as when he penned them over 150 years ago. Our lives are often unnecessarily complicated by a lot of clutter that confounds us and adds worry and extra hurry to our lives. Most of the clutter I am referring to comes from our activities and our possessions. We frequently make bad choices in these areas based on two faulty assumptions: (1) more is better, and (2) always get the best. I would propose that you rethink these two assumptions, as I am trying to do, and realize that more stuff is more trouble, and better stuff means even more trouble. Or to paraphrase Voltaire, the enemy of *good* is *better*.

The First General Rule of Things

The First General Rule of Things is pretty simple: the more things you have to deal with, the more you worry. Many women play a large number of roles simultaneously these days—mother, daughter, wife, employer, employee, professional, and volunteer—in a society that prides itself on speed, which only heightens the pressure they feel.

When you are at your maximum capacity to handle stress, the effect of adding a small stressor is much more pronounced. Relieving even small amounts of stress may have a very beneficial effect if you have Hurried Woman Syndrome. Don't underestimate the value of removing what you might consider to be the source of only a small amount of stress. The benefits may be remarkable.

The Second General Rule of Things

The Second General Rule of Things states that the more personal investment you have in an object (in terms of time, money, or emotion), the more you will worry about losing it. Worry comes from fear of loss. If you have nothing to lose in a given situation, then you don't worry about what happens. Alternatively, in a situation that has two possible outcomes where one costs you something and the other costs significantly less (or perhaps, nothing at all), you'll obviously prefer the solution that costs less. If the difference in cost between the two alternatives becomes large enough to reach your own personal level of significance (it matters to you), then you will worry that the more costly outcome will occur. I know this point is a bit philosophical, but it's an important concept to grasp.

If you had to leave your car on the side of the highway overnight, you would be a lot more worried about a brand-new BMW convertible out there with its top down than a 1989 Toyota Corolla with no hubcaps, back windows that don't work, and a tendency to only start on Thursdays. Actually, you'd probably hope someone would steal the old clunker so you could get a new car! And when it comes to people, you would be a lot more stressed out if your husband told you he was leaving and never coming back than if your gardener told you the same thing. The thought of losing your husband and all that goes with him would most likely prompt a great deal more worry and stress than the notion of replacing the guy who takes care of your lawn. The more you value something, the more you want to keep it.

After decreasing the hurry in your life by realizing your limitations and reordering your priorities, another way to decrease your stress levels is by simplifying and organizing what you own. By simplifying, I mean decreasing the quantity of things you have to deal with in your life and reducing the amount of money and emotions you have invested in them—particularly the things that aren't that important to you any longer (based on your reordered priorities). Organizing will also free up resources that you can use elsewhere to greater advantage. This is particularly true when it comes to time.

I often find it difficult to separate simplifying life from organizing it in the examples I give, so the distinction between them may not always be clear. What follows are several practical suggestions for removing unnecessary stress in several of the major problem areas identified by my patients, friends, and family through the years.

THROW OUT THE CLUTTER

Most of us hesitate to throw away anything that we think may have some value. If it might have any life left in it, we tend to keep it. The problem with this strategy is that through the course of time, we accumulate a whole bunch of stuff that we can't possibly use and that clutters up the house, filling up all of our available storage space. Have you ever seen a house with an empty closet? Here's a good rule of thumb: if you haven't used something in a year, get rid of it. (This may not hold true for keepsakes or for children's clothes that you may wish to pass on to someone else.) You can sell it, give it away, have a garage sale, or donate it to charity for the tax write-off. Whatever method you choose is irrelevant to this discussion. Just get rid of it. It's obvious that you don't really need it or you would have used it within the last twelve months. I'm not suggesting that you sell everything and live in a tent. If something brings you pleasure, don't feel obligated to part with it. But if you can't find a good reason to use it during the year, just let it go.

SHOPPING

Sit down before you go grocery shopping and plan out meals for the next week. If your partner does some of the meal preparation, do this together. Look at the calendar to be sure you accommodate for nights when you'll be eating out or you know some other family member will not be eating with the family.

After deciding on a meal plan, mark your master grocery list for the items you need. Your master grocery list is a complete listing of all the items you might buy when you go shopping—including dry goods, fresh fruits and vegetables, beverages, cleaning products, frozen food, and so on—perhaps even arranged in the order in which their respective aisles are laid out in the grocery store. Create a master copy, then make several photocopies for future use. Then, when you sit down to make your shopping list each week, you can just check off the items you need on the punch list. This will help you remember to get everything you need when you go shopping, and you won't waste time wandering through the store wondering what you really need at home or constantly going back and forth to the store during the week.

I would also recommend that you never shop without a list and never go to the grocery store when you are hungry. When I do either of these things, I come home with a lot more stuff than I'd planned on buying, and it's usually the fattening stuff. I also recommend buying items in bulk if you have enough storage space and can use up the product before it spoils. This allows you to take advantage of volume discounts, and once you get the stuff home, you've got a lot less to pick up each week. Encourage your more mature family members to take on the responsibility of helping to keep the list current. Post it on the refrigerator or someplace prominent, so it's handy for everyone. When someone uses the next-to-last whatever or finishes a bottle or box of something, he or she should check it on the list. So if one roll of paper towels is left in the pantry when you take one out, "paper towels" gets marked on the list. If your partner or children will sometimes be enlisted to do the shopping, don't forget to specify brand names and sizes (8 oz., 16 oz., etc.) for items where this information would be helpful.

LAUNDRY

Wash big loads whenever possible to save on water and detergent, and try to buy clothes that don't need ironing. At my house, kids seem to make a disproportionate amount of dirty laundry. When my middle son was younger, he would change clothes two to three times a day for no apparent reason. In fact, we would make a mental note of what he was wearing at breakfast to discourage him from changing clothes midmorning and sometimes again in the afternoon. You'll have to keep reminding younger children to hang up or refold clothes they've worn briefly but haven't gotten dirty yet. This way, they can wear the stuff again later, until it really does need washing. Make bringing the dirty laundry to the laundry room one of the children's chores, and let them all share in it by rotating assignments on a regular basis. This will give them an appreciation of just how much dirty laundry there is each week and perhaps encourage each of them to do their part to keep it under control.

I also recommend having a policy that everyone gets one bath towel each week. My mother used to wash bath towels every Saturday and would issue my brother and me a new towel for the week. Have everyone in the house change towels on the same day so you can keep track. And if you have a swimming pool or visit one frequently, find an out-of-the-way place to let towels air-dry for reuse. Assign the children their own towels for swimming so they can use one all week. Perhaps a towel hook with each child's name on it would help them cooperate. Another useful system is to color code each child and issue each of them two towels in their color with instructions not to put the towel in the dirty clothes hamper until their other towel is clean. If they don't follow the rule, they will have no towel to use. This cuts down on the amount of dirty laundry and gives the kids a nice, colorful bathroom.

Clean out your closet and give away clothes that don't fit anymore, are worn out, or that you just haven't worn in a year. They are cluttering up your closet, and they might do someone else some good. Don't buy a lot of extra clothes that you will only wear rarely, and try to simplify your wardrobe. Try to get by with as little wardrobe as you need to be happy.

HOUSEWORK

This is another duty in which children should actively participate. Obviously, small children aren't going to be much help at first, but as they grow up, kids can help a lot. Emptying wastebaskets from bedrooms and baths, straightening up their rooms by picking up their toys and making their beds, and keeping pets clean are good tasks for children. As soon as they can hold a vacuum cleaner or power a bottle of window cleaner, kids should participate in keeping the house clean. They won't be able to do it as efficiently or as effectively as you can, but if they can get it 80 percent clean, the other 20 percent won't take you nearly as long or stress you out as much as doing 100 percent of it by yourself.

If you can afford it, you might consider getting a housecleaning service to do the stuff you absolutely hate to deal with but can't trust the kids to accomplish. Even having someone for half a day each week would free you up to spend time on more important activities with the family and help you have more energy at the end of the week. You'll have to decide for yourself what's best for your situation and budget.

TELEVISION

I recommend turning your TV off when possible; at least place reasonable and firm limits on the time your kids spend in front of the television. I think television saps smaller children of their creativity and makes them want a lot of things they normally wouldn't even care about if they hadn't seen it on high-powered television ads. Madison Avenue has gotten very smart about how they advertise to their target markets, and kids are a huge market. My children ask for a lot less when they watch less television—I'm convinced it's the effects of advertising.

During the school year, we turn the TV off when the kids get home from school. Before we did this, we had a lot more struggles with them about getting their homework done. They would get home from school and go immediately to the television by way of the kitchen. Then, after letting them unwind a bit, we would attempt to start on homework. With four kids, you have to start on homework early to get it all done. The fussing, squawking, and even temper outbursts were really unbearable some days. That's when LaNell and I decided to change things and turn the TV off every day before it became an issue. It's amazing how much quieter and calmer our house became without it. Sure, there are still protests; not too many children relish doing their homework. Once in a while we loosen up and let them watch a show here and there, but sticking to this rule has really lowered the anxiety levels at our house where homework is concerned.

I'm not totally against television; it is one of the greatest inventions to come out of the twentieth century. It has made the world a smaller place, brought different peoples and cultures closer together, and informed us as well as entertained us. But like mineral oil, it is best taken in moderation. I believe parents should carefully screen what their children are watching and limit the amount of viewing time each day. Encourage your kids to read and play outside when the weather allows. Play games as a family rather than subjecting yourself and your loved ones to prolonged mass hypnosis in front of the "one-eyed monster." And don't forget that many adults substitute television for conversation, exercise, or doing something more productive. Turn it off!

ENTERTAINMENT

Going to the movies used to be a big event at my house when I was a kid. We probably went four or five times each summer and maybe two or three times during the school year. I remember going to see *Mary Poppins* as a child; the tickets cost 90¢ each, which my mother complained was inordinately high at the time. I wonder what she thinks now when she takes her grandchildren to the movies at $7.50 apiece. If you buy popcorn and drinks, you can spend a small fortune taking your family out for a show. We have been attempting to become more patient and wait until a movie comes out on video before seeing it. To take my family of six to the theater costs about $55 to $65 if you include snacks. However, at the video store, even one of the high-demand movies only costs about $3 to rent, and you can watch it twice if you wish. Throw in another $2.50 for microwave popcorn, and we're set. That's a big difference in cost. We still like to go to the movies just for the sake of going out as a family, and some movies are just better viewed on the big screen, but we think twice before heading out to the show, and we often eat dinner at home or on the way to the theater to cut down on excessive snack costs.

MEALS

Most mothers find mealtimes difficult. In fact, even the Hurried Woman who is in deep denial will usually admit mealtime is stressful, particularly with small children. One big problem in our hurried culture is finding a time when the whole family can consistently gather together to break bread. Either the kids complain about eating out too much, or they don't like the food you cook for them. And they often love something one week only to hate it the next. To sum it all up—coordinating meals for a busy family is a real hassle for most women. Here are a couple of hints to make some of these common mealtime worries less stressful.

If you find that there's just not enough time to get a meal ready between getting home from work and the evening's activities, consider preparing meals—or at least the main dish—in advance. There are two good ways to do this. One is to cook ahead when you see a busy week coming up. Perhaps on Saturday morning or Sunday afternoon when things are quieter, cook a pan of lasagna, bake a casserole, or roast chicken and freeze it in the appropriate freezer-proof storage bag or plastic container. Then when the tight part of the week's schedule hits, you can put the frozen main dish out to thaw when you leave for work and be able to pop it in the microwave or oven when you get home from work with minimal prep time. You can then heat up a few veggies and/or bread to go with it, and be ready to feed the masses with less hassle. Alternatively, you may occasionally want to prepare twice as much of a main dish as your family usually eats and freeze half of it for a future meal. This will work just as well as the first scenario and may suit your schedule better.

I also think that you should teach your children—boys and girls—how to cook when they are old enough to learn effectively. My mother had two boys, and she taught both of us how to cook a variety of dishes. I'm certainly no chef, but I can make most casseroles, cook chicken and beef, and prepare most breads and vegetables. This has come in handy on numerous occasions. Let your children help you get meals ready early, particularly if they get home in the afternoon before you do. They can start warming things and opening cans for you, saving time and lowering your stress levels. Admittedly, it sometimes seems that training them isn't worth the effort, but the time spent teaching your kids to help you in the kitchen and around the house can pay back big dividends for you and your family.

Also, don't forget to ask your husband to cook more often if he can do it. Lots of men actually like to cook or fire up the grill. At least you won't be responsible for the main dish quite as often, which will help you cope better with a busy schedule. Try to limit the consumption of fast food, which is how many Hurried Women typically attempt to provide meals in a hectic schedule.

MEALS OUT

We've already discussed the vagaries of fast food when it comes to your healthy eating plan. The general rule is that any place with a drive-through window is not a good choice. Some fast-food chains are responding to the obesity epidemic by offering lower calorie meals as an alternative to their traditional fare. A money-saving trick one of our friends with a big family uses when they go out to eat is to order water for everyone with their meal. Since there are five of them, they save about $7 to $9 each time. It's also healthier to drink water instead of soft drinks. Simplifying your lifestyle doesn't always end up being less expensive, but it often saves money to "go simpler," and lessening your money worries helps lower your overall stress levels.

Also, as part of your meal planning each week, decide which meals you will eat out and account for this in your calorie counting. This will help you stay within your limits and plan your calorie intake for the day in advance rather than being surprised at dinnertime that you're going out to eat that evening, in which case you either blow your diet by overeating or have to go hungry that night to stay on track.

JUNK MAIL

At my house, junk mail is a royal pain. We must get close to a thousand catalogs each year, and virtually all of them are unsolicited. Direct marketers share our names and addresses among each other just like hobos share a cheap bottle of wine. Actually, mail-order companies buy lists of names from credit card companies and other direct-mail retailers. Stop junk mail by getting your name off the numerous mailing lists that you are undoubtedly on. You can write to Stop the Junk Mail, P.O. Box 9008, Farmingdale, NY 11735-9008 and request that your name (and all variations of your name that appear on mailing labels) not be sold to mailing list companies. Afterward, if you do request a catalog, ask the company not to sell your name. Consider sorting your mail over the waste can or right into the recycling bin, if your area recycles mixed paper of this kind. Unless you really feel that there's something in a particular catalog that you've been looking for, throw it away. Otherwise, old catalogs will stack up and clutter your house. I can testify personally to the importance of throwing this type of correspondence away immediately unless you have a specific need. Leaving catalogs lying around my house encourages needless consumption—particularly if they're for toys or clothing—and makes keeping the house clean and orderly more difficult.

I also recommend stopping your junk e-mail. I recently returned to my PC after a five-day vacation to find 429 e-mail messages waiting for me. It took me well over an hour to sort through them all. More than three-fourths of the e-mail messages I receive are jokes, most of them forwarded to me by friends, who are actually friends with each other, too. This means I get the same joke from two or three different people. I have started telling my friends (nicely, of course) to be a little more selective about the messages they forward to me to avoid cluttering up an hour of each day sifting through a bunch of lame jokes just to get my messages.

SCREENING PHONE CALLS

It used to make me mad when I called someone and got an answering machine. I hated to leave a message, often hanging up a few times until I practiced what I wanted to say. Now that I've learned how to leave a coherent message, I don't mind them anymore. My family uses our answering machine to screen our calls, particularly during mealtime. Unfortunately, when I am on-call for my practice, I can't do this, but on most nights the answering machine allows us to use our family time together better and avoid annoying interruptions.

BEEPERS AND CELLULAR PHONES

When I first started medical school, only the faculty members and chief residents carried beepers on their belts; no one else had them. Back then having a beeper was a status symbol; you were "somebody." Now, everyone has a beeper, even the janitor at church. And, after nineteen years of carrying one, I wish I could get rid of mine. However, beepers can be very convenient, and many a mom has gotten one so she can be more mobile but still remain accessible to her family. Cellular phones allow for the same mobility as a pager and also quick access to a "safe" phone, particularly on the highway. My only caution is to not give your cell phone or beeper number out to just anyone. Once someone has your number, he or she has quick and unfettered access to you at all times. Using your voice mail to screen your cell phone calls makes a lot of sense and will guard your personal time from intrusions by unwanted callers.

I am amazed at the number of children who now carry cell phones and beepers. When my children were lobbying for cell phones, they told me that a cell phone would allow them to go anywhere they wanted and still stay in touch. Of course, that's what worried me. I still like the old-fashioned but effective method of "call me from your friend's house when you get there," because your kids know that you can verify if they are there by simply calling them back after they hang up or by using caller ID. I know it's more convenient to issue and use a cell phone, but who said that being an effective parent would ever be convenient? Your children may think you're behind the times and don't trust them enough, but just smile and agree with them and keep providing them with firm, loving guidance, because they are not born knowing the right choices to make in life. You have to watch them and teach them.

I'm not sure anymore whether our technology actually serves us or we serve our technology. There are military aircraft that fly so fast and maneuver so quickly that if the plane is turned too sharply at high speed, the pilot will literally pass out. Pilots are trained to do certain physiologic maneuvers to stay conscious during a sharp turn but will often black out for brief periods because the g-forces are so great that the blood in the brain actually stops flowing; our technology has taken us to the edge of what our bodies can handle. Could it be that we are beginning to see a similar situation in Hurried Woman Syndrome?

Our hurried lifestyles provide us with so many inputs for the brain to process constantly—pagers; cell phones; e-mail; PDAs; fax machines; computers; television; radio; newspapers; and interactions with people at work, at home, and on the go. These inputs are available virtually without interruption—news, television programming, and the Internet are all accessible 24/7. These inputs greet us when we wake up in the morning and bombard us incessantly until we go to bed at night. The downtime that was once built into our schedules has essentially vanished.

In years past, if we wrote someone a letter, it took a day to process it on our end, two to three days for the postal service to deliver it, a few more days for the recipient to respond, and at least another two to three days to receive their response; the whole process took more than a week to complete. Now, we can use e-mail and fax machines to make the same type of communication almost instantaneous. This seems a great improvement because we can now get a quick response to our inquiries, but it's also bad because we are now expected to respond the same way—quickly. This nearly subliminal sense of hurry pervades almost every facet of our lives. Twenty years ago, if you put dinner in the oven, it took thirty minutes to a couple of hours to cook; now we can microwave almost anything in under ten minutes. It saves us time. But do we use that time to make ourselves healthier or tend to the important things in our lives, or have we become slaves to the speed at which these devices force us to work—and use the extra time to do more work and receive more stimuli that we must process and respond to? Little wonder that many view Hurried Woman Syndrome as a symptom of a bigger societal problem—the fast-paced, high-tech way we live is causing us to suffer physically because our technology has outpaced our physiology. It's a reasonable notion.

FINANCES

This is the number one problem area for married couples in America, and surveys show that it is the primary issue over which husbands and wives argue. Money is important to people in almost every facet of their lives—sometimes too important. Learning how to handle your money effectively, rather than letting your money handle you, is a vital key to being happy in life. I wish I had more space to devote to this topic, but here are a few key steps to achieving peace and harmony with your spouse when it comes to finances.

SET REASONABLE LONG-TERM FINANCIAL GOALS

Traditional financial wisdom says that we should work hard during our lives with the goal of saving enough money along the way so that when we retire the following will be true:

- We won't have to work at all.

- We can maintain our present lifestyle (home, travel, cars, clothes, and so on), which most experts estimate will require about 70 percent of our present combined salary.

- We will not deplete any of the principle in our retirement account but will get the money we need to live on from the interest and earnings of our retirement savings.

- We can pass all the principle on to the next generation.

Although I am also a certified public accountant and love to discuss this subject in depth, to fully develop the proper strategy for setting financial goals and implementing them is beyond the scope of this book. However, I want to show you some important points about setting the right personal financial goals for you and your family, particularly on the issue of retirement, because it impacts everything else you do.

I think that one of the most important things you can do to lower stress levels is to plan adequately for your retirement. There are too many grasshoppers out there who think somebody else— particularly Uncle Sam—is responsible for taking care of their needs during their golden years. I agree with the original concept of Social Security—to act as a buffer against inflation and economic downturns and to supplement the savings of retired people, particularly those who, through accident or illness, couldn't save enough for their own retirement. But I don't agree with its present goal of providing enough income for everyone to retire and do nothing after age sixty-five or so. This is an impossible feat, considering the demographics of the baby boomer generation. Whether you agree with this statement or not will soon be irrelevant, because the Social Security system is hopelessly underfunded and will no doubt go bankrupt at some point in the future. I suspect those of us who are currently under the age of fifty will need to find a way to save more for our own retirement while still being taxed to pay for the retirement of those who are older than we are, because it is extremely unlikely that we will receive a full share of Social Security when we finally do retire. Simply put, if you are younger than fifty, don't factor Social Security into your retirement savings because it probably won't be there. But to all you ants out there, I still have much good news about planning for retirement.

If you look at the four traditional goals of retirement planning and do some calculations, you quickly realize that you will need a substantial sum of money to accomplish them all and that you are probably woefully behind in your efforts to save for this goal. For example, if you and your spouse are both forty years old and your combined salaries total $80,000 a year, your income after taxes is about $60,000. Traditional financial planning would suggest that you will need 70 percent of your current income to maintain your current lifestyle in retirement beginning at age sixty-five, or $42,000 a year. If you're planning to live off only the earnings from your retirement savings (which, after factoring for inflation and taxes, will be about 4 percent), you will need a retirement nest egg of $1,050,000 to make it happen. Let's say you have managed to save a total of $200,000 thus far for projected retirement at age sixty-five. This means you will need to accumulate another $850,000 before you retire. If you can average a 6 percent return on your future savings, you must budget about $2,800 each month from now until retirement to meet your goals. This is 42 percent of your current earnings, a true budget crusher.

But before you give up on retirement altogether, let's rethink those four traditional retirement goals. First, let's look at the "70 percent of your present income" assumption. Will you really need that much money to maintain your lifestyle in retirement? If your house is paid off, the kids are out of your home and your wallet, and you are willing to drive an economical car, you can probably easily trim down to 50 percent of your present income and still travel and have fun. Adopting this step alone drops the required nest egg from more than $1 million down to less than $750,000.

Second, rather than retiring and doing nothing at sixty-five, why not plan on you and/or your partner working part-time for a few years afterward? The statistics on people who retire to sit in rocking chairs are abysmal, with death rates in the first year approaching 30 percent. It's probably not only healthier to work part-time for a few years, but if you work at jobs that pay just a fourth of what you make now, it would take some of the heat off of you now to save more than you can afford.

Third, living off of only the interest earned by the investments in your retirement account may make you feel more secure about not running out of money in a pinch, but you can obtain this security another way without forcing yourself to work harder now to save the extra money. To continue our example, if you are willing to expend the principle in your retirement account as well as receive the interest earned, you will only need about $430,000 in your nest egg. Since you have already saved $200,000, you will only need to accumulate an additional $230,000 by age sixty-five, which amounts to saving less than $800 per month from now until retirement. Compared to the original $2,800 per month needed under the traditional retirement planning assumptions, this looks a lot more palatable.

To alleviate your worries about running out of money, most pension plans offer retirees an annuity that they can purchase at retirement. An annuity is simply a promise by the annuity company to give you a steady payment each month for the rest of your life in return for a portion of your pension funds. Life insurance protects you from dying too soon, whereas an annuity protects you from living too long. Since the annuity will pay out the money each month for as long as you live, it guarantees you will not run out of money. An annuity should be a part of virtually everyone's retirement planning. Vendors can calculate the amount of money you need at retirement to purchase an annuity sufficient to fund your cash flow needs. They can also show you how much you will need to start saving now to reach this goal.

Many people also don't want to plan on spending all of their retirement funds because they want to pass something on to their children and heirs—a legacy. Death taxes used to approximate 60 percent of the money in one's estate. This meant that only less than half of what you intended to leave behind would actually go to your relatives. Congress suspended these taxes a few years ago, but they are due to return in 2010 unless there is another vote to suspend them further. But even if death taxes stay "dead," I propose that you reconsider the strategy of attempting to leave your children a lot of money when you die. According to Stephen Pollan in his book, *Die Broke* (HarperCollins, 1997), expecting an inheritance changes the relationship between family members: "Suddenly, every dollar spent by the parent, whether on a new dining room set or a month-long vacation in France, is a dollar coming out of the child's pocket. . . . The child is put in the position of being hurt by the parent's pursuit of happiness and pleasure. And the parent is forced to choose quality of death over quality of life. This can lead to an endless cycle of guilt." Pollan's solution to this dilemma is to die broke—or at least nearly so—and don't promise your children anything. If there's money in your estate, fine; if not, they were warned. However, if you have the financial wherewithal to do so and wish to leave them something, I think it's a great idea to do something like buying your kids a paid-up whole life insurance policy when they graduate from college. They can borrow against it in the future if they need money—for a down payment on a new home, for example—and it guarantees them some amount of life insurance into the future should they become uninsurable for health reasons. A $50,000 life insurance policy purchased at age eighteen would typically cost you about $5,000 and be worth about $30,000 by age forty and almost $250,000 by age sixty-five. This gives them a gift while you're alive yet also prepares them for the possibility that there may not be anything else coming when you die.

Traditional retirement assumptions require a much more intense and sustained effort to save than adopting the new set does. Following the proposals of working part-time after you retire, looking at a more realistic estimate of what you will need to live on, planning to "die [nearly] broke," and giving up the need to leave your children (and Uncle Sam) a lot of money when you die, can save you a lot. It saved our fictitious couple in the preceding example about $2,000 each month in forced savings. These savings could be translated into more happiness now in several ways. They don't have to work as hard to save adequately for retirement—this could mean working part-time or taking more time off. They might consider slowing down to part-time work earlier than age sixty-five. They could also divert the extra money to other financial needs, like saving for college and paying off debts, or more fun spending, like better vacations or home improvements. No matter how you choose to "spend" your savings, adopting a more realistic set of retirement goals will lead to less worry about the future and perhaps the present.

One area of great concern these days is the rising cost of health-care insurance and nursing-home care. Long-term-care insurance covers nursing-home care and assisted-living (living with other seniors who need assistance with medications and some simple life tasks but don't need to be in a nursing home), neither of which is covered by Medicare/Medicaid. This type of care can be very expensive (between $1,000 and $5,000 per month today), so many financial planners are now recommending it to their clients. The best time to purchase this coverage is usually in your late forties or early fifties, *before* you develop some chronic illness like heart disease or diabetes.

GET OUT OF DEBT

This is the single most important step you can take to reduce stress in your life when it comes to money. You ought to hate going into debt and try hard to avoid it when you buy anything other than your house or a car. Paying interest to a bank or credit card vendor is basically money you have given up for the privilege of purchasing something when you want. Depending on the interest rate on your card, this "own-it-now" privilege can cost you anywhere from $10 to $25 for every $100 you charge. Instead of the familiar "20 percent *off* sale," using your credit card to buy something is like having a "20 percent *on* sale" if you don't pay the balance quickly; the interest charges add up to a lot of money over time. For example, if you carry an average balance of $500 over five years at 20 percent interest, you will have given the bank over $500 in interest payments. Was what you bought worth doubling its total cost just so you could have it right away instead of waiting until you'd saved up enough cash?

Besides interest charges, the monthly payment obligations can start to stack up if you have more than one credit card, and most of us have several. In fact, we often decide whether we can afford a new purchase based on whether we can meet the monthly payment rather than what the item actually costs or what the total cost of the item will be when we finally pay off all of the interest charges too. Most credit card companies know that we view our capacity to buy things in this fashion; that's why they schedule our monthly payments as low as they can. On average, a credit card with a big balance may take several years to pay off if you send in only the minimum required payment each month. You might be thinking, "If I make my monthly payments on time, then I'm okay." This is true to a point, but look at all of the extra interest expense you had to pay to do it that way. What will happen if you have a big, unexpected repair bill, like replacing the air conditioner; or get sick and are unable to work; or are suddenly laid off from your job? Your bank account will very quickly look like the *Hindenburg* going down in flames. Furthermore, what about saving for retirement, your kid's college expenses, a financial safety net for your parents, or even early retirement for you? You cannot adequately prepare for any of these possibilities if you are floundering in debt. Dave Ramsey, in his book *The Total Money Makeover: A Proven Plan for Financial Fitness* (Thomas Nelson, 2003), provides a system for getting out of debt and back on track. It is not a quick fix, but there is no easy way to get out of debt except through discipline and determination. His book offers you a good shot at fixing the problem by yourself.

If you think you're in over your head, seek the help of a professional credit counselor. Many offer their services at no cost because they are either subsidized by the credit industry or make a margin off the discounts they get from your creditors. Most of these services are listed in the yellow pages of your phone book under "Credit [or Debt] Counseling Services." They will advise you to go to a bankruptcy lawyer if you need one, but this alternative should be used as a last resort. Bankruptcies tend to hang around like bad tuna; it takes a long time for the smell to go away—seven years to be exact.

CUT UP ALL BUT ONE CREDIT CARD

Some people do better with no credit cards at all, but most of us need one for catalog, online, or phone purchases and to avoid carrying around a lot of cash. Pick a card with a low interest rate, no interest penalties if you pay off each month's purchases on time, and perhaps some extras—such as air miles or points toward the purchase of a new car—for using the card and paying off the whole balance each month. However, there is no such thing as a free lunch. To some extent, you are paying for the card's bonus program. However, most of the bonus you get is predicated on the fact that the majority of people don't pay off their balances in a timely fashion. So if you do, you are probably gaining something from the bonus schedule. However, if you let balances stay on your card for more than a month or two, you will be paying extra for the bonus you ultimately receive. And don't forget that many of these credit cards charge a hefty annual fee. Just be honest with yourself and go for the card with the lowest interest rate rather than the one that pays a bonus if you don't think you can keep it paid off each month.

If you decide to use a credit card, budget the amount you are going to charge and pay it off each month. Be disciplined and don't make charges over your self-imposed spending limit. Put a sticky note in the front of your checkbook to keep track of your current month's charges or use a portion of your checkbook ledger to do this. Jot down the date, the vendor, and the amount of the charge, and keep a running total if you charge a lot of little things. When you hit your budgeted amount, stop using your credit card until the statement comes and you pay the full amount. This system will keep you within your budget and out of trouble with interest and fees.

I have some friends with high incomes who use their bonus-style credit cards like checking accounts. They buy everything with their credit card, including groceries and the like, and rack up big bonus points each year. In fact, one of our good friends flew his whole family to Hawaii, first class, last summer on the air miles he got from his bonus program. But he makes a lot of money and can afford to overcharge sometimes or even make mistakes keeping track of his charges without getting busted. He's got the earning power to overspend once in a while and not get into trouble. Most real people can't afford to do this, so keep track of your spending if you intend to use your credit card this way.

CHANGE YOUR BUYING HABITS

Don't be an impulse buyer. Only buy what you set out to get in the first place and learn to be patient before you purchase. Going to the mall, looking for "nothing in particular," with no budget and room on your credit cards is a recipe for financial disaster. It's like going to the grocery store when you're hungry; there's no way you're going to get out of there economically. If you stumble on something you think you need, ask yourself, "Do I really need this, or do I just want it now? Is it worth what I'm going to have to pay to have it?" If you're not really convinced that you need the item at this point, you probably don't. Go home and think about it. Sometimes the excitement of engaging in "retail therapy" (buying something to feel better about yourself) clouds our rational thinking. If you really need it, you can pick it up the next time you go to the mall. If you follow this wait-and-think-about-it method, you'll be surprised by how many things that you would have previously thrown into the shopping cart (and ultimately, the back closet) stay at the store and off of your credit card statement.

Delay any major purchases for at least one month. This will give you time to think them through and shop around for the best deal, should you decide to buy. You might also look into borrowing or renting the item rather than buying it, or perhaps you can purchase it secondhand. This is especially true of equipment used for leisure or hobby activities. I know people who have owned more exercise equipment than World Gym but have rarely used any of it for more than a few weeks. Once they discover that however advanced it is they still have to do exercise (you know—hot, sweaty, and no fun), they immediately stop using it and declare it ready for their next garage sale. I recommend that you not purchase any new exercise or sports equipment without first trying out a friend's gear or consulting the trainer at a health club.

Rethink Your Big-Ticket Items

Bestselling author Elaine St. James recommends that you "get a smaller house . . . drive a simple car . . . and get rid of the damn boat." Of course, what she says makes a lot of sense if you can detach your emotions from the decision. Remember the Second General Rule of

Things: the more it costs you, the more you worry about it. A simple car is less expensive to operate and maintain than a fancy sports car. A smaller house usually costs less and has lower property taxes and fewer things that need repair than a bigger home. Also, a smaller house has less room for stuff than a bigger house, thus lowering your stress through a corollary to the First General Rule of Things (the more things you have to deal with, the more you worry). Of course, this is not always the case, but it usually is. Most of us have to make this mistake for ourselves before we can really appreciate the importance of following this rule.

After I had been in private practice for about four years, we decided to build a house. We had two kids at the time and wanted more room. So we made the mistake a lot of people who are new to money make, we spent too much of it on a huge home. It was a positively splendid, well-built home, and we really liked it because it had been built for us from plans we had drawn up ourselves, and all of our neighbors were very good friends. However, the mortgage that went with this big house was huge, too.

We lived there very happily for about two years when we began to realize that our big, wonderful home was really a lot more house than we needed and that perhaps it sent the wrong signal to others about our values and what we thought was important. It also came with high monthly electric bills and property taxes, big rooms full of expensive furniture and ornate light fixtures, and several hundred dollars each month of repairs and "improvements." This house illustrated both of the General Rules of Things and caused us a lot of extra worry. Eventually, we realized that what we needed a house to be was a shelter from the weather, a secure place to keep our belongings, and enough room to live in and raise our children in reasonable comfort. So, after much prayer and a lot of soul- and goal-searching, we sold it. Except for missing our neighbors, we have never really regretted it.

Rethink what you need in a house; if you can downsize, a smaller home will probably provide the same shelter, security, and comfort you have now with a lot fewer worries and less cost. Perhaps you've been thinking about getting a bigger house or buying your first home. Just be sure to think about it and order your priorities carefully before making the move. A good rule of thumb is not to tie up more than 30 percent of your monthly after-tax income in a home. Unfortunately, this is not just the mortgage at the bank (principle and interest) but also the property taxes, homeowner's insurance, flood insurance, maintenance, and repairs. Many couples with two incomes look at what they currently bring home monthly to make this decision. But once you sign the papers and buy the house, you are locked into making those payments every month without interruption for the next fifteen to thirty years. Are you both planning to work full-time until it's paid off? Are both of your jobs secure for the time needed to pay off the house? Many couples buy their first home based on their combined income but forget that when they have children, one of them may want to stay home with the kids for a time. They forget to factor this into the decision. Where and how you choose to live are two of the most important and far-reaching decisions you will have to make in your life.

Recreational items like boats (I'm talking about big boats), travel trailers, and beach or lake homes are wonderful things to have if you use them enough to warrant the time and expense involved with maintaining them. Most people I know who have owned boats, for example, fall in love with them at first. They can't wait to get through the week and "get on the boat." They may spend three out of four weekends each month joyously on the boat: swabbing the decks, blowing out the bilge pumps, and keeping her in tip-top shape. However, after a few months to years of this activity, the weekends spent on the boat become fewer and farther between. This is when, if the people are smart, they finally sell it. I propose selling the boat now if you're not really using it, because it's costing you a lot of money, concern, and time away from home. I also propose, for those of you who don't presently have a boat, don't get one unless you're absolutely sure that you and your "crew" are really going to use it.

You can always charter a boat if you occasionally like to go deep-sea fishing, or perhaps you can find a fishing buddy who has a boat. You can offer to bring the food and pay for the gas each time you go out together. This is a whole lot cheaper than buying and maintaining a boat yourself. The same is true for recreational vehicles (RVs) and other vacation items.

Get in the Habit of Saving Money

A wise cowboy once said that the best way to double your money is to fold it over and put it back in your pocket. After having invested in a few too many "dumb doctor deals" (doctors have a reputation for being extraordinarily astute businesspeople), I think this is good, albeit a little oversimplified, advice. We have all been told to learn to live within our means, but what does this advice really mean? I think it means you must learn to save some of what you make now for later and not buy things with money you don't have, which we call credit. You can't look at your paycheck and think, "This is how much money I can spend this month." You have to condition yourself to take the total on your paycheck and first subtract what you give to charity and religious organizations (I recommend about 10 percent), then take out the amount you will set aside for savings and debt reduction (20–25 percent is good), and then learn to live off the rest (about 65–70 percent). You may wonder how you could live on only 65–70 percent of your current salary after taxes. But if this is true, you are already living beyond your means and need to cut back on spending. You need to look at your savings as another bill that must be paid each month. The good news is that this bill is paid to *you*. This is the money you will need later to use for retirement, cover education costs for your kids, care for your parents if needed, and provide rainy-day protection against unexpected expenses. It's easier to start this new approach to savings when you're young and haven't yet committed yourself to a lot of financial obligations. But even if you think you're up to your eyeballs in debt, you can still change things now. You may have to use most of the 20–25 percent savings for debt reduction at first, but decide right now not to take on any new obligations, and you will slowly but surely be able to pay your way out of debt.

As your debt load decreases, you can begin to shift more of the 20–25 percent portion of your money into savings. A credit counselor or a financial planner (mentioned later in this section) can help you set up a schedule to pay off your debts and begin your savings program now.

As parents, we owe it to our children to teach them how to manage their money effectively and learn how to save for their future. Encourage your children to establish the saving habit now so it can become ingrained before they get into trouble with overspending and debt as adults. Besides, we need to be sure they become good savers so they can help us with our retirement if we didn't save enough!

DON'T PAY TOO MUCH FOR COLLEGE

Most of us want to be able to pay for our child to go to the college of his or her choice. But is this a realistic goal? For most families, the costs are prohibitive. The College Board estimates the average cost to send a child through four years of college—tuition, fees, room and board—is as follows:

	2002–2003
Public university	$51,400
Private university	$110,800
Public (out of state)	$76,800

Tuition continues to rise about 6 percent each year, and the cost of living in most areas of the country has increased about 4 percent each year. If these rates of inflation continue, the projected cost for four years at each type of institution will be as follows:

	2007	2012	2017
Public university	$65,600	$83,700	$106,900
Private university	$141,400	$180,500	$230,400
Public (out of state)	$98,000	$125,100	$160,000

It is impractical for most families to make this level of sacrifice even for a college education, particularly if you have more than one child. It is unwise to borrow liberally from your retirement fund, gut your life insurance policies, and give up family vacations just to send your son or daughter away to college. But before you give up on sending the kids to college or resign yourself to a life of working to pay for it all, consider the following ways to lower the costs:

• **Consider your local college or university.** You can cut the cost of a public college education down by about two-thirds (a 65 percent decrease) if you keep your child at home during college. Of course, most kids want to go away to school because it's more fun than staying at home, and it promises them freedom (a lot of parents feel the same way). But the added cost of doing this is tremendous—about $33,400 on average for four years at a public university. If nothing else, consider sending your child to the local community college for the first two years and then off to the big-name university to complete his or her degree, particularly if he or she doesn't have clear career goals. Changing majors is quite common and certainly preferable to getting trained for a job your child doesn't want, but it usually guarantees you'll be paying for five years of school instead of four, which means 20 percent more cost to deal with.

• **Forget going out of state.** Unless your state doesn't have a reasonable option for college (which is highly unlikely regardless of what your child says), don't waste your money on out-of-state tuition. That being said, if you are still committed to doing it anyway, the following discussion may prove helpful. Some schools will waive the extra cost for better students from other states, and you can also look into purchasing property near the school and using it to house your child as well as to establish his or her state citizenship—this usually takes one year—to stop paying the extra cost after the first year. Residential property near major universities is generally appreciating in value. This means you should be able to sell it for a profit after your child graduates, but consult a tax expert before adopting this strategy.

• **Ask grandparents to help.** Most grandparents are glad to help send grandchildren to college. They can contribute to Section 529 plans that are transferable among family members. When the first child finishes school, the plan can be changed to benefit the next child in line. It makes more sense for grandparents to gift money to grandchildren now than to wait until death to transfer these assets— after the need has passed. This is another good area in which to seek expert advice before diving in.

• **Think twice about an expensive private school.** Unless it's a family tradition to graduate from a specific private institution, it will be hard for most people to justify the additional $92,800 in cost to attend a private college versus staying at home or the additional $59,000 in cost over leaving home but going to an in-state public university. Most job recruiters and graduate school admissions directors will verify that graduating from a big-name school carries a lot less weight than it used to. They are much more impressed by an applicant's performance in school than by the name of the school they attended. What most employers and graduate schools are looking for are students who rose to the top of their class, students who stood out from the crowd—both academically as well as through their involvement on campus—because these are the people who can handle the workload they are given and also have good people skills. These are the "big fish" who rose to the top of the food chain in their respective pond. The big fish always tend to do better when it comes to a job interview or finding a place in a professional school or graduate program because they have demonstrated their competitiveness, ability to interact with people, and desire to stand out from their peers. Now, here's the hard part for a lot of eighteen-year-olds and their parents to realize when they are making the important decision about where to go to college—it's easier to become a big fish in a little pond than to become a big fish in a big pond. In fact, a fish in a little pond will appear larger than the same size fish in a big pond because perspective is critical when it comes to assessing size. For example, my alma mater—Lamar University in Beaumont, Texas—is a medium-sized public university that you may have never heard of, but it has managed to have the highest placement rate of students into medical and dental schools among all universities in Texas for over twenty-five years. Although it has rarely made any of the "Top Universities in America" polls run by several national magazines, it still manages to place more of its students in professional schools on a percentage basis than any other institution of higher learning in the state. Why? Because professional schools know that what I'm telling you is true—smaller schools turn out high-quality graduates just like big schools do, but unfortunately students don't want to believe it and parents often don't know any better.

At its most basic value, a college degree is a ticket to the next level. The next level after graduation for most students is an interview for a job or a spot in a professional school or graduate program. But once you get to the interview, it's all about you. Not what school you attended—just you and how you present yourself as a candidate for the position you're seeking. And after your first job, no one really cares that much about your academic background anymore—except that it was adequate. Then it's *really* all about you and what your previous employer thought about you. The average price today for a "ticket to the next level" is $18,000 at your local college, $51,400 at the public university that's too far away for commuting, and $110,800 at a private school. Which one appears to be the best deal? Many people will still argue that the bigger school or the one with the better name recognition will get your child a better career in the long run, but let's look at it another way.

Take two high school graduates with approximately the same skills and talents, and give each one of them $110,800 to cover the cost of their education. Student A will go to a prestigious private university that costs $110,800 for four years, while Student B will attend a local college while living at home at a cost of $18,000. After graduation, Student A has no money remaining, while Student B has $92,800 left over. If Student B invests this money at 7 percent interest when she graduates, she will have $1,834,000 at age sixty-five. Do you think Student A will be able to outperform Student B over their respective careers to a point that justifies the original investment in the higher priced school? I think it's very unlikely. In fact, the notion is absurd. What if Student A were your son, and instead of sending him to the private university, you had kept him at home to attend the local college and kept the $92,800 in your retirement account earning 7 percent interest. If your son graduated when you were forty years old, you would have an additional $531,000 in your retirement account when you hit sixty-five. This is the amount of money you would be giving up at retirement to send your son to the private university rather than the local school.

Most of us don't think about the long-term consequences of these decisions at the time we make them, and consequently we often make a poor investment choice when it comes to buying a "ticket" for our children. It's exciting for child and parent alike to be accepted to a big-name school. It feels good to tell your child the sky's the limit and you'll send her anywhere she wants to go. None of us want to say "no" to a child who has worked hard in high school to get accepted at a prestigious university, particularly when we can brag about it to our friends. But the joy fades quickly after the initial announcement when we are left paying the bills. Don't get caught buying a seat in first class when you really wanted one in coach—they all ultimately arrive at the same place at the same time. Why pay more unless you really feel it's worth it and can afford it?

Rather than letting your child peg the institution she wants to attend at the start of her senior year and then scrambling to make it work—a setup for a disappointed child or a bad monetary decision for you—sit down with her when she enters high school or soon thereafter. Give her an honest estimate of how much money will be there for her at graduation and what the cost of each type of school is expected to be when she graduates. If she is nearing graduation now, sit down with her now. Let her know this is what you have to spend on college given the fact that you can't work until you're ninety-five and that you have to be fair to the other children in the family as well. If there's a wide gap between where she wants to go and the money available, tell her that working hard in school might provide a scholarship that could make up the difference. Let her know that student loans are also available and that, within reasonable limits, she could expect to borrow some of the money or work while in school to help close the gap. This process will give your child realistic expectations about her choices for college early in the decision-making process and avoid a big disappointment later—yours and hers.

INVESTMENTS

An in-depth discussion of investment strategies to minimize stress and maximize wealth is beyond the scope of this book, but I will make a few suggestions.

Have a Plan

Even if you think you don't have much to plan for in regard to your retirement, kid's education costs, long-term-care insurance, and the like, you can still benefit from the advice of an independent certified financial planner (CFP). Keep in mind that many CFPs were life insurance agents first and then became financial planners. So they often look to insurance first when trying to implement a plan because it is familiar to them and they know it will get the job done. They may also use insurance for a financial plan because they receive commissions from the insurance you buy. Most of these financial planners are reputable people who honestly want to help you achieve your financial goals, but I recommend that you use a CFP who is paid a fee and/or is independent of an insurance company or stock brokerage rather than one who receives commissions. When you call to make an appointment, ask how they are reimbursed for their services. If they won't tell you this information upfront, try someone else. You can find a listing of CFPs in your area on the Internet from the Certified Financial Planner Board of Standards (cfp-board.org) or the Institute of Certified Financial Planners at (icfp.org/plannersearch).

A financial planner will help you think through your short- and long-term financial goals, then show you different options for achieving those goals and help you outline an action plan. They also offer periodic reviews, usually yearly, to monitor your progress, offer advice on how you are doing, and update the plan as needed. Good financial planners will earn the fees they charge, if you let them help you.

Use Low-Maintenance Investments

Once you have defined your overall financial goals, have your financial planner help you meet those goals with investments that don't require a lot of direct maintenance from you. For example, the investment portion of most variable life insurance policies is basically a group of mutual funds, just like a 401k retirement plan. Mutual funds are professionally managed stock portfolios classified by the type of return expected and the amount of risk the investor wishes to bear. They are low maintenance because a financial services professional manages the money in the fund for you. Your financial planner can give you the details of the various types of mutual funds and the mix of fund types that will best suit your investment needs. Trying to pick individual stocks to adequately diversify your portfolio and effectively manage risk and return is difficult even for seasoned market veterans. Unless you enjoy constantly monitoring the stock market and the economy in general, it will be difficult for you to manage your investments more effectively than a professional money manager. Of course, if you really enjoy watching the market and running your own show, then go for it. Otherwise, lower your stress level about three notches by investing your money in mutual funds and let the pros handle it.

Similarly, don't get involved in unconventional investments that can't be monitored easily or are difficult to sell when you get nervous or tired of worrying about them. Don't invest in Cousin Lenny's reindeer farm, any unsolicited investment (you didn't call them, they contacted you and won't tell you who gave them your name), or anything sold over the phone. You might occasionally miss out on the deal of a lifetime, but most likely you will keep your money and keep it growing steadily and safely. Most get-rich-quick schemes only work for the guy selling them to you. You are the one who usually gets left holding the bag. Stick to investments that are tried and true.

Reevaluate Your Plan Annually and Stick With It

At least once a year, take some time to sit down with your most trusted advisor and review the progress you've made toward reaching your financial goals. Don't be upset that in the first few years it looks as if you'll never make it. The power of savings and investing comes through the compounding of interest, which builds slowly at first and then finishes strong. If you invest money at 10 percent compounded interest, it will double every seven years. So if you have $5,000 dollars invested at age thirty that is earning 10 percent interest, when you are sixty-five, you will have over $160,000! The power of interest compounding is huge. Here are the numbers:

Age	Amount Saved
30	$5,000
37	$10,000
42	$20,000
49	$40,000
56	$80,000
63	$160,000

This is the amount of money you would have at age sixty-three from the initial $5,000 you invested without having to add any more money to it. Think how much more savings you would have if you added a little money to the initial investment on a monthly or even yearly basis. If, on the other hand, you waited until age thirty-seven to put the $5,000 into savings, you would only have $80,000 at age sixty-three—half as much money than if you had started seven years earlier. This is why it's so important to start saving now!

WORK

Few topics stir a woman's emotions as much as work. Women who work outside the home are often defensive about their time away from their family. Women who stay at home with children are sensitive about not having a career outside the home. When the subject of work comes up, both camps draw their swords, ready to defend their positions. Let me start out by making a couple of affirming statements and then discuss work and how it affects the Hurried Woman.

I think women who want to stay at home and raise their children should feel free to do so. The presence of a caring parent in the home during a child's formative years is very beneficial. Children raised this way are much more verbal (an early sign of intelligence), perform better in school, and tend to stay out of trouble with the legal system more often than children raised by others outside the family. Similarly, women who seek a career outside the home should feel equally free to do so. Work is honorable, and women who have the skills and abilities to work should enjoy the same opportunities as men in the workplace.

Partners must decide for themselves the place work holds in each of their lives and how to balance their work goals with the goals of the family. However, this is not always an easy task. My observation has been that many women suffer from "the grass is always greener on the other side of the fence" perception of how the other half lives. Women who work full-time often wish they could stay home more, and women who stay at home, particularly those with small children, frequently long to get out and work with adults.

The best way to sort out the question of work is to answer the three questions discussed in Chapter 11 for evaluating other activities:

- What are your goals for family and career, and how will working outside the home serve these often competing goals?

- What are the benefits and costs associated with working?

- How does working as you do now affect your schedule?

Many women who have chosen to be stay-at-home moms often complain of the monotony of life and feel that they are trapped by their circumstances. For them, being a "good mom" means they should stay home, but they feel they are missing something by not working. If these women can arrange for economical child care, they often feel rewarded by working part-time. Part-time work allows them to earn money they can call their own, get out of the house for a while, interact with other adults, continue their career, and still have quality time at home with their family. I have several friends who are accountants and job share, splitting a position between two people. Both work about twenty to twenty-six hours each week and can go in more frequently in a pinch.

Hurried Women who work need to be honest with themselves about why they work, the importance of the money they bring home to their family, and how much time they need to work. Could they be happier working fewer hours, perhaps part-time or in a job-sharing arrangement? Would a less stressful job make life at home easier? Would they be happier working in a job that pays less but gives them more time off or allows for more flexible working hours? Would a significant break in employment, such as six months to a couple of years, give them time to feel better, sort things out, or accomplish some personal goals that work has blocked through the years?

If you are a single parent, you probably don't have as many viable alternatives, but if work is adding a lot of extra hurry to your life and you don't need the money or don't feel the need to work full-time, you might have more energy and feel better about yourself if you cut back your hours. Ask yourself these questions: "Am I working so I can have a bigger home, a better car, or more and better things? Are these benefits worth the extra hurry and anxiety my current workload is causing?" A wise pastor, Bob Bateman, said that in his many years of service he never once heard anyone on their deathbed say that they wished they had spent more time at the office. What are you getting from work, and what is it costing you? If the benefits outweigh the costs, work is appropriate. You might still benefit from lowering stress levels at work through a change in job assignment, hours, or employer.

These can be deep, soul-searching questions that require concentrated mental effort to sort through. There is no single perfect answer to these questions that will fit every woman's needs, and the right answer is not always obvious at first glance. However, because answering these questions correctly is so important to you and your family, I strongly recommend getting away for a few days to think about the answers. Pray or meditate about them if you have a spiritual connection. Read through this information again, because it contains some of the more important "thought tools" you will need to work through these decisions for yourself. There is no "cookie-cutter" life that every woman should aspire to; if there were, there would be consensus on what that life looked like and everyone would have it by now. Time invested in answering the questions I've posed will reap big benefits when it comes to being happy and healthy.

13

STEP 7:
ORGANIZE YOUR WORLD

Now THAT YOU'VE RESET your priorities and simplified your life as best you can, it's time to organize what's left. This is not an exhaustive review of all the ways you can create more order in your world to lower your stress levels, but it will cover the major areas that most women request help fixing. Once you get started organizing, you'll probably see other areas where you can make improvements.

KEEP CONTROL OF EVERYONE'S SCHEDULES

Get a big family calendar and post it where everyone can look at it, but make it clear to everyone in the family that only Mom and Dad can write on it. Some people find it helpful to use different colors for different people's activities, including one color for whole-family activities. Everything the family needs to concern itself with when it comes to scheduling should be there. As soon as the dates for major events such as vacations, trips, school events, recitals, and rehearsals are announced, they should be placed on the calendar. This will identify scheduling conflicts as early as possible and avoid later confusion about the family's time commitments when the world starts trying to put in the "sand and gravel."

A few years ago, my wife told me in April that there were several day trips and activities that she wanted to do with the kids that summer. We even spent a few nights talking about them and mentally planning the events. However, when August 15—the day before school started—rolled around, we realized that summer had flown by and we had actually done very few of the things we had both thought were so important back in April. We had made a priority list in our heads for summer activities, but we didn't schedule them. If you don't make a habit of planning family activities in advance and keep an accurate calendar of events, your schedule won't accurately reflect your priorities and it will be difficult to maintain reasonable limits on activities.

SET LIMITS ON CHILDREN'S ACTIVITIES

It's important to set reasonable limits on children's activities because they don't know how to do this by themselves. I discussed this in depth in Chapter 11, so I won't go into great detail here, but do remember this one point because it's crucial in organizing your time. I'm not saying that organized sports and after-school activities are a waste of time. On the contrary, participation in organized sports is exactly what some kids need to feel a sense of belonging, learn teamwork, and acquire discipline. Music lessons, gymnastics, art lessons, and the like may provide a route for creative expression and personal growth that cannot be found elsewhere. But I encourage you to take a long, hard look at what allowing your children to play multiple sports and participate in other activities costs you in terms of scheduling hassles, time away from home, and lost opportunities for other activities that might be important to you and your family as a whole. What does all of the hurry do to your energy levels, weight-loss efforts, and sex drive? Be sure the benefits of the activity outweigh the costs when you evaluate it in the long run—how it all fits into the big picture.

ASSIGN CHORES AND RESPONSIBILITIES

Make out a written list or schedule of each child's duties and responsibilities—jobs can be assigned daily, weekly, or monthly—and post it on the refrigerator or someplace else where it will be seen frequently. Sit down with each child and review what his or her duties are and what you expect each day. Discuss what you consider to be good and bad performance and how you are going to reward good performance or deal with poor performance. Our family finds that a set allowance works. The kids get it each week for good performance, and we withhold some or all of the allowance for poor performance. People need incentives to modify behavior, and your children are no exception. If you decide to do this, give each child an allowance that is appropriate for his or her age and spending needs, and pay them on time. That's what you expect from your employer, right?

Some people do not like to make allowance contingent on chores or to feel that they are "paying" their children to do what they should be doing for the family. That's naturally up to you, but I recommend you come up with some kind of carrot-and-stick plan, because people respond best when they are rewarded for good performance.

Anticipate that you will have to frequently remind your children to do their chores. This is probably one of the single most frustrating features of parenting. Why do you have to continually stay on your kids to do their work? Many parents get tired of pushing their offspring to do chores and finally give up, saying, "It's easier to just do it myself." We get tired of reminding our kids over and over again to do what we've asked. But if you don't force kids to follow through and complete their work, they will never learn to do it and it will become your job again. But if you take the long-term view instead, calling them back one more time and making them do the job right, this process will help them in several ways:

- It will establish a work standard for them to follow indefinitely ("A job isn't done until it's done right").

- They will learn how to manage their time better ("Don't put off till tomorrow what you can do today").

- It will help them realize that there are consequences for their actions or lack of them ("You don't work; you don't get paid." Or get to play with friends, or whatever other consequences are appropriate.).

Before you give up on them, remember they are going to be forgetful, preoccupied with their own concerns, and have a short- rather than long-term focus in their decision making. This is what makes them children. But being able to accept responsibility and learning how to handle work are important areas of their development that require diligence on your part. Besides, once they get the hang of doing their chores, they can help you get the work done.

HAVE A PLACE FOR EVERYTHING

Many of us accumulate stuff more quickly than we can find a place for it all. While it's best to cut down on the stuff, some of it is inevitable. Where do all the baseball bats and mitts really belong?

How about the kids' shoes—do they really have space for them all? If everyone's things don't have a specific place, you can bet they'll never be put away.

Take a look at all of the categories of things in your house, and be sure you have a place to store everything. It doesn't have to be expensive; the in-season sports equipment can all be kept in a big cardboard box in the hall closet, for example. It's better there than loose on the closet floor, someone's bedroom floor, or the middle of the doorway.

Shoes can be a big issue. Kids tend to kick them off when they come in—and if they're dirty, that's probably a good thing. But do they ever get put away? Unlikely. If you have space, try setting up some kind of mudroom area with a bin for shoes. Then each night, have the kids take all the shoes out of the bin and put them away. Same for jackets, coats, backpacks, purses, and other items that are used repeatedly through the day but tend to clutter up the house if they don't have a specific place to stay.

It seems that for weeks after a birthday or Christmas the house is literally flooded with toys. In fact, when our kids were young, they would get so many new things for Christmas that they didn't know what to play with first. One trick my wife would use immediately after the holidays was to spirit away a few of the new toys when the kids weren't looking and put them up in our closet. Then when the kids would complain about being bored, she would pull out one of the forgotten playthings and let the kids enjoy them as a "surprise." This technique also cut down on the clutter from the holiday influx. She also made a point of encouraging the kids to view spring as a good time to let go of old toys they didn't play with anymore—a spring-cleaning for toys—which were usually donated to charity or sold in a garage sale.

Children's toys, particularly when they are little, always seem to clutter up the family room. If you have a playroom, this may not be as big a concern. Consider designating a low cabinet in the family room for the kids' toys. This allows a quick place to put them out of sight if someone's coming over and also makes cleaning up an easy chore for the little ones at the end of the day.

You may also find organizing your kitchen to be helpful using a few key principles:

- Store items near where they are used—pots near the stove, knives near the cutting board, dish towels near the sink.

- Stock your pantry by type of food—vegetables in one area, canned fruit in another. Consider labeling your shelves so that you remain organized and family members can help unload groceries.

- Reserve counter space for food preparation—move canisters and cookbooks to a handy shelf instead. Store appliances that aren't used daily in a cabinet. Consider under-the-cabinet mounting for appliances, if practical.

- Frequently used items like spices and spatulas should be located conveniently near the food-preparation area and organized so you can quickly find the one you want.

- Use a cleaning caddy for storing cleaning supplies (usually under the sink)—pick one that can easily be carried around the house.

Larger families may benefit from color coding laundry, sheets, towels, and so on. Permanent markers can be used on the clothing tags or hidden inside the garments. Assigning each family member a specific color can help in sorting certain types of clothing—pajamas, underwear, and socks—as well as towels and washcloths. Using sheets with easily identifiable patterns linked to each child will eliminate confusion at laundry time. It may also help to assign a laundry basket to each member of the family. Older kids can take their own dirty clothes to the laundry room on request and take clean clothes back to their rooms in these baskets. You may even wish to assign a specific day for each child to take their dirty clothes to the laundry room, should daily washing fit more easily into your schedule than a single laundry day. If you find certain clothes items are always short—particularly underwear and socks—consider buying more of them. The decrease in hassles, as well as the money saved from washing fewer small emergency loads, will more than make up for the additional cost of the extra items.

Most of us accumulate a vast stockpile of old medications and first-aid items over time. It's important to sort through and update these things at least once a year. Take everything out of the medicine cabinet, bathroom drawer, or whatever storage area you use, and lay it out where you can look at it. Throw away any expired medications and any that you cannot identify by name and purpose. All prescriptions should have a label with the patient's name, drug name, date, purpose (such as "for pain," "for cough"), and instructions. If a bottle doesn't have an appropriate label, make one yourself or throw it away. Then organize your cabinet space just as you did the pantry with labels for items with a similar purpose to be kept together. Also, consider purchasing a simple first-aid kit and keep it stocked, or get a larger plastic tray or caddy to keep all first-aid items together.

The following is a recommended list of first-aid supplies everyone should have, particularly with kids around:

- Small bottle of syrup of ipecac (This is used to induce vomiting in case of accidental poisoning; however, be certain to call your doctor or poison control hotline before using it.)

- Antibiotic ointment or spray (Neosporin)

- Baking soda for insect bites (This can be kept in the kitchen.)

- Band-Aids (Usually an assortment of sizes makes the most sense.)

- Burn ointment or spray (Something with aloe is best.)

- Calamine lotion or Benadryl for bites and rashes

- Elastic bandage (3″ Ace wrap)

- Eyewash solution (Get sterile contact lens solution, *not* the cleaning solution.)

- Heating pad

- Hydrocortisone cream

- Hydrogen peroxide

- Ice bag

- Insect repellant (Keep this in the cabinet near the door the kids use most often so it's handy and won't be confused with other medications in the first-aid kit.)

- Oral thermometer (You'll also need an ear thermometer and/or a rectal thermometer if you still have a baby at home.)

- Petroleum jelly

- Sterile cotton balls, 4″ × 4″ pads, and a sterile roll dressing

- Sunscreen (Keep this where kids can get it before playing outside or going swimming.)

- Tweezers

Additionally, most of us would benefit from keeping the following over-the-counter medications available at home:

- Antacid (TUMS tablets or a liquid)

- Antidiarrhea medication (Imodium)

- Acetaminophen (Tylenol)

- Antihistamine (Benadryl)

- Decongestant (Sudafed, Drixoral, and so on)

- Ibuprofen (Advil, Motrin) or naproxen (Aleve)

- Laxative (Milk of Magnesia)

- Nasal (saline) spray

More helpful hints at improving your stress levels through better organization can be found in *Organize Yourself* (Macmillan, 1997) by Ronni Eisenberg and Kate Kelly.

ENFORCE DISCIPLINE IN YOUR HOME

There are few things harder than being a "parent" to your parents. The role reversal that many adult children experience when their parents get older is frustrating for both the adult child and the parents as well. Because this situation is so difficult for everyone involved, I would suggest not starting it now while your child is still in grade school or perhaps even in diapers!

If your two-year-old child decides where he will sleep at night—like your bed—he's in control of your life. (If you have decided this is your preferred way of parenting, then it's your choice. Just be sure that you are the one choosing it.) If your seven-year-old decides when, where, and what she will eat, then she is in charge of the situation and you're not. If your four-year-old son throws a temper tantrum in the grocery store, demanding a toy, and you give in and buy it when you didn't want to, you have not only taught him that bad behavior is acceptable, but that it will be rewarded. If you let your strong-willed child run the show at your house, she has in essence become your parent and you have become her child.

Noted child psychologist Dr. James Dobson has written several books on how to discipline children lovingly and effectively. I highly recommend starting with the first book in the series, *The Strong-Willed Child: Birth Through Adolescence* (Tyndale House, 1992) and read more as needed. Dr. Dobson takes a very practical approach to childhood discipline and gives lots of useful recommendations and anecdotes to guide you through the process. Another resource that many parents have found helpful is *Setting Limits with Your Strong-Willed Child: Eliminating Conflict by Establishing Clear, Firm, and Respectful Boundaries* (Prima Lifestyles, 2001) by Robert J. Mackenzie.

Sit down with your husband first, and then with the kids, to set rules in trouble areas such as television, shared toys like video games, homework, bedtime, chores, and allowances. You'll have topics such as cars, dating, and curfews for older kids. Enforce the rules consistently and as a unified parental team. Never argue with each other in front of the kids on the issue of discipline. Retire to a quiet place, just the two of you, and discuss any disagreements until you can come up with a compromise. If kids, especially teenage boys, respond more to Dad's disciplinary style, use this to your collective advantage. Remember that consistency is one of the key elements to successful parenting.

CONTINUALLY MONITOR THE PROCESS

Nothing in life stays the same. Things are constantly changing—sometimes for the better and sometimes for the worse, but always changing. In fact, the only thing consistent in life is inconsistency. Unfortunately, no matter how well you've mapped out your strategy to solve the problems that bring hurry into your life or how "in control" of the situation you are now, you are aiming at a moving target. What worked well for you last year or even last month may no longer do the trick. You must constantly reassess your limitations, rethink your goals, reorder your priorities, and attempt to simplify and organize your life based on those evaluations. It will be an ongoing process and one in which you should continue to seek perfection although you will probably never attain it, at least not for long. Unhurrying your life is not an event; it's a process. Review your priority list at least twice a year—the start of summer and the end of the year are good times to do this—and reflect on your successes and problem areas. Revise the list if needed and plot your strategy for the next six months.

SUMMING IT ALL UP

Surviving Hurried Woman Syndrome is about *balance* and *choices*. We all need balance in our lives; it keeps our body, our mind, and our spirit healthy. A life in balance is one that is happy and fulfilling. But balance doesn't just happen by itself. Keeping your life in balance is an active process, one that requires thoughtful planning, diligent execution, and constant reevaluation and adaptation to ever-changing circumstances. Finding balance also requires you to make choices—choices about how you will define yourself, what you want out of life, what you're willing to give up to get it, who you will love, and whose love you seek.

In most cases, Hurried Woman Syndrome is the result of a life that is out of balance. The symptoms of fatigue, moodiness, weight gain, and low sex drive come from an imbalance in brain chemistry that can be corrected with antidepressants, but the imbalance in the brain is caused by an imbalance in life; restoring the proper balance in your life will cure the syndrome as surely as any medication— and for much longer. But for many people, restoring balance to their life appears to be a much harder task than taking a pill every day or ignoring the pain and hoping it will somehow magically go away by itself. Restoring balance requires you to make some changes in the way you view things and how you live, and no one relishes change. It scares us; it's unsettling. In a lot of cases, it often appears impossible to make change happen; you feel locked into doing things the same old way, trapped by circumstances and powerless to make things happen differently because you've fought this fight before and couldn't see any meaningful progress. For the most part, these are all rationalizations, excuses for maintaining the status quo.

The fact is you do have the power to change things for the better, to take back control of your life, and to find the happiness and sense of fulfillment you once knew but thought was lost. Yes, you will have to make some tough choices, but they are choices you would have made a long time ago if you had only known what it was ultimately going to cost you in terms of your physical and emotional health. It's not too late to make this work, but you must choose to do something about it now. Change won't just happen or fall into your lap one morning at breakfast; you must make the decision to act.

Although you've thought about doing something and perhaps even tried a few times to make things better without much success, this time will be different. Now you know what you're up against, and you have the tools necessary to make the changes that will lead to victory. You know that you have to make your personal growth a priority in your life. It's not selfishness; it's self-preservation. You can now recognize that negative thinking, false beliefs, and errors in logic have hamstrung your decision making in the past and instead can choose a new, more positive perspective. Those old cognitive distortions that led you to conclude that you were in a hopeless situation, one that you were just going to have to tough your way through, can be replaced with a renewed sense of purpose and the energy to face your demons and defeat them.

Choosing to get the best of stress will provide you with new-found physical and emotional energy that, along with your new perspective, will allow you to rethink your goals and priorities, simplify and organize your life, and help you properly manage your resources—time, money, and energy—to meet your goals and nurture your important relationships. Choosing to spend energy on your relationships will be much more fulfilling than wasting it on unnecessary clutter and accumulating "things" that in the long run don't really matter anyway. Most of us will not be canonized in history books nor have monuments built in our honor because of what we owned or the things we accomplished at work. Our legacy will be found in the lives and endeavors that were enriched while we were passing through this life. Some of the choices won't be easy, particularly when many people around you say that you're "doing it all wrong." You may have to shun the world's definitions of material as well as personal success. But don't be afraid to do it your way, to personalize your life. After all, it's *your* life, isn't it? Choosing to take the road less traveled can be scary at times, but don't hesitate to do it. The payoff will be living your life to the fullest and sharing your joy with those who love and need you. What could be better?

APPENDIX A

Scoring Guide for the Attitude and Mood Self-Assessment Quiz

POINTS FOR ANSWERS

Question	A	B	C	D
1.	5	4	2	1
2.	1	2	3	5
3.	4	3	2	1
4.	1	2	3	5
5.	1	2	3	4
6.	1	2	3	4
7.	1	2	3	4
8.	7	5	3	1

9.	1	2	3	4
10.	4	3	2	1
11.	4	3	2	1
12.	5	4	2	1
13.	1	2	3	4
14.	1	2	3	4
15.	5	4	2	1
16.	5	4	2	1
17.	1	2	4	5
18.	1	2	3	4
19.	1	2	3	4
20.	6	5	2	1

APPENDIX B

Using the Food Diary/Calorie Counter

USING A FOOD DIARY can be very helpful when you're trying to watch your weight, and they are easy to use. Simply follow these five steps. A blank food diary/calorie counter can be found on page on page 335. Make photocopies that you can use throughout your weight management program.

1. Write down everything you eat—everything—as soon as you eat it. Give a brief description of the food eaten as well as the amount and the total calories. Break down the total calories into the number of calories from protein (P), carbohydrates (C), and fat (F). Subtotal each of these columns at the end of the day.

2. Record your exercise calories out. You have a minimum exercise requirement of three half-hour sessions each week. When you complete your first session, circle the number 1 under "Required Calories Out"; circle the 2 when you finish your second session, and

so on. If you exercise longer than half an hour at your first session (say one hour), you can either circle numbers 1 and 2 when you finish or write in the extra calories in the "Additional Calories" area of the "Calories Out" column.

3. Calculate your net calories in for each day by subtracting any additional exercise calories from your total calories in. This will show you how you are doing on a day-by-day basis. Remember though, you have the flexibility to move calories around during the week or to earn calorie credits from additional exercise.

4. At the end of the week, you can add up your total weekly calories in from each of the daily subtotals. This is a good time to see whether you have maintained the recommended ratio of 40 percent protein, 30 percent carbohydrates, and 30 percent fat. You can also add up your additional exercise calorie credits and subtract these from the total calories in to arrive at your net calories in for the week. This is the best time to analyze how well you are sticking to your diet plan and to make any necessary adjustments if you have reached a plateau.

5. We haven't discussed how to calculate your target calories per week, but it's easy to do. Just take the recommended target calories in per day (formula given in Chapter 9) and multiply that number by 7:

Target net calories in per day $\times$ 7 = Recommended net calories in per week

⚜ THE HURRIED WOMAN FOOD DIARY/ CALORIE COUNTER

Week # _____	*Calories In* Description & Amount	Total	P	C	F	*Calories Out*	*Net Calories In*
MON / /						REQUIRED 1 2 3 ADDITIONAL CALORIES:	
	Sub Tot						
TUE / /						REQUIRED 1 2 3 ADDITIONAL CALORIES:	
	Sub Tot						
WED / /						REQUIRED 1 2 3 ADDITIONAL CALORIES:	
	Sub Tot						
THU / /						REQUIRED 1 2 3 ADDITIONAL CALORIES:	
	Sub Tot						
FRI / /						REQUIRED 1 2 3 ADDITIONAL CALORIES:	
	Sub Tot						
SAT / /						REQUIRED 1 2 3 ADDITIONAL CALORIES:	
	Sub Tot						
SUN / /						REQUIRED 1 2 3 ADDITIONAL CALORIES:	
	Sub Tot						
		Total	P	C	F	Calories Out	Net Calories In
	Weekly						

WEEKLY WEIGHT_____

INDEX